D1105228

# THE ECONOMIC
# DEVELOPMENT OF
# MEDIEVAL EUROPE

# THE ECONOMIC DEVELOPMENT OF MEDIEVAL EUROPE

## ROBERT-HENRI BAUTIER

with 158 illustrations, 23 in colour

THAMES AND HUDSON · LONDON

*Translated from the French by Heather Karolyi*

© 1971 THAMES AND HUDSON LTD, LONDON

*Printed and bound in Great Britain by Jarrold & Sons Ltd, Norwich*

*ISBN 0 500 32021 7 Clothbound*

*ISBN 0 500 33021 2 Paperbound*

# CONTENTS

The period we call the 'Middle Ages' covers more than a millennium in the history of civilization. From the fall of the western Roman empire to the outbreak of the Italian wars, from the end of the fourth century to the end of the fifteenth, forty generations shaped and moulded Europe. These forty generations settled its population, stabilized its landscape, built its towns, and determined the course of its economy. In so doing, they also decided its future. It is, in fact, imprecise to subsume such a long, diverse, and decisive period under the single label of the 'Middle Ages', as is emphasized by the fact that the nature and importance of the sources are extremely uneven for the different epochs. From the baptism of Clovis to the imperial coronation of Charlemagne, only a few comparatively unimportant documents span a period as long as that separating us from Cromwell; and it is worth remembering that a shorter period of time has elapsed between St Louis and ourselves than that between the establishment of the Merovingian dynasty and St Louis's accession.

If the evolution of Europe is considered from the economic and social point of view, in terms of population, land, trade and technology, a number of different epochs should be distinguished in this vast period.

The first period may be called the early Middle Ages. It continues up to the end of the tenth century and is characterized, on the whole, by a considerable slowing-down of all economic activity in the barbarian west, and by its retrenchment in the face of the brilliance of the Byzantine and Moslem east. Various sub-phases of opposing tendencies can also be distinguished: first a pre-medieval period which in many respects only feebly prolonged the declining ancient world, and then two 'renaissances' alternating with profound crises of economic depression. One of these renaissances, which has been ill understood because of the scarcity of texts, is in the seventh century; the other, in the ninth, is known as the Carolingian Renaissance; it was protracted in the eastern part of the Holy Roman Empire by the Ottonian Renaissance.

We may call the next period, from the end of the tenth century to the middle of the fourteenth, the classical Middle Ages. In this period, we come first upon an era of great significance, lasting from the tenth century to the middle of the

7

twelfth, when a new system developed and the whole framework of life in what was to be western civilization was set up. At this time the west was tending to raise itself to the level of eastern civilizations and economies. Subsequent advances took the form of a more or less general improvement in the quality of all aspects of material life, with the conquest of wasteland and forest for cultivation, with industrialization, the development of towns, the expansion of trade, and the appearance of credit and banking methods. It was a time when communications extended freely from the far west to the far east, and when Europe secured the advantages that led to its pre-eminence over the east in the fields of industry, technology and finance.

The last period may be called the late Middle Ages. This period opens a little before the middle of the fourteenth century with a very severe demographic and financial crisis. Proceeding through a series of crises which severely shook those regions that had been the most favoured in the preceding period, it reached its climax in the second half of the fifteenth century with a new and very rapid growth in population which continued to the middle of the sixteenth century, and a development of European techniques and manufacturing processes.

It goes without saying that in a geographic area as vast as the one we are considering, developments were not always synchronous, and the rate of evolution varied greatly from one region to another. We shall therefore confine ourselves to two main areas: (a) the Mediterranean basin, where the centre of gravity passes, as the period unfolds, from the Levant to Italy, but where developments in Central Asia and their economic consequences are always of considerable importance, and are transmitted in successive waves to the heart of the west; (b) the region of northern Europe, that of the North Sea and the Baltic, which was isolated at first but came to be connected with the first area in certain favoured zones of north-west Europe, southern Germany, and northern Italy. Developments in this second region begin with a revival first of Atlantic and then eastern Europe, which existed for a long time in great obscurity and was subjected to the repercussions of the great changes in Asia, but finally enjoyed one of the most remarkable renaissances of the late Middle Ages.

As this essay is largely based on personal research, its bias towards the economic history of the Mediterranean region will perhaps be forgiven.*

* A first (abridged) draft of the work was published as a chapter of Vol. III, *Le Moyen Age* (ed. M. François), in the series *Civilisations, peuples et mondes* (Editions Lidis, Paris 1966). Thanks are due to the publisher, who has kindly authorized republication and translation.

# I THE MIDDLE AGES:
# THE ARDUOUS SURVIVAL OF THE WEST

The chief problem presented to the historian by the early Middle Ages is that of knowing under what conditions and at what moment the west passed from a broadly based and relatively prosperous organized economy, that of the Roman empire, to a state of almost total recession. The economy of the Roman empire had been founded on maritime trade, supported by the network of cities and towns, and backed up by a bimetallic currency with gold predominating. The era of the barbarian kingdoms, on the other hand, and even in some respects that of the Carolingian empire, is characterized by obliteration of towns and industries, introversion of each region, quasi-autarchy of the rural estates, a debased silver coinage and barter trade. This problem of the transition from antiquity to the Middle Ages is one which historians have found particularly absorbing. In spite of much research, however, the problem is still unresolved because of the dearth of sources and their wide dispersal in both space and time. The limited interest of ancient historians in economic life, at least by comparison with their very thorough studies of politics and legal institutions, is another difficulty, as well as the shortcomings of medieval archaeology, which has paid little attention to the history of 'material culture'.

FROM THE LATE EMPIRE TO THE PRE-MEDIEVAL PERIOD

In the first century, and, under the Antonines, in the second, Rome experienced its golden age in the political and economic sphere. The *pax Romana*, although relative, more or less guaranteed the equilibrium of the empire and its institutions, and gave rise to a remarkable development of urban civilization across the vast areas ruled by Rome. An abundant labour force made possible the cultivation of extensive tracts of country. Roman currency circulated well beyond the frontiers, and Roman merchants hurried along the amber and tin routes to the far-off countries of the north, and along the silk routes across the boundless expanses of Asia, with their gold, their *objets d'art*, and their manufactured wares. Lying at the centre of the Mediterranean basin which it dominated, Rome was indeed the heart of its empire.

From the end of the first century, however, Italy had begun to experience a degree of economic lassitude, which was the first sign of later crises. There

1 This Roman road map, preserved in a medieval copy known as 'Peutinger's Table', is the most important source for our knowledge of the network of Roman roads and

was a drift from the countryside towards the towns, which became swollen with an undernourished proletariat. When the wars of conquest ended, the supplies of slaves dried up, with the result that labour became scarcer in the rural estates. In order to bind their dependants (*coloni*) to the soil, the owners made over to them parcels of land which they worked without much initiative, and primarily with a view to maintaining their own families. Romans and Italians emigrated in large numbers to the provinces to seek their fortune; certain regions (the Tuscan Maremma and the Pontine Marshes) were abandoned. For its own provisioning, Rome had ever greater recourse to foreign sources, notably Africa, Spain and Gaul for corn, oil and wine. Industrial

landmarks. The original was probably drawn up towards the end of the fourth century, in the reign of Theodosius I. The detail shown here centres on Rome.

competition from Gaul, western Germany, and also from Spain, with their manufactured pottery, glassware, metal objects, and textiles, became brisk, and objects originating in Italy apparently no longer reached the Danubian countries, Bohemia and northern Germany, as they had before. Oriental luxuries flooded Italy, resulting in a drain of gold to eastern Mediterranean lands. Rome became a great consumer-centre provided for (and the excavations at Ostia confirm this) by merchants flocking in from the whole empire.

More significantly, the continued expansion of Rome in political and military fields was brought to an end, and the empire forced on to the defensive on all its frontiers. It was attacked simultaneously for the first time by the

Germans on the Danube and the Rhine, by the Moors in North Africa, and by the Parthians in the east. From the year 174, during the reigns of Marcus Aurelius and Commodus, the consequences of this were seen in the rapid deterioration of gold currency, and then under Septimius Severus (193–211) of silver currency.

The provinces, however, continued to experience a discernible economic development. Toponymy and excavations have proved that in the second and third centuries, on the virgin lands of the west, large numbers of *villae*, or rural estates, were built up from nothing. In these regions, which had scarcely known urban civilization, many cities (*civitates*) and boroughs (*vici*) were founded, or developed rapidly. Military requirements helped to bustle up business in the frontier regions, while contacts with the barbarian peoples in the process of organization gave rise to new movements of trade.

In the east, the economic climate was apparently even more favourable. The towns were revitalized, and, in this renewed life, thousand-year-old commercial traditions found new vigour. Control of the trade routes in the direction of the Red Sea and the Persian Gulf, and the meeting-up of the Roman and Chinese silk-routes in the heart of Asia, opened new perspectives to merchants for the products of the eastern part of the empire: direct contact was established with southern Asia and China, to which a more or less official mission made its way in 166. Ivory, incense, pepper and silk were readily available in the markets of the Roman world; and the intermediary caravan cities, Palmyra or Petra, and still more the great markets of Alexandria and Antioch, Laodicea and Beirut, were made wealthy through it. Hence from the end of the second century, and during the course of the third, the power of the east, of its businessmen, its resources in gold, and its religions too, began to preponderate in a world which was politically unstable. The capital city, Rome, had become, in the political arena, a military stake, and economically a dead weight.

Following upon the decay of Italy, the whole of the west in its turn began, in the middle of the third century, to undergo a decline. The causes of this are not entirely clear, but the chief of them were certainly of a political and military nature, such as the military anarchy of the years 255–68, the repeated if not annual invasions, starting in 254, of the Franks and the Alemanni, and the Saxon raids on the coast of Gaul. Defensive measures were rendered still more difficult by the attacks of the Goths and Persians in the eastern territories. But the demographic depression was no less serious. Spain, for example, was apparently emptied of its population. Cádiz, its chief port, fell almost to the level of a village, and its export of oil to Rome declined to such an extent that

4 The great Roman commercial and strategic route, between Antioch and Aleppo (beginning of the second century), which crossed the desert in northern Syria. This is probably the best-preserved road fragment from the whole Roman world.

2 Palmyra, principal point of contact between the Roman commercial world and the caravans that came from the Orient across the Syrian desert in the second and third centuries. This monumental arch lay across the city's great central road (*c.* 220).

3 Petra was a caravan depot in the desert south of Jordan, near the Red Sea. These tombs (first–third centuries), carved out of the mountains encircling the city, give Petra a monumental setting.

the 'Testaccio', Rome's huge rubbish dump, contains no fragments of Spanish earthenware jars dating from later than 256.

Owing to various factors, a large proportion of the population became pauperized and this led to a concentration of land in the hands of big landowners or the imperial treasury. Among these factors we may list the first great barbarian military expedition across Gaul, the havoc it wrought, and the settlement of the marauders in the devastated areas. There was increasing fiscal pressure to face up to the requirements of defence, while measures taken to reimpose taxes failed. Prices in the last third of the third century continually rose: there was a corresponding weakening of the silver currency and poor coinages, minted with base metals in repeated issues, became inflated. There were attempts at monetary reform. Gaul underwent an appalling social crisis, which culminated in the *Bagaudae* revolts of the third quarter of the third century. Most of the money-hoards discovered in modern times date from this period, as does the abandonment or destruction of a large number of Gallo-Roman *villae*. Inadequate agricultural production and the disruption of transport brought famine to the towns. The economic function of the cities, which were ruined by the unreasonable demands of the treasury, declined at the same time as their political role came to an end due to their loss of autonomy. This decline of the urban system in the west, where the cities contracted within considerably diminished walled areas, was of great significance for the economy and the entire civilization of the early Middle Ages. By contrast, the oriental cities were still thriving. No doubt they were weakened but they still kept up a certain cultural brilliance out of their own productive resources.

For the whole empire, the reforms of Diocletian and of Constantine, following those of Gallienus, delayed the effects of the economic slump, if not the political and military decline. The currency was restored, a rigid fiscal system was universally imposed, agricultural and industrial prices were controlled and pegged by the 'maximal' edict of 301. These measures guaranteed that the indispensable taxes were collected and that industrial productive power survived, while after the law of 332 agricultural labourers were kept on the land by force. In fact, economic activity was state-controlled: vehicles and factories (mills, textile workshops, potteries, arms factories), whether intended for supplying the army or not, were considered as public utilities to which men should be attached by heredity. Even municipal administration was deemed to be a hereditary civic duty. Yet the official freezings scarcely had any effect on the rise in prices, and inflation continued in spite of the minting of the Constantinian gold *solidus*, the silver *siliqua* and the bronze *miliarensis*.

Consequently when the authority of the state collapsed under the blows of military disasters, the continual infiltrations of barbarians (official or illicit), and the evasion of their responsibilities by the traditional élites, everything broke down simultaneously. From the middle of the fourth century, the Roman west was already in the pre-medieval era. Soon there was nothing left, in the west, but a Roman administrative system virtually empty of content. Many of the cities of Britain, Gaul, Germany and Spain were abandoned at the end of the fourth century and during the fifth; the others stagnated and most of them saw their populations fall to village level. When they were able to do so, *curiales* established themselves in their country properties. State factories were destroyed or abandoned. Roads were no longer maintained. Trade disappeared, where it did not fall into the hands of merchants from the east, Greeks, Syrians and Jews. When the barbarian kingdoms were set up, the impression was of a land already ruined; it had been emptied of a large proportion of its inhabitants, ruralized, and allowed to revert for the most part to waste ground. Life was concentrated on the estates of the big landowners, from whom the peasants sought protection at the price of their freedom, and who took advantage of the dissolution of public authority to impose their patronage and power on the villages that still existed. The tendency towards concentration of land increased, to the benefit of the magnates, whose authority over the enslaved *coloni* was substituted *de facto*, if not *de jure*, for that of the state.

From the third quarter of the fourth century, lower Germany and northern Belgium from the Boulogne-Tongres line were abandoned to the Franks, and in 382 the Goths were allowed to set up a federal state inside the Danubian frontiers of the empire. Such settlements very quickly became common. The 'barbarians' were given allotments of land, but they also apparently drove some of the former inhabitants from their homes, while wars among their chiefs tended to reduce the warring peoples to slavery. The situation was particularly dramatic in the more distant regions. Under the Huns, who drove out the romanized Goths, east-central Europe was turned into a no-man's-land into which the Slav tribes began to make their way. Contact was broken off between the continent and the British Isles, which were left to fend for themselves from then on. Roman Africa suffered terrible disasters under Vandal rule.

In Gaul, the rift between north and south deepened. The decline was felt less in southern Gaul, which was occupied by barbarians who had been romanized for some time. Arles kept its prestige as an imperial town, and this was reinforced by the installation of the prefect of the Gauls, who was withdrawn from Trier. As well as Arles, Narbonne and Marseilles still kept up contacts with the rest of the Mediterranean. Even as late as 475 Sidonius Apollinaris witnessed the last burst of activity of the port of Marseilles, practically on the eve of its capture by the Visigoth Euric.

In spite of growing anarchy, Italy too experienced a decline which was less pronounced, or at least a little delayed. It is true that, from the end of the fourth century, Rome collapsed politically. Its pre-eminent role did not survive the sack of Alaric (410), though the city still possessed some renown up to the middle decades of the sixth century. The texts and excavations of the port of Ostia, the window of the *Urbs* on the outside world, clearly illustrate the decline of the ancient metropolis. Northern Italy was able to preserve an urban life which retained a certain glamour, thanks to the maintenance of a façade of imperial power and the resulting economic activity; but from 403 Ravenna superseded Milan as the capital, and this more than anything indicates the decisive importance of the direct maritime link with Constantinople; the land routes had become too dangerous and had to be abandoned. Even Aquileia suffered greatly, although it was one of the vital centres of the empire, and, with its colonies of oriental traders, maintained the commercial land routes connecting the Roman world with the countries of eastern and central Europe up to the end of the third century. Public works were neglected, the countryside

was inundated and the lagoons and marshes spread out; the city-port did not survive the invasion of Attila's Huns in 452.

The east survived the crisis, and its powers of endurance kept it going in spite of the pressures brought to bear on it in the course of the fifth century by Germans, Huns, Slavs and Bulgars, Persians and Arabs. Understandably the empire and its institutions became progressively orientalized. New religions – cults of the Sun, of Mithras or of Isis, and Christianity itself – gradually made their mark on the Roman world; missionaries were sent from the east to found churches among the Gauls; and Syrian traders ensconced themselves in everything that remained worth while in the western economy. Diocletian drew the obvious conclusions in establishing the Diarchy (286), and then the Tetrarchy, but the decisive moment came when Constantine established at Byzantium (330) the city which bore his name and which was intended to maintain the heritage of ancient Rome. The rise of Constantinople, the 'New Rome', whose institutions were borrowed from those of the old, was immediate; but it was not the only brilliant centre of economic and cultural activity. Once the worst of the crisis was over, all the other cities of the east, and particularly Alexandria, had a share in this revival.

5 Mosaic in S. Apollinare Nuovo, Ravenna, showing the walls of the city and ships in the port of Classis (mid-sixth century).

6 Aquileia was the principal home-port of the imperial navy during the late empire. Shown on the right are excavations of the port.

Faced with the vacuum in the west, the Roman world looked to the emperor. Though he resided in the east, he considered himself as the sole legitimate heir of the whole empire, and he was able to plan the economy of the late empire without any major setbacks. The end of the fourth century, the fifth and the beginning of the sixth, are marked by prosperity. The 'Byzantine' navy held absolute mastery of the sea. Egypt and Syria were linked by trade with Nubia, China and the Indian Ocean, and gold, silk and spices were brought by overland caravans across Arabia and Nubia, and by maritime convoys from Ethiopia to Egypt, through Berenice or Eilath. After an interruption lasting for a century, Roman coins reappear here and there among Indian hoards. Situated right at the heart of the empire, at its strategic and economic crossroads, Constantinople, whose population is said to have approached 800,000 inhabitants – making it by far the largest city of the time – profited by this general prosperity, thanks to a relentless taxation.

## SIXTH- AND SEVENTH-CENTURY RENAISSANCE

The re-establishment of a strong and thriving state in the east encouraged the last of the 'Roman' emperors, Justinian, to attempt the reconquest of the whole empire, beginning with the small barbarian kingdoms of the west. The power of his fleet and armies, as well as his gold and his diplomatic expertise, enabled him, after securing his eastern frontiers by a treaty with Persia (532), to recapture the whole of North Africa from the Vandals (533), then Dalmatia (536) and Italy (536–55) from the Goths, and finally southern Spain from the Visigoths (554). In August 554, he affirmed the reconstitution of the empire by the 'Pragmatic Sanction'.

This great edifice was not destined to last long. Though Italy had been temporarily set on its feet again in the time of Theodoric, it emerged debilitated from the tooth-and-nail struggle between Goths, Lombards, Franks and Byzantines. Epidemics (the 'plague') made their appearance in 543 and recurred periodically for half a century. The efforts of Justinian and his successors up to Heraclius, however, secured a very marked economic revival which benefited the Mediterranean world, and no doubt in consequence the whole of the west. With its unrivalled historic monuments, Ravenna bears witness today to the undeniable prosperity it experienced at that time. Buildings like the church of San Vitale in Ravenna (about 550), following upon St Sophia of Constantinople (532–37) as well as other sumptuous architectural works at Rome and Jerusalem, are powerful witnesses to the new vitality. The fame of the Italian masons was such that the bishop of Turin, in 550, sent some to work for his colleague at Trier.

7, 8 Justinian's architectural achievements still attest to the wealth of the empire in the mid-sixth century. Right, a capital from St Sophia in Constantinople (note the imperial monogram in the centre); below, view of the arcade in S. Apollinare in Classe at Ravenna.

The ports came to life again: coins minted at Carthage under Justinian in 539–40, and no doubt lost in a shipwreck, have been found near the Atlantic coast in the Gironde at Bec d'Ambès.

The revival affected Gaul indirectly, but not until other political events of the utmost significance had occurred. In the middle of the sixth century the Avars, a small tribe of Manchurian origin related to the Ouïgours, came on the scene. After settling in central Europe, the Avars collided with the Slav peoples who swarmed round the frontiers of the empire, and abruptly severed the direct links that had traditionally existed between Byzantium and the countries of the north, as attested by the gold ornaments discovered in the tombs of Schleswig and by Italo-Byzantine treasures found in Scandinavia.

The Lombards, a formidable group of Germanic tribes, were swept along by this *Völkerwanderung*, and in 568 they crossed the Alps; within a few years they took possession of a large part of northern Italy, where they wrought slaughter and destruction. From then on, Byzantine trade was barred from its northern outlets and the Italian ports were consequently ruined. But this development was beneficial to Frankish Gaul, and all the evidence now points to an economic renaissance, parallel with the revival of prosperity round the Mediterranean, which it experienced for a good half-century. Franks and Byzantines drew closer together in the face of the Lombard threat; the Franks

made expeditions over the Alps on behalf of the Byzantines, and in return received huge sums in gold from the emperor.

Oriental merchants, notably Jews, Greeks and Syrians, set themselves up again in Marseilles and in other cities of Gaul, as well as in Visigothic Spain. In spite of the official ban on the export of gold currency, money hoards show that Byzantine coins circulated in Gaul in the reign of Justin II (565–68); these were exceptionally numerous under Maurice (582–602), but disappeared with the second issue of the *solidi* of Heraclius (613–29). Marseilles and several other cities of the Midi minted coins, which turn up in places as far away as Friesland and England, in imitation of the imperial currency. These coins are so numerous for the reign of Maurice that numismatists have sought to account for them by supposing that they were issued to back the rebellion of a Merovingian pretender, Gondobald, which originated from Constantinople and was supported by Byzantine gold. In fact, the issue was necessary in order to float Provençal trade in the Mediterranean; there is also evidence of a fresh minting of imperial currencies at Carthage, Syracuse and Catania at this time (582–83).

Although historians have unfortunately been all too careless about the exact chronology, it seems clear that almost all the widely heterogeneous signs of economic activity of which we are informed in the Merovingian period can be dated to this half-century of renaissance. The former system of communication

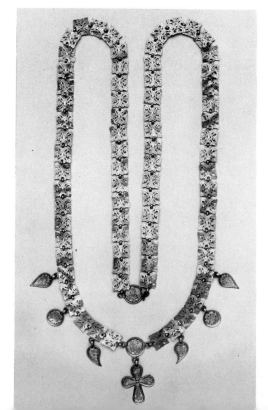

9 Silver earrings of Slav origin and Byzantine influence, seventh century (left).

10 Byzantine coin showing the head of the emperor Maurice Tiberius (above).

11 Sixth-century Byzantine gold necklace (right).

was apparently about to be restored, running from the east (Syria, Egypt, Constantinople) towards southern Italy, Sicily and Carthage, to Marseilles; from this point it went by way of the rivers towards the northern parts of Frankish territory and England. Around 600, after two centuries when there had been a complete suspension of monetary economy, England minted gold coins again, and, soon after that, silver too. The greatest pope of this pre-medieval period, St Gregory the Great (590–604), planned and effected the conversion of England to Christianity, sending St Augustine, the founder of the sea of Canterbury (597). Contacts became so frequent between Rome and the British Isles that St Aunaire, the father of a bishop of Auxerre, built a hospice (*xenodochium*) in the heart of Puisaye near the middle Loire, which was wild country at the time, specially to lodge the English on their way to Rome. At this time, too, Columban and his Irish monks established themselves on the continent, from Luxeuil to Bobbio. Quentovic was founded at the mouth of the Canche, on the site of the present port of Etaples, to maintain contacts between England and the Frankish seaboard; thus it took over the role pre-viously played by Boulogne and Vechten, which had been eclipsed in the fifth century.

As for the Mediterranean region, the letters of St Gregory indicate that in his time sea traffic from Rome and Naples to the islands, Africa, the Levant, and Provence, was fairly brisk. After a plague and famine, he himself had the population of Rome reprovisioned with Sicilian corn, and he bought slaves at Marseilles. During the same period, Gregory of Tours found nothing strange in the fact that a monk of Nice should subsist exclusively on a diet of bread and dates; date-stones (probably used as charms against evil spirits) have also been found in Merovingian tombs. Gregory was only surprised to learn that the monk in his piety had contented himself, during Lent, with roots that traders had brought him from Egypt. Gregory of Tours also tells of a theft of seventy jars of oil from a Marseilles trader in 573. (Was the oil used for manufacturing soap, a trade carried on by the people of Piacenza a few decades later?) The jars came from overseas, perhaps from a part of northern Syria where, at precisely this period (as the researches of G. Tchalenko have shown), there was a remarkable development of olive cultivation, indicated by the ruins of Roman *villae* in what is now the Syrian desert. Whatever the exact provenance of the oil, it was also to Marseilles that the monks of Saint-Denis regularly made their way, according to the *Gesta Dagoberti*, to obtain the oil necessary for lighting their church. About the year 629, Dagobert himself granted them the means to buy six wagonloads of oil a year out of the revenues of the Marseilles customs office. We may further recall Gregory of Tours' joke about the bishop of

12, 13 A Roman ghost town in the north Syrian desert: the *xenodochia* (hostelries) at Deir Seman, at the foot of the sanctuary of St Simeon Stylites (sixth century).

Nantes: if he were bishop of Marseilles, he said, the ships would not transport oil, but papyrus to enable him to write many fine works.

The customs warehouse at Fos, on the Rhône delta near Marseilles, also appears in various Merovingian records. In 661, goods required by the abbey of Corbie, which had just recently been founded, were exempted by the king from customs dues payable there; and a royal ratification at the beginning of the eighth century informs us that these goods included not only 10,000 pounds of oil, but a great number of oriental spices (pepper, cumin, cloves, dates, etc.). Finally, at the beginning of the seventh century St Eligius, if his biographer may be believed, purchased the freedom of slaves of both sexes, Moors, Saxons and others, who were crowded together in cargoes of up to a hundred persons. Other documents, including the letters of St Gregory and the life of St Bonet, confirm that there was a large-scale trade in human flesh, which was partly in the hands of Jewish merchants. A regular supply reached Marseilles from Spain, too, since we learn that in 588 a ship returning with its 'usual' cargo (*cum negotio solito*) brought the plague to the city.

The great trade-route from the shores of the Mediterranean to the interior was by way of the Rhône and the Saône. It is certainly no accident that an entry in the Marculf formulary, which was compiled towards the end of the first half of the seventh century, notes the following succession of towns as places for gathering traffic or market-toll taxes: Arles, Avignon, Soyons (not Sorgues, as some writers have maintained), Valence, Vienne, Lyons and Chalon-sur-Saône. From this point, travellers and traders might reach the Seine, or the Meuse, and, beyond that, the North Sea lands, England and Frisia, which were themselves in contact with the countries of the north. There is no room for doubt here: coins from Marseilles and Arles, for example, are found on English soil; and coins from Marseilles, Arles and Viviers are found in the Frisian hoards that form one of the most valuable sources of information about the economy of this time – for example, that of Escharren, which dates from about 600. Conversely, the treasure-hoard of Buis, in Saône-et-Loire, of about 631–41, contains coins originating from mints in the Rhône, Saône and Meuse valleys, and especially from Maastricht.

At about the same time, Atlantic trade revived. We find signs of this in the fact that coins from Nantes appear in Frisia around 575, and coins from various cities of the south-west (Agen, Oloron, Comminges) at Canterbury about 580; the currency of Marseilles penetrated as far as Nantes. The famous funeral ship dating from a little after 625, which was discovered at Sutton Hoo in Suffolk, has yielded, as well as pieces of Byzantine and Frankish silverware, a whole hoard of coins from Orléans and western and central France.

14 Silver dish from the Sutton Hoo ship burial (first half of the seventh century).

The next regions to experience the revival were those of the Loire and the Seine. Exploitation of the salt-marshes in the bay of Bourgneuf started (or revived); no doubt it was with this source of supply in view that, before the middle of the seventh century, the abbey of Stavelot received a royal licence exempting it from paying taxes at the mouth of the Loire. The cities of Orléans, Paris and Rouen expanded beyond the walls which had enclosed them in the late empire, giving evidence of a revival of urban life. At Paris, which was beginning to play the role of capital city, fifteen chapels, the nuclei of the future parishes of the medieval town, were founded outside the walls. The same feature is found at Clermont in Auvergne and in other cities; these appear to have been linked with the Mediterranean zone again by a land route, which is marked out by a series of mints.

Twenty years after the reawakening of the Mediterranean, the whole northern region in its turn came to life again. The institution by Dagobert of the *Lendit* fair at Saint-Denis, probably in 634–35, would appear to mark a peak in the revival; merchants flocked to it from Provence, England and Italy. This economic recovery perhaps has something to do with the legend of the 'holy' king, although Dagobert's generosity towards the abbey of Saint-Denis no doubt also helps to explain his flattering portrait in the *Gesta Dagoberti*. The northern and eastern regions gained most from this revival. The treasure-hoard of Escharren in Frisia, dating from about 600, contains not only southern coins but also pieces originating from two more distant sources, one around the middle and lower Rhine (Bonn, Cologne, Nijmegen and Tiel), the other around the middle reaches of the Meuse (Huy and Maastricht); the Sutton Hoo treasure, too, contains coins from Huy and Dinant.

Other finds in Friesland, in the Isle of Walcheren and as far away as Holstein, corroborate the expansion of the Meuse towns. When the Frisian port of Duurstede, which came to be the hub of a large-scale trade with Scandinavia in the Carolingian epoch, fell into the hands of the Franks under Dagobert, a moneyer from Maastricht set himself up there (about 629–39). The Meuse river-axis became vital at this time: below Verdun the 'river-ports' (*portus*) spaced out along its banks quite clearly superseded the old Roman cities sited inland, at the road junctions. Swords and glass objects from the Rhine and the

15 Merovingian coins from the Sutton Hoo treasure.

16 Frankish grave-goods, fifth–sixth century.

Meuse make their appearance in northern Germany and in Scandinavia. Natron has been found in sixth- and seventh-century glass vessels in the cemeteries of Lorraine, and this can only have been imported from distant Egypt, which confirms the existence of a commercial route connecting east and west by way of the Rhône, the Saône, the Meuse or the Rhine. Further evidence is supplied by the little 'Coptic' vases in cast bronze, originating in Egypt, which have been discovered in tombs along a route extending from northern Italy to England, by way of southern Germany and the Rhine valley.

The opening-up of the land route to the east, which is connected with the political and military expansion of the Franks, is also of some importance. Frankish merchants pushed forward well beyond their own frontiers, and supplanted the Byzantines as dealers in Slav and Avar slaves, mounting raids or making deals among the tribes, and then sending their captives to Spain and Constantinople. We have a good picture of the exploits of these 'traders' in the story of Samo, a native of Sens (in Burgundy), who arrived among the Slavic Wends with a caravan of merchants. He intervened so effectively in his hosts' quarrels with the Avars, that they chose him king in 623–4. Later he massacred another group of Frankish merchants who had also been attracted by the trade of these regions, and Dagobert had to lead an expedition against him – which in the event failed.

Verdun apparently played an essential role in this slave-trade from eastern lands, which it retained during the following centuries. Gregory of Tours tells of the *domus negociatorum* or 'great bazaar' of the city, and of a loan of 7,000 gold *solidi* solicited by its traders from king Theodebert in order to save their businesses, which were at a low ebb at this time. Ferdinand Lot has disparaged this loan, which, he said, would represent only a million francs at 1913 prices (200,000 dollars). But it was a vast sum in the context of the early Middle Ages: according to the tariffs of the Ripuarian Law in use in Austrasia, it was the equivalent of 3,500 adult oxen (valued at the time at two *solidi* apiece) or 2,300 mares (valued at three *solidi*).

The commercial recovery may have been accompanied by efforts to repair the Roman roads, which had gradually fallen into disrepair (As early as the end of the third century, one of the authors of the Panegyrics had written of Autun: 'the military road is full of holes . . . so that one can only drive half-loaded wagons on it; sometimes indeed it will only carry practically empty ones.') It is notable that legend or popular tradition pays tribute to Brunhilda (later thought to be the mother of Julius Caesar!) in connection with the network of Roman roads; in the north, as well as in Quercy and Languedoc, there are still roads called 'Brunehaut Way' (*Chaussée Brunehaut*) or 'Bruniquel Way', suggesting that in her time there was a concern with their maintenance. (Some roads are also called 'Queen Julietta's Way' – Julietta being another name for Julius Caesar's 'mother'.)

17, 18 Frankish coins of Byzantine influence showing heads of Theodebert I and Dagobert. Theodebert (534–48) was the first Merovingian sovereign whose name appeared on a coin.

Markets and mints, necessary for supplying metal currency for local trans-actions, were set up. Many historians have regarded the appearance of con-siderable numbers of local mints as evidence of growing anarchy, and issues by moneyers using their own dies as a symbol of the abandonment of the royal prerogative. But the establishment of close to 700 mints in the space of less than a century might also suggest that, after a long period of decline, there was now a pressing need for currency. In the more important cities and towns, the money-merchants eagerly launched out into new transactions, which could not fail to be remunerative, and the dissemination of their wares is the sign of a trade of some extent, at any rate locally. Although of debased quality, gold *solidi* and the third of a *solidus*, or *triens*, did in fact circulate: between 625 and 650, the abbey of St Peter's near Ghent negotiated cash purchases of land for considerable sums (6 pounds' weight in gold and 150 gold *solidi*), and in 680 the abbey of Moissac acquired vast estates for a payment of 700 gold *solidi* in specie and 200 in kind.

At the same time the country areas began to be repopulated. The great Benedictine and Columban abbeys of the north, which had received by royal grant largely wooded lands of considerable extent, began their pioneer work. As a result of their labours, the Brie region, which had been one vast thicket, was opened up to agriculture; in Beauce and in Picardy place-names ending in *-ville* and *-court* bear witness to *villae* and *curtes* founded by the efforts of the monks of Saint-Germain-des-Prés, Saint-Denis, Chelles, Faremoutiers, Jouarre, Saint-Wandrille, Saint-Vaast, Corbie and Fleury; their frequency indicates an increasing population which was once again searching for land to till. Small peasant holdings were formed here and there by clearing the land, in the region of Ghent and in Campine, in what became Normandy and in lower Auvergne. A recent study has suggested that Germanic place-names ending in *-heim* and *-weiler* also date from this period.

The picture which emerges from all this is of a revival originating on the Mediterranean coast, and more especially in Marseilles, around 568. It developed towards the west, the centre and the north of Gaul, with some ups and downs as time passed, and brought these areas back to life once more.

THE HALT IN THE DEVELOPMENT

The halt in economic development also began in the Midi. During the reign of Heraclius, Byzantine influence came to an abrupt end: the last counterfeit Byzantine gold coin minted in the west (before 629) bears his name; and the last exchange of missions between Constantinople and a Frankish king also took place in 629. The last Byzantine gold coin found in a western hoard was

one of Constans II (641–68), and it came from Syracuse, not from the east
proper. Without assuming a radical break with the east in all fields, we may
conclude that gold no longer reached the west and that Mediterranean trade
no longer felt the need of a supply of coins with the imperial stamp.

The reason is clear: the eastern empire was engaged in a fresh phase of its
age-old struggle with Persia. The Persians first deprived Byzantium of its
sources of precious metals on the slopes of the Caucasus. Then, taking advantage
of the Avar encirclement of Constantinople, they advanced as far as the Yemen,
and seized the spice route; in 613–14 they captured Damascus and Jerusalem,
thus dividing the empire into two. The destruction they wrought was extensive and sometimes irreparable; hundreds of ruins in the region of Aleppo and
Antioch still bear witness to the dramatic struggle and final surrender of a
land which was doomed from then on to become desert.

Although it had successfully resisted the waves of nomads from the steppes
and furthest Asia, the eastern empire was no longer capable of opposing the
advance of other tribes, appearing this time from the Arabian deserts. These
invaders began by ousting the Ethiopians, who were in close contact with
Syro-Byzantine traders, from the Red Sea and Arabia, while in Africa yet
other tribes cut the trade-routes between the Nubian gold-mines and the
Syro-Egyptian world. Then, in the second quarter of the seventh century,
Islam rose up at the behest of the Prophet to conquer the southern part of the

19 Window in the Umayyad palace of Khirbat al-Mafjar, near Jericho.

20 Mosaic of Byzantine influence under the west gallery of the Great Mosque of the Umayyads at Damascus, begun by Caliph El-Walid in 708.

21 Ruins of the fortified palace of the Umayyads at Andjar, at the foot of the Anti-Lebanon.

Byzantine empire, which had scarcely recovered from the Persian war. After the battle of the Yarmuk in 636, the Moslems took possession of these areas with little difficulty, since this served the interests of the Egyptian and Syrian merchants, who no longer felt loyalty to the imperial see as a result of the Monophysite schism and the disputes between the Patriarchates.

With Syria and Egypt the empire lost the richest of its territories between 636 and 656; even its navy no longer held mastery of the sea since the Moslem fleet asserted itself in the Cyprus and Rhodes expeditions. At precisely this moment a highly significant event occurred in the west (as we have already noted): Byzantine coins disappeared, the imperial stamp was no longer copied, and gold was no longer minted. This happened during the reign of Dagobert, when the western economy had apparently reached the zenith of its revival, and a little after England had been brought back to a monetary economy, which she had abandoned completely during the 'dark ages'.

To explain this fact, historians have postulated a drain of gold from the west to the east from the time of the late empire onwards: in the middle of the seventh century, it is said, large-scale trade petered out for lack of gold reserves, and the whole western part of the old Roman empire was from then on inexorably dragged down into total recession. Most historians apparently believe that the trade deficit of the west was permanent and that the drain of gold went on for well over a thousand years. In my view, this is not at all likely: Byzantine gold came to the west in the sixth century despite official bans, and indeed these bans testify to such a traffic since their purpose was to oppose it. The slave-trade, an extremely profitable business, counterbalanced imports of luxury products (spices, silk, textiles, ivory), which were necessarily limited. Moreover, contemporary sources indicate that, more than once, the *Basileus* sent Frankish kings large sums in gold. Gregory of Tours tells us that king Chilperic I showed him a bowl, weighing fifty pounds, made from gold which the emperor had sent him, as well as gold medals stamped with the imperial likeness, each weighing a pound. Childebert II received 50,000 gold *solidi* from the emperor Maurice in return for his intervention against the Lombards in Italy; on another occasion he was offered 3,600 gold *solidi* as compensation for the murder of two of his envoys in the course of a brawl at Carthage. The pretender Gondovald came from Constantinople with 'treasures', and we know that the Lombards paid Clotaire II a tribute of 12,000 gold *solidi* annually. In an economy which was relatively depressed, such injections of precious metal were certainly not negligible. In any case, the region cannot have been quite so bereft of gold in Dagobert's reign as has been alleged, since, as we have noted, abbeys bought property against payment in gold *solidi*, and the mint-master Eligius, among others, made his famous solid gold reliquaries and crosses intended for presentation on behalf of the king to churches and abbeys.

Hence we cannot say that the west fell back on its own resources and passed over to a silver-based economy because it no longer had gold to pay for its purchases in Byzantium. We must remember that there was a widespread political and economic crisis in Byzantium, due to the Arab conquests which cut it off from its principal trading areas and from its supplies of gold and other merchandise. According to the most recent study, the Frankish monetary reform which resulted in the introduction of the silver penny, or denier (*denarius*), would appear to date from the years 660–70: it is therefore difficult not to connect it with the complete collapse of the political and economic *status quo* in the eastern Mediterranean: it was, after all, in 661 that Muawiya founded the Umayyad Caliphate at Damascus.

Silver *denarii* seem to have appeared simultaneously throughout Gaul, while at the same time gold *solidi* and *tremissi*, or thirds of *solidi*, disappeared. This was preceded by a debasing of the gold pieces, which became progressively paler due to the use of silver alloy. It has been established by numismatists that the Frankish gold coins had already broken away from the official standard of Mediterranean countries, based on the late empire *solidus* weighing 24 *siliquae* or carats, in favour of another standard, at a weight of 21 and later of 20 *siliquae*, which was that of the northern countries. Marseilles alone remained faithful to the traditional weight as well as to gold currency up to the beginning of the eighth century.

This new orientation of the Frankish west's monetary policy is of great importance: it marks a break with the region's Roman past, since during the late empire Rome had given priority to minting gold above silver and bronze. It indicates a rupture with the Mediterranean economy, dominated by Byzantium, without adopting that of the Arab world. The west turned decisively towards the countries of the north, where silver coins – *sceattas* – were minted in profusion. These came quickly to dominate the currency. The West proved to be in an excellent position as regards the production of silver, since the silver mines of Melle in Poitou, which had been worked in the Roman era and were then abandoned, could provide a reliable supply; Poitou coins have been discovered in fairly large numbers all over the European west.

Here we see one outcome of the commercial contacts cultivated in the course of the preceding half-century among the countries of the North Sea, the Meuse and the Rhine. Silver currency is not in itself a sympton of recessions, as we can see, for instance, from the case of the Persian empire, which had a mono-metallic currency in silver, and where gold was simply provided as the standard for big business. From the time of the late empire onwards, the Roman world had been progressively denuded of silver coins, and subsequently of bronze, and this must have made retail trade singularly difficult; the acquisition of daily provisions, in so far as one did not produce them oneself, involved recourse to general barter. This system corresponded to an economy where each region, each locality, and indeed each group of estates or even each holding, was forced to be self-supporting because of the recession in trade. An augmentation of the silver coinage, together with the proliferation of mints, might therefore spell a return to an economy based on a wider circulation of goods.

If the system based on silver was in fact deliberately planned by the rulers of the time (which is doubtful), it was bound to fail. It was established at the moment when anarchy reappeared in the Frankish kingdom and the west was going through a fresh commercial recession. But the return to silver was a most important event in economic history: the silver penny, finally sanctioned by the reforms of Pepin and Charlemagne, determined the course of the whole western economy for nearly six centuries, from the second half of the seventh century to the middle of the thirteenth.

From this time forward we are faced with two distinct worlds: the Frankish world, where gold plays no part in economic life, but for all practical purposes is withdrawn from circulation and is no longer used for anything but jewellery; and the Mediterranean world, divided between Byzantium and Islam, the two heirs of Rome, where gold circulates freely and where the supply of precious metals is suddenly augmented by the plundering of the Syrian monasteries and by the iconoclast crisis.

From the point of view of their economies and cultures, they were clearly two separate worlds. With the last Merovingians and the first Carolingians the Frankish kingdom turned away from the sea towards the interior of the continent. Even though political troubles at home led Pepin in 755, and Charles in 774, to launch out into Italian adventures, they confined themselves to the conquest of continental Italy, contributing to its ruralization and leaving it almost wholly unprovided with a fleet, since they had scant interest in large-scale maritime trade. The entire economic and political centre of gravity passed to the north and east of the kingdom, shifting towards the rivers which led to the Frisian and British Isles and to those opening the way to the Danubian outposts. Under the new dynasty, military affairs became the main pre-occupation. Everything was sacrificed to administrative efficiency, purely with a view to territorial acquisition: Charles Martel put an end to Moslem

22 Frankish jewels of the seventh century.

23 Byzantine gold *solidus* showing the emperor Heraclius and his two sons, and an Arab copy on its right.

expansion, autonomous Aquitaine was forced to submit, and there was a lunge towards Bavaria (which was cut off from southern influences), Saxony, and the Slav and Avar territories. The most striking result was ultimately that the foundations of the feudal system were laid: the great estates were enlarged and their owners acquired increased powers, while small private estates and freehold properties were progressively liquidated. From this time trade was extremely limited, in spite of a renewed issue of the silver penny by royal command. The decline of the majority of the old Roman cities was complete by the beginning of the eighth century, while new sites were developed in a modest fashion along the rivers.

In complete contrast, the cities to the south and east of the Mediterranean basin, and especially those in the Moslem world, went through a period of remarkable brilliance, notably Damascus, Baghdad and Cairo, as well as Constantinople. Byzantium had at one time been thrown back on her own resources, after suffering the shock of the Arab impact. Now she profited by the eclipse of the Persian empire to recover her power in the Black Sea and on the vital trade routes towards the east and the north. In less than a century Islam came to dominate all the great markets from the shores of the Indian Ocean to the Atlantic, as well as the routes used by traders in Nubian and Sudanese gold and Asian silver. Goods circulated freely from Morocco and Spain to India and East Africa. Although the traditional coinage was respected in conquered lands and the zones where Sassanid silver and Byzantine gold were current remained more or less the same under Arab rule, the Caliphs minted their own gold dinars from 694. Even when their empire was on the point of breaking up politically, their lands constituted the most extensive market which had yet existed, and the Arab and Persian navy was augmented to guarantee communications with their foreign trade-partners.

It has not always been acknowledged by modern historians that at this time northern Italy was again linked with the Mediterranean economic region, in spite of acute crises in the political relations of the Lombard kingdom with the Byzantines. About the year 584 the Lombards minted gold thirds of a *solidus* (*tremissi*) with the head of the emperor Maurice Tiberius, as well as smaller silver and bronze denominations of the Byzantine or Ravenna type; this fact helps to explain a letter in which the suffragan bishops of Aquileia pleaded with the emperor Maurice in 590 for peaceful co-existence between Romans and Lombards, while Gregory the Great lamented the flight of Roman taxpayers towards lands under Lombard rule. But there was also a much more significant development: whereas the counterfeiting of Byzantine gold coins had ceased in the Frankish west by about 629, and a little after the middle of the seventh century the exclusive minting of silver pence commenced, king Rotharis (636–52) coined gold currency of his own at Pavia and in several towns of the Lombard kingdom. Here the middle of the century saw the end of silver coinage. This indicates that the lands of the Po had once more been absorbed back into the Byzantine monetary system.

With its navigable tributaries, the Adda and the Lambro, the Po provided an ideal entry-point for trade, and as a result a balance was struck between the Lombard country inland and Byzantine territory. This had been rendered infertile and unhealthy by the spread of lagoons and the meanderings of rivers, which the inhabitants had been unable to contain over a long and unhappy period. The two economies became complementary: from the interior came the characteristic products of Lombard craftsmen, gold objects and weapons,

24 An example of Lombard art: the altar erected at Cividale by the king Ratchis (744–49) in memory of his son Pemino.

which no longer passed over the Alps as they had at the beginning of the century, while in the other direction there was a realignment of trade between the mouths of the Po and central Lombardy. About this time a canal was dug at Brescia and a quay (discovered in 1959) constructed with the aid of flagstones taken from a neighbouring Roman cemetery. In 715, the treaty of Comacchio regulated commercial transactions: salt from the Adriatic marshes, oil from southern Italy, textiles, weapons and spices were to be exchanged for Lombard grain; this trade was carried on especially at Cremona and Piacenza, where we hear of a corporation of soap-manufacturers paying rent to the royal court.

If Ravenna and the Exarchate were in economic decline from the beginning of the eighth century, former refugees from the mainland now living on the little islands of the Venetian lagoon, at Rialto and at Torcello, experienced a great upsurge in their trade, by providing a link between Lombard and Byzantine lands. In this context the Veneto-Lombard rapprochement of 727 is significant, as well as Venice's attitude to king Aistulf's attempt against the Exarchate in 751. No doubt it was at this time that Venetians were granted permission to visit the fairs of Pavia.

The consequences of this new configuration were widespread. An agricultural development took place in Lombard lands, indicated by the clearing of ground and the increase of smallholdings grouped in new villages, forming new parishes, as well as by the better-known works of those great amassers of property, the large monasteries and churches.

In the place of oriental merchants, who had set themselves up in most of the towns only recently and, with the exception of the Jews, finally disappeared at the time of the Arab conquests, native traders became established: these are the *negotiatores* who appear in the law of Liutprand in 720, and to whom a special role is allotted by the laws of Aistulf of 750, which considered them as a distinct social class, just under the great landowners. They were apparently numerous in the various northern towns in the eighth century, as well as in Tuscany.

The evolution of Italy was, then, very different from that of the Frankish kingdom: the Byzantine centres of the Adriatic stimulated a renaissance of urban civilization based on the prosperity of traders, boatmen and craftsmen. Pavia, the seat of the court, became an important consumer centre, trading with Cremona, Piacenza, Milan and Venice. In the towns building increased. From the time of king Liutprand, the *magistri commacini* acquired a privileged position in the Lombard economy: as building entrepreneurs, they contracted with their clients, paid their workmen by the day, moved round all over the kingdom and signed their works – for instance, Master Ursus set his name on the *ciborium* of San Giorgio di Valpolicella. Churches and monasteries were built in great numbers; those at Pavia were ever dedicated to saints honoured at this time by the Greeks, for example St Eusebius, St Agatha, St Nicholas, St Michael, etc. It is perhaps significant that in the middle of the eighth century Paul the Deacon went to Pavia to learn Greek from a 'Roman', the teacher Flavianus. Among buildings of the seventh and eighth centuries we may note particularly the 'hospitals' or *xenodochia* founded in the northern towns and Tuscany, notably at Pavia and Lucca, to welcome pilgrims and travellers, who flocked to Rome in great numbers: this phenomenon also gives evidence that land traffic was reviving.

We have startling proof of the recovery of Lombardy and of the links between Lombardy and Byzantium in the fact that in 725 king Liutprand possessed the diplomatic and material means to enable him to carry off from Sardinia, which was Byzantine but in the process of yielding to the attacks of the Saracens, the relics of St Augustine, in whose honour he built the church of San Pietro in Ciel d'Oro at Pavia.

It therefore seems fairly certain that it was the Carolingian conquest which drew Lombard Italy away from the Mediterranean economic region. It contributed to making her less receptive to the Byzantine influences near at hand. It linked her more decisively with the economy of the continent, and, politically, it led to her incorporation within the framework of the empire, while reinforcing latent tendencies towards the establishment of a feudal system. No text is more revealing of the general deterioration of the living conditions of the people than an inquiry conducted in Istria in 804: as a result of popular pressure, imperial *missi* heard grievances of the patriarch of Grado and 172 'captains' representing each of the cities and boroughs, who compared the burdens imposed on them to those they had borne 'in the time of the Greeks'. The forests where wood-cutting rights might be exercised had been confiscated, horses and cattle requisitioned, lands had been seized for settlements of slaves who cultivated them on the duke's behalf, the inhabitants had lost their legal rights, they were forcibly conscripted into the army with their serfs, and their freemen were taken from them; they had to endure forced labour on river ships, and on sea voyages to Venice, Ravenna and Dalmatia; their freedom to fish in the sea was restricted and they were obliged to build palaces and houses for the duke and his retinue. The situation was so serious that men were prepared to leave their homes in order to reach areas under the control of Byzantine authorities. Even if matters had not come to such a pass in other regions, one cannot fail to note in the attitude of the Carolingians a total lack of comprehension of the economy and institutions of Italy.

These thoughts on the situation in Italy at the beginning of the Carolingian period bring us to a question which is hotly disputed by historians, that is, whether or not there was an economic revival in the time of Charlemagne, corresponding to the intellectual, literary and artistic renaissance.

Henri Pirenne, in his well-known thesis, lays great stress on a contrast which he saw between the Merovingian era as the successor of Rome, and the Carolingian period, marked by total recession. Alfons Dopsch has maintained the opposite viewpoint and has undertaken to rehabilitate the Carolingians and the efforts of the man who attempted to restore the western Roman empire. More recently, Jean Lombard has put forward the paradoxical theory that the Arab conquest, far from cutting the west off catastrophically from the Mediterranean world, enabled it to revive, thanks to the miracle of Moslem gold. None of these theses pays enough attention to the sequence and changing spectrum of events, for the situation in the middle of the eighth century has little in common with that of the first half of the ninth, and still less with that of the tenth. Insufficient interest has also been taken in the fundamental differences in development between the various parts of the empire.

If, as has been claimed, Italy was the scene of considerable economic activity from the beginning of the eighth century, owing to her links with Byzantine areas, quite the opposite was the case with the rest of the Frankish empire, which did not achieve any kind of revival until at least three-quarters of a century later. Only in the last years of the eighth century, or more likely in the first years of the ninth, does a moderate economic recovery become apparent in Frankish lands, when the Carolingian state, after incorporating Frisia (which thereafter became converted to Christianity), pushed on southwards beyond Barcelona and as far as Venice, northwards to the heart of Schleswig, and eastwards as far as Slav and Avar territory. From then on, contacts were inevitably made with neighbouring societies and relative political stability helped the situation to improve in the reign of Louis the Pious; this progress was maintained until after the middle of the ninth century.

There are references here and there in the texts to merchants who are not solely purveyors to the court or the abbeys, as was formerly supposed to be the invariable rule, since they were called upon to make independent contributions to the Norman tributes. Those of Verdun, following their traditions, continued to traffic in slaves bound ultimately for Spain. In 811, Charlemagne restored the ancient lighthouse at Boulogne; Quentovic, at the mouth of the Canche, and Duurstede on the Meuse delta, both expanded thanks to their contacts with England, which became fairly extensive.

At Rouen, in April 841, Charles the Bald requisitioned twenty-eight merchant ships from the mouth of the Seine to transport his army to the gates of Paris; in the following September, Lothair requisitioned twenty ships at Saint-Denis so that his troops could cross the Seine. The Annals of Fulda record that in the winter of 860, as the Adriatic was frozen over, traders arriving at Venice by boat had to use horses and wagons to transport their goods. The Alpine passes, notably that of Mont Cenis, were put in order. Roads were repaired and bridges rebuilt, some of them in stone, making wagon traffic possible again. The texts mention a large number of toll-taxes: *rotagium*, on wheeled vehicles; *pulveraticum*, on carriage by land; *pontaticum*, at bridge-crossings; *portaticum* or *portus*, ferry toll; *cespitaticum* or *ripaticum*, mooring fee; *raffica* in the Mediterranean, and *mute* (*Maute*) on the rivers of Germany.

The tenants of Saint-Germain-des-Prés continued to act as carriers for the abbey to Angers, Blois, Orléans, Troyes and Quentovic, and we know that at the end of the eighth century they were exempt from tolls at Amiens, Duurstede and Maastricht. These lists of places clearly show that the river routes were still the main thoroughfares for all traffic. The Po, the Rhône and the Saône, the Loire, the Seine, the Somme, the Scheldt, the Meuse, the Moselle, the Rhine, the Main and the Danube were all used for freight, apparently involving quite large numbers of boats; in the first half of the ninth century, towns and *portus* came to life along their banks. The affluence of Paris, 'divitias regum, emporium populorum', was celebrated. Her trade in the wines of the Ile-de-France, Burgundy and Champagne, and in grain provides corroboration that the economy was essentially linked to agricultural production. Salt from the bay of Bourgneuf and the Adriatic lagoons was also of great importance. Even at this early date, Frisian cloths from Artois and Flanders, no doubt woven in estate workshops, anticipate the remarkable role that textiles from this region played in later centuries; abbeys such as Saint-Wandrille or Ferrières-en-Gâtinais obtained their monks' clothes from this region.

The products of Carolingian industry, notably weapons and jewels, as well as coins, have been found in the north, beyond the frontier, in excavations at the busy city of Haithabu on the Schlei, at the base of the Danish peninsula;

25 Ninth-century bracteates, probably struck at Haithabu.

41

we also learn from capitularies that barter-posts were set up on the eastern frontiers for dealings with neighbouring Slav and Avar peoples.

Further evidence of the increase in wealth is provided by texts which describe a noble emulation in the building or embellishment of cathedrals and abbey churches, and the palace of Aix-la-Chapelle itself.

On the border between the Carolingian and Byzantine empires, Venice (Rialto and Torcello) continued its commercial role: in 829, the will of a magnate, a great landowner, mentions an important legacy of 1,200 pounds to be drawn from sums which he had invested in maritime trade in accordance with a contract system, to which the *Pactum Lotharii* makes another reference in 840, when laying down the procedure to be followed in case of dispute. Luxury goods from the east reached the west by way of Venice, especially the textiles, of which some examples have survived among church treasures; in many cases they made their way into the empire via Pavia, which was still a great market. It was at Pavia that, on the occasion of the baptism of the emperor Lothair's daughter in 839, the archbishop of Ravenna obtained a gold cloth at the fantastic price of 500 gold *solidi*, which Agnellus, the official historian of the church of Ravenna, found very remarkable.

It would be a mistake, however, to lay too much stress on the commercial activities of the Carolingian era, for land undoubtedly remained the real source of wealth. The great were what they were only through the importance of the produce of the estates which they owned; practically the whole population lived by agricultural labour.

Whereas hardly anything is known of the true situation in earlier periods, round about 800 we have a few hazy glimpses of rural life, at any rate in certain favoured areas. We owe them mainly to the famous capitulary *De villis*, which consists of instructions sent by the emperor for the administration of his own

26 The palatine chapel of Aix-la-Chapelle, built under Charlemagne and consecrated in 806; represented here in a panel of the emperor's reliquary (end of the twelfth century).

27 Silk textile from Syria or Egypt, found in the tomb of Charlemagne, showing a charioteer in the Hippodrome.

estates, together with a few concrete descriptions of fiscal lands. Our knowledge is filled out by a few inventories of church property in France, northern Italy and Germany – the polyptychs. These documents come right in the middle of a period of great obscurity as regards the rural economy, lasting until the twelfth century. They have been carefully scrutinized by historians and have yielded precious information, although they have given us more insight into the judicial system than into agriculture.

The royal estates, like those of the abbeys and no doubt the aristocracy, were formed – at any rate in the region between the Loire and the Rhine – from *villae*. These usually comprised two distinct parts. The first, the *mansus indominicatus* or manorial demesne, consisted of land which the lord reserved for his own use (fields, vineyards, meadows, orchards and gardens), as well as a large part of the woods and waste land; it included the master's house, the usual outbuildings (barns, sheds, stables, various storehouses and cellars), and huts provided for the *familia*, the slaves (*mancipia*) who had the task of maintaining the house and cultivating the land within the demesne. The second part of the estate was made up of *mansi* or holdings worked by the master's dependants, that is, parcels of land which had been made over to them, together with a family dwelling. In theory the 'manse' was a one-family working unit, and it was also the unit on which the calculations of the estate and ultimately of central and local government were based.

From the beginning of the ninth century, however, there is evidence of considerable variation in the sizes of manses on the same estate (they ranged from 5 to 40 hectares), as well as in the obligations and duties required of them. The legal status of the manses, and their origins, were also marked by the same diversity. Among them there were manses called *serviles*, made up of rather mean parcels of land, cut off from the lord's demesne and given to slaves (*servi*) whose labour was required on the demesne throughout the year, while the women were often allotted the tasks of grain-milling, or cloth-weaving in the manorial workshops. Other manses were called free, *ingenuiles*; these were worked by freemen, perhaps small private landowners who had thought it best to put themselves, their offspring and their property under the protection of a lay or ecclesiastical 'magnate'. In exchange for this protection, they had to pledge certain services to the master – forced labour with their yokes of oxen, or carriage or cartage of the manorial crops to granary, store, or woodshed, or even to the nearest market. Forced labour was generally done in teams under the direction of a steward or *villicus*. The lord's demesne was also sometimes divided up between the dependants for tillage, on condition that the produce, or part of it, was brought to the master's barn.

44

28 Typical plan for a monastery, with its annexes and notably its manorial workshops. Known as the 'plan of St Gall', this was sent to the abbey of St Gall *c.* 820.

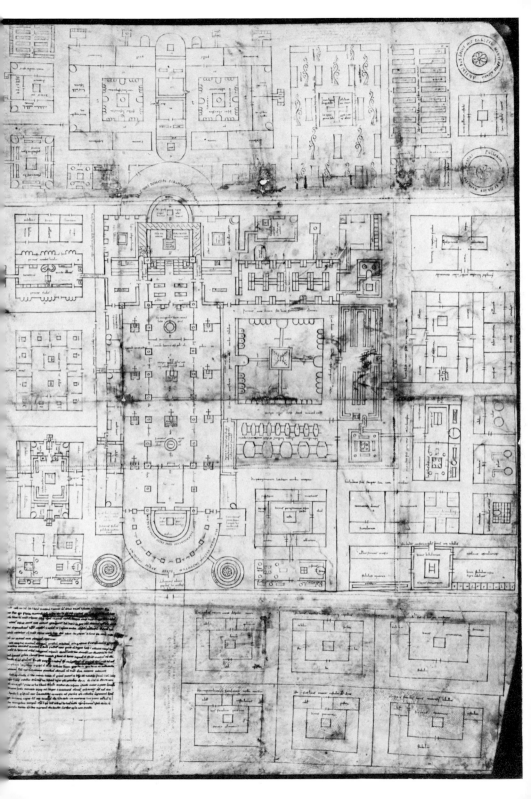

Apparently the system differed from *villa* to *villa*: sometimes all the manses were *serviles*, sometimes free manses were attached to the demesne in varying numbers or even other manses of an intermediate category. The demesne itself might be larger or smaller than the manses. Occasionally more distant plots, acquired in the course of time through purchases or inheritances, became linked with it. Sometimes the estate was all in one piece, sometimes its parcels were scattered and intermingled with those of other estates and with property belonging to freemen. As early as the Merovingian period landowners began the practice of establishing a place of worship, and earmarking land and revenue for its upkeep. The tenants' cottages, crowded round the master's house and the church, tended to form themselves into a village.

To contributions in kind (cereals, poultry, eggs, etc.) and the performance of duties, which were already fairly diverse, were added minor dues in cash. Thus we find that even slaves were able to obtain some money by selling off the surpluses, however small, from their own production.

For seasonal work some *villae* recruited additional temporary labour, rewarded by a minimal wage or by emoluments in the form of meals or benefits in kind; this labour was provided either by men working overtime, or by neighbouring freemen who were happy to supplement the meagre income from their land in this way.

As far as possible, the *villa* tried to be self-supporting. It always combined the production of cereals, the staple food of the time, with fairly extensive stock-raising in the demesne's woods, which were still considerable at this period when the villages were often closely hemmed in by forest. The stock was also commonly run on the fallow and waste ground which made up a large part of the land; the weed-burning system was customary, as well as intermittent working of fields which were cultivated until the soil was exhausted, and then abandoned for several years. Biennial or triennial rotation also seems to have been practised at this time, though we have no details of the methods used. The flocks and herds were relatively large, especially those of pigs, which lived half-wild in the forests, and of sheep; in fact the increase in the numbers of sheep was the basis for the cloth-trade, which was one of the most important sources of wealth in the medieval west.

During the Carolingian period water-mills were built; these had been known in ancient times, but were not very common until this time. It was a significant development in agricultural life; one of its important consequences was that menial labourers were freed from one of their most time-consuming tasks. Only in the eleventh century, however, did the use of the mill become general, and this brought about another radical change: the lord's mill –

together with the bakehouse, brewery and manorial church – gradually forced the peasants in the neighbourhood into the system that has been called 'banal seigniory'.

The *villa* tended to form an economic unit; its inhabitants did their best to produce clothes, shoes and pottery on the spot, and also agricultural tools – usually of wood, for iron was still used only rarely and almost entirely reserved for weapons. The great landowners who possessed many *villae* formed their various estates into a kind of super-unit, obtaining their wine here, their hemp there; and all the great abbeys of the north apparently pursued a deliberate policy of acquiring lands in the vine-growing regions so as to obtain the wine they lacked. The king made or ratified gifts to abbeys of this or that estate, whose specific function was to provide the monks with clothes, shoes, salt, or oil for lighting the church.

While at one time historians tended to emphasize this classical picture of the economy of the Carolingian estate, the opinion now is that it is unsafe to extrapolate to all properties in Gaul, or even to those in the north, information culled from the polyptychs of the great abbeys, especially the most famous of all, that of Saint-Germain-des-Prés, which was compiled by order of the abbot Irminon at the beginning of the ninth century. It is by no means certain that all the landowners administered their estates in the same way as the great abbeys of the areas round Paris and along the Rhine. Certain regions, such as Maine or Auvergne, do not appear to have known the *villa* system, with its manorial demesne and manses. Virtually throughout the Carolingian state, the *villa* was surrounded by a network of 'allodies' (freehold properties), that is, lands owned by *pagenses*, *rustici*, *mediocres*, who supported the public authorities and fell under the sway of the lords only when central government was usurped – especially in the administration of justice – with the rise of feudalism. In the southern parts of the empire in particular, at the end of the ninth century, dozens or sometimes even hundreds of free peasants took part in judicial inquiries.

This new line of historical research must not, however, be overemphasized, and the existence of occasionally very extensive estates in the Midi cannot be denied: at the end of the sixth century a great landowner, whose property was near the abbey of Moissac, gave the abbey no fewer than seventeen *villae* and kept five for himself, among which there was a single plot of several thousand hectares. The origin of many of these estates may perhaps be sought in the estates of the late empire, and they may be compared with those which existed in other parts of the Mediterranean world. The Carolingian *villa*, at least in certain cases, might well be a relic of the past in the process of transformation, rather than a phenomenon characteristic of the period. In northern Italy, the enlargement of the great monastic estates seems to have gone on from the seventh century to the ninth: this tendency may have gathered strength in the Carolingian period, but it had certainly started much earlier.

Even in areas where the *villa* had imposed its sway, the manses by no means remained unchanged in the hands of the tenants. As early as the beginning of the ninth century it was not unusual for a distinction to exist between the nature of the manses and the rank of their owners: *serviles* were held by free men, and *vice versa*, which had the incidental effect of confusing the various classes of dependants and levelling their legal status. Some tenants sold parts of their holding to others, with or without the lord's authorization; others were able to acquire allodial plots or lands belonging to another estate bordering on their own. The increase in population noted by the polyptychs also had the effect of destroying the primitive identity of the manse with its family working-unit: sometimes several families lived on the same manse, so that 'half-manses', or even 'quarter-manses', became common, to the point where the 'manse' came to mean simply a unit of agrarian measurement, having no direct link with the way it was worked.

The self-sufficiency of the estates should also not be overemphasized, as has been done in the past: the Carolingian economy was not entirely home-spun. The fact that a cash rent was paid for every dependent homestead is enough to show that money played some part in affairs, even at the lowest level of the social scale. The texts also mention markets, even in the villages, in Aquitaine as well as in northern Gaul and Germany. A hagiographical narrative of Fleury-sur-Loire, dating from the middle of the ninth century, speaks of a weekly market attended by peasants from the villages round about, and describes the scene for us. These markets, which were exceptional under Pepin and Charlemagne, seem to have become more widespread towards the middle of the ninth century and in the following century. Outside the regular markets, there were transactions enabling abbeys, and no doubt also many other large landowners, to acquire the commodities they needed. The texts mention 'abbey purveyors' who looked after certain supplies. Other abbeys sold the surpluses from their vineyards far and wide. There were also *officine* attached to abbeys, some of whom must have sold the various products of the abbeys. In the monastic borough of Saint-Riquier, there were artisans grouped by whole streets according to trade (blacksmiths, shield-makers, shoemakers, carders, fullers, furriers, etc.); they evidently carried on a fair amount of business, both on behalf of the abbey and on their own account. The same feature is found in northern Italy and along the Rhine.

The market was sometimes connected with a mint, which supplied it with currency. The first Carolingians had aimed to concentrate the minting in a very small number of places, but from the end of the ninth century, with regional fragmentation and the division of authority, the number of mints increased, benefiting the bishops in the first instance, and after them some of the magnates.

To keep level with the population explosion, which is indicated by the overcrowding of manses at the beginning of the ninth century, more land was cleared in central Gaul as well as in eastern areas, where inroads were made on the territory of Germanic and Slav tribes. Here the Carolingian revival was certainly most marked and most prolonged. In south and east Germany it continued until the very end of the ninth century, up to the Hungarian invasions; it was quickly renewed from the middle of the tenth century onwards, when the second restoration of the empire took place with Otto the Great.

On the other hand, in the south and west of Carolingian Europe the benefits of the revival were already in jeopardy a little before the middle of the ninth century, and definitely lost in the last quarter of the century, which saw the complete economic collapse of all that had been essential to the Frankish empire, under the double onslaught of two maritime powers, the Saracens from the Mediterranean, and the Vikings from Scandinavia.

THE ECONOMIC COLLAPSE OF THE FRANKISH WEST

Charlemagne had hoped to contain the territorial ambitions of the Umayyad emirs of Córdoba by establishing a strong Spanish frontier against them, and by making an alliance with the distant Caliph of Baghdad, Harun al-Rashid, while at the same time lamenting, according to the Monk of St Gall, that a real 'gulf' divided their states. The northern and eastern frontiers were also settled, and strongly fortified against the Danes. But it was from the sea that the danger came. Time after time, from the North Sea to the Mediterranean, it was found that the initiative belonged not to the rulers, the kings of Denmark and Norway or the emirs of Córdoba or Kairawan, but to bands of warriors and pirates, who succeeded in plundering the wealth of the Frankish empire.

It was fortunate that the Arabs did not attack directly. With its obvious maritime limitations, the west could have done little against the Fatimids of Egypt or the Aghlabids of Tunisia; even the Byzantine fleet was forced on to the defensive to protect the imperial possessions in southern Italy. The resources of the Carolingian state were small compared with those of the Caliphate of Córdoba, for instance, whose treasury was regularly financed by taxes rising

49

to more than six million gold dinars in the middle of the tenth century, when the Medina of Córdoba far outshone the 'capitals' of Aix or of Paris.

The first consequence of the Moslem offensive – the closing of the Tyrrhenian Sea – was much more ominous for the west than the sixth- and seventh-century conquests. Moslem forces seized all the islands essential to navigation, from the Balearics to Crete (827), by way of Sardinia, Corsica, Malta and, most important of all, Sicily, which was wrested from Byzantium with some difficulty during the years 827–902. From then on every Christian coast was the target for destructive raids: Marseilles was pillaged in 838, Arles in 842, and Rome was sacked in 846. From 837, the Saracens involved themselves in rivalries among the Lombard princedoms of southern Italy, and snatched sovereignty over them from the *Basileus*. By the middle of the ninth century, the Frankish empire was completely cut off from the sea and from the Byzantine empire, whose largest central Mediterranean port, Bari, was occupied by the Arabs from 841 to 871.

At the end of the ninth century and at the beginning of the tenth, Marseilles, Aix, Arles, Fréjus and Genoa were abandoned, and their bishops took refuge in the interior, as did the archbishop of Embrun. The Moors settled in Campania, to the south of Salerno, and from this point fanned out all over the Apennines; about the same time, they established themselves near Saint-Tropez, where they presented a sufficiently severe threat to Byzantium for the Byzantine fleet to be sent out against them twice, in 932 and 941. They drove far into the interior, between the Rhône and the Alps, cutting the land routes between France and Italy: they ransacked the abbey of Novalaise on Mont Cenis, which the monks apparently abandoned for nearly three-quarters of a century; they brought terror to St Gall in 939, and they held up Mayeul, the abbot of Cluny, on the Great St Bernard pass in 972. Destitution followed in their wake. When the countryside was later reoccupied, the pattern of settlement was no longer the same: the villages left their traditional sites and perched on the hilltops. The same situation existed in Italy, where many ancient cities which had survived the great crisis of the sixth century, such as the metropolis of Luni, the capital of Lunigiana, and Civitavecchia (*Centumcellae*), Cumes, etc., disappeared at this time.

The state of affairs which confronted the Frankish empire (or what remained of it) in the western and northern areas was even more serious, in view of a terrifying new phase of the expansion of the Scandinavian peoples. Charlemagne had hoped to defend the empire against them by fortifying the frontier. In the past regular streams of 'barbarian' tribes, from the Cimbri and the Teutons to the Burgundians and the Lombards, had come from Scandinavia

29 Ornamental hilts of swords found in a bog in Denmark and possibly of Frankish origin, dating from the earliest part of the Migration Period.

30 Interior of an early royal tomb under a tumulus at Kivik, in southern Sweden.

to the continental mainland, but this time the danger to the empire came exclusively from the sea – though it must be emphasized that the empire was not alone in being threatened.

The Eruli (Heruli), Jutes and Angles had already shown the way; in the last years of the eighth century the Norwegians started to colonize Iceland, to establish themselves in force in Ireland, and to penetrate into northern Britain in large numbers.

The equilibrium of the Frankish kingdom was even more seriously menaced by the Danish threat from the interior than by the danger from Norway. The Danish king had requited Charlemagne's land attacks in 810 by plundering Frisia, the centre of Frankish trade, and perhaps advancing even further. Clearly the emperor feared the worst, since in that year he had a fleet built by his son Louis at the mouths of the Loire and the Garonne, and the following year he himself fortified the Rhine delta. These efforts were followed up by individual initiatives: around 820 the first skirmishes began. A fleet of Northmen attempted a landing in Flanders and at the Seine estuary, and then destroyed various settlements to the south of the Loire such as Noirmoutier and Bouin, which were centres for the manufacture of salt. These areas subsequently continued as the principal target of the Northmen's raids.

From 834 the Danish fleet, which grew with each successive expedition, evidently had complete supremacy in the North Sea and the Channel, if not the Atlantic, at the same time that the Saracens, as we have seen, were operating in the Mediterranean area. The efforts of the Danes were directed alternately towards the continent and England. Plunder was the essential, if not the sole, object: only the ports, the main economic centres, and the salt-works were affected. Every year from 834 to 837 Duurstede, the principal port for Frisian trade, was pillaged, as well as neighbouring ports, and also the island of Noirmoutier and the Thames estuary. Rouen was taken in 841, Quentovic (the chief Frankish port) and London in 842, Nantes was sacked in 843, Paris in 845, Bordeaux in 848.

In 841, the emperor Lothair ceded some Frisian territory and the Isle of Walcheren to the 'Normans', and a Norman duchy was established in the region of the Rhine delta, including within it the town of Duurstede. The main outlet of the empire was thus in the hands of the northerners, and this accounts for the discovery in Scandinavian hoards of certain coins from the Rhine and Meuse, to the almost complete exclusion of those of all other Frankish territories.

About 850, after an internal crisis in Denmark, the Vikings stepped up their raids and set to work in a more systematic fashion. From the mouths of the

Thames, the Scheldt, the Seine and the Loire, they pillaged the hinterland, ravaging and plundering every place of any economic importance: the silver-mining centre of Melle in Poitou (out of 956 pieces of French origin in a treasure-hoard found in Cuerdale in Lancashire there were 565 pieces minted at Melle), Ghent, Rouen, Orléans, Toulouse, etc. The abbeys (Saint-Martin in Tours, Saint-Germain-des-Prés, Saint-Benoît in Fleury-sur-Loire, etc.), with their treasuries and store-houses, offered tempting booty, and these too were pillaged.

From 866 onwards the Northmen undertook the systematic conquest of England: within twelve years they had seized the whole of the island to the north and east of a line from London to Chester. Successive expeditions set

31 The most famous Norse ship of the Viking period. Found at Oseberg in 1903, it had been used as a royal tomb around 800; thanks to the objects found on board, we can, to a large extent, reconstruct the Scandinavian civilization of that period.

out from the Frankish coast across an exhausted, ravaged country, where towns, abbeys and imperial palaces were successively burnt, including even Aix-la-Chapelle. The Northmen settled permanently in camps, using these as bases for raids, the dates of which are difficult to establish. Fortifications were built round the towns and monasteries, in which the country people sought refuge. New cities were created in this way since after the invasions the people did not resume their former patterns of settlement. It must have been increasingly difficult to take up the threads of life again after each expedition; the kings paid tribute to the pirates as a ransom for this or that region, which contributed to the financial ruin of the country. Taking advantage of growing anarchy, the Bretons and the Gascons withdrew to the limits of civilization on the frontiers of the kingdom. The Northmen finally began to form permanent settlements in the Low Countries, and in what became 'Normandy'; they also settled in England, in the Danelaw to which king Alfred managed to confine them.

The repulse of the Northmen at the siege of Paris in 885 marks a turning-point in the people's resistance: from then on many encounters turned out to the advantage of the Franks. In 892 the country was in such a devastated condition and experiencing a famine so serious that, after twenty years of military occupation, the Northmen decided to abandon Gaul, which was now greatly weakened. They returned in 896, but were decimated in battle. At the same time they had become progressively civilized by contact with the countries they had plundered, and to some extent lost their bite: conversion followed shortly, as well as official recognition of their settlements in the 'Duchy of Normandy'. Under their energetic administration, and thanks to their economic contacts with England, this region had a new lease of life from the middle of the tenth century onwards.

In the rest of the kingdom, and as far away as Christian and Moslem Spain, the Northmen continued to make sporadic forays, which finally ceased only when the duke of Brittany, Alain Barbetorte, expelled them from Armorica and the Nantes district in 936.

At the end of this long period of crisis, the economy was in a state of collapse: ports such as Duurstede and Quentovic were destroyed, never to recover; trade was at a standstill; there was no circulation of coinage; villages were razed to the ground; monasteries were in ruins; there was serious depopulation. Such was the situation at the beginning of the tenth century, in the north and west as a result of the Viking attacks, and in the Mediterranean south following those of the Saracens and occasionally also of the Northmen, who sometimes managed to pass beyond the Pillars of Hercules.

In studying medieval economic history, one must not neglect the problems posed by the expansion into eastern Europe of a third Scandinavian people, the Swedes. During the period from the ninth to the eleventh centuries they established a direct link between the east and the west, behind the back, as it were, of the Frankish and Ottonian states, and this actually contributed further to the isolation of western Europe from eastern countries. East met west at the frontier town of Haithabu on the Schlei: in the middle of the ninth century this was a place of considerable economic importance, and excavations have revealed oriental, Carolingian and Anglo-Saxon objects. But it appears that western merchants scarcely had access to Birka, which was another busy commercial centre in Sweden itself, on Lake Mälar. More than ever, large-scale trade slipped through the fingers of the Franks, who were already cut off from the east by the activities of the Saracens in the Mediterranean.

The Swedish expansion presents the historian with problems which are difficult to solve on the basis of the evidence at present available. Taking advantage of the vacuum created in eastern Europe by the eclipse of the Avar kingdom, Swedish bands originating in the remotest parts of the Gulf of Finland spread over the European land-mass separating the Baltic from the Black Sea. From Lake Ladoga, and from Pskov and Novgorod, where they settled before the middle of the ninth century, they worked their way along the great rivers, in particular the Dnieper and the Volga, towards Kiev and

32 'Block houses' in the excavated north Russian trading station of Staraya Ladoga.

the Caspian Sea. In 860 they appeared at the walls of Constantinople with the name of 'Varangians', and here they finally provided an imperial guard; they colonized Kiev, at the centre of Slav territory, which they built into a powerful princedom; eventually at the beginning of the tenth century other bands made their way as far as the Iranian borders of Turkestan.

The Varangians were above all warriors and plunderers; but they were also merchants, and they roved over eastern Europe in a zone indicated by more than a thousand treasure-hoards. These hoards, which extend from the Scandinavian peninsula and islands to the Russian steppe, passing through Pomerania and the Baltic countries, constitute one of the enigmas of economic history. Side by side with Abbasid gold bezants and gold dinars, about 100,000 silver dirhems have been found. Three-quarters of these had been minted in the Samanid princedom of northern and eastern Iran, which broke away from the Caliphate and remained faithful to the silver mono-metallic currency of the ancient Sassanids. Two-thirds date from the first half of the tenth century, the others from the last quarter of the ninth or the third quarter of the tenth. Perhaps they were the spoils of foraging raids, similar to those which brought the Danes to western Europe: and in fact the largest hoards have been discovered in the islands, pirate-lairs like Gotland, Oland, Bornholm, or the Aalands, not in the trading centres like Haithabu or Birka. Or should we perhaps see them as evidence of a large-scale international trade conducted by the Varangians on behalf of the Swedes, as some historians have thought? The objection to this second theory is that such a movement could not have originated in the Scandinavian peninsula, which had practically nothing to offer in exchange for money: owners of the hoards had little idea of what to do with surplus coins since they could only think of burying them.

Apart from being the proceeds of the sale of furs from the north and particularly from Russia, the money must surely have been spoil from raids made by pirates among the Slav population, augmented by the consequent sale of large numbers of slaves in the rich markets of Samarkand, Bukhara, Merv, etc., which were stopping-places for caravans on the great silk route between the Chinese and Arab worlds. At any rate we know from a reliable source that in 922 Swedish slave-traders were very active on the shores of the Caspian; we know too that in 944 the 'Rus' went on a foraging raid as far as Berda'a in Azerbaijan. These pirate operations, coupled with those of the Turko-Mongolian tribes on the borders of the Arab-Iranian world, had a disastrous effect on the economy of this region and necessitated a redirection of communications with the Far East, which for a long period had to use the sea route via the Indian Ocean and the Red Sea.

The view of some historians that the Swedes must have been instrumental in injecting Arabian gold into the economically depressed west thus seems to be unfounded. Other evidence also points in the same direction: no Arab coins of this period have been found in western Europe; as has been said, gold practically disappeared from the Frankish empire, and the texts are silent on the subject. To sum up, the most immediate effect of the Swedish expansion was to contribute to the further isolation of the west from the east.

During the same period, the Bulgars were pressing on the northern frontiers of the Byzantine empire. Once they succeeded in severing the great intercontinental land route, this also contributed to the isolation of Byzantium from the Germanic countries. The Germanic peoples were themselves grappling with the most terrible invasion they were forced to endure, that of another people from the steppe, the Hungarians.

The Hungarians crossed the Carpathians in 895, and with them a final scourge reached the Carolingian empire, dealing the economy its death blow. The eastern part, which until then had escaped relatively lightly, was completely overrun by these marauding horsemen, and northern Italy was devastated; everywhere it was the fields that were laid waste rather than the towns, against which the bands rarely risked an attack. As the booty began to give out, the raids became more and more far-ranging, reaching Bremen in 915, Pavia in 924, Orléans in 937, and Otranto in 947. Throughout Germany and Italy castles were built as a defence against the invaders, as they had been built in the west against the Northmen, and the abbeys surrounded themselves with fortifications. It was only in 955 that Otto the Great succeeded in gaining a victory over the Hungarians at the Lechfeld near Augsburg, one of the decisive events in European history.

From the middle of the ninth century to the middle of the tenth, there was a total collapse of the European economy as a result of the Saracen, Viking and Hungarian attacks. Little by little a new world emerged from the general chaos, and from the systematic destruction of all that had made western and central Europe a going concern economically. It was, however, a very different world from its forerunner, which still had links with ancient Rome. The process of recovery lasted for two centuries, from the middle of the tenth century to the middle of the twelfth, before the remarkable flowering of the classical Middle Ages could come about.

# II THE CLASSICAL MIDDLE AGES

Western Europe had been the region most seriously affected by the invasions of the ninth and tenth centuries: it was very slow to recover its human strength and its economic impetus. France in particular was thrown back on its own resources. Germany suffered much less from the invasions: with a few exceptions, the bands of Northmen, coming up against a relatively strong power, scarcely advanced beyond the lower Rhine. The Saracens, too, were satisfied with a few strongholds in the Alpine regions. Thus until about 900, Germany continued to live within the political, institutional and economic framework of the Carolingian empire. Then the Hungarians began their catastrophic raids.

In Germany the great estates resisted for longer than in other areas: the feudal system which they embodied even went on gathering strength up to the twelfth or thirteenth century, and, when they eventually succumbed, they had been undermined by the schemings of imperial or manorial agents, the *ministeriales*, who tried to encroach upon their masters' rights and infiltrate the system. Internal colonization continued in Bavaria, Hesse and Saxony. After the crisis had passed, agriculture slowly resumed its development; the greatest progress took place in the regions between the Saale and the Elbe, and well beyond the Elbe, in the direction of the Oder, in moorland and woodland inhabited by Slav and partly Baltic tribes. The growth of agriculture made possible an expansion of the marks (border states) of Misnia (Meissen) and Lusatia (Lausitz), and pioneers flowing in from the whole of Germany, including the western areas, provide evidence of a continuing increase in population. The effects of this population explosion were felt from one end of the eastern frontier to the other, from the coasts of the Baltic to the hills of Bohemia, and from the Danubian plain to the limits of Carinthia and Carniola, near the Mediterranean. It was one of the most important features of German political and economic history throughout the Middle Ages.

The Hungarian raids utterly devastated the countryside, but, on the whole, they spared the towns. Reconstruction was therefore infinitely easier in Germany than in the western kingdom after the havoc wrought by the Northmen, and it proceeded along the lines of the economy and institutions of the Carolingian state. From the middle of the tenth century the region resumed its advance, and the development was swifter and more effective here than elsewhere; under the Ottonian dynasty it led to what has been called the German golden age of the early Middle Ages.

As early as 918, Conrad I had granted a market to Würzburg, and subsequently the Ottos were anxious to build up trading centres in most of the important towns: twenty-nine acts granting market concessions have come down to us, mainly dating from the third quarter of the tenth century. New rights were established: in 946, when a market was set up for two estates of the abbey of Corvey, it was proclaimed that the *pax* would protect it, and this affirmation of peace – foreshadowing the 'Peace of God' – is significant. Similarly, when the emperor built a market at Bremen in 965, he declared that he would take under his protection (*patrocinium*) the merchants who came there, who stayed there or who returned there.

These markets were often established with an eye to long-distance trade. The market of Rorschach, granted in 967 to the abbey of St Gall, was provided expressly to facilitate communications with Italy and Rome; the market of Worms was founded in 947 to receive Frisian craftsmen; that of Bremen existed for the purpose of trade with Scandinavia. A charter was granted by Otto the Great to the corporation of traders in Tiel, the great port of the Waal, which specialized in transactions between England and the Rhineland; the document has not come down to us, but we know of it from a chronicler of Metz who complained bitterly that these men judged according to their own law and not according to the usual customs. This is the first evidence of a merchant guild and of the famous merchant law which played a vital role in the development of the medieval market-towns.

To supply the markets with currency, the emperor established mints, or rather he granted minting rights to a number of sees and abbeys – Corvey, Osnabrück, Magdeburg, Herford, etc. – without in any way relaxing imperial control over the manufacture of coins. This development was made possible by the exploitation of rich deposits of metal (silver and Harz copper) at Rammelsberg in the Harz mountains and in the Goslar region.

The most economically active part of the Ottonian empire, the area between the Rhine and the Meuse, including Verdun, Mainz and Cologne, directed its activities on the whole towards the North Sea countries. But as the central and eastern areas were stabilized and converted to Christianity, there was a distinct realignment of trade towards Italy, and beyond, to the Mediterranean and Byzantium. This trend fitted in very well with the political ideology of Otto the Great, who had himself crowned king of the Lombards at Pavia, and received the imperial crown at Rome in 961. The Ottos managed to achieve much more than Charlemagne's ephemeral and incomplete 'revival' of the empire: they brought about a real restoration of the western Roman empire, which lasted for half a century, despite internal disturbances and the increased prestige of the Greek eastern empire at this time. Otto married his son Otto II to the famous Theophano, daughter of the *Basileus* Romanus II; Otto II went on campaigns as far as Calabria and Apulia, before his death at Rome; Otto III settled in the palace of Ravenna where, under the influence of his mother, he lived more like a Byzantine ruler than a Roman or German, and when he died he too was about to marry a Greek princess, brought back to him by his ambassador from Constantinople. The interest of this dynasty was centred on the Mediterranean: in 956 Otto I sent an ambassador to the court of the Caliph of Córdoba; ambassadors visited Constantinople, and in 999 Otto III went incognito to Venice to negotiate secretly with the Doge.

It is not surprising that the eminent scholar Gerbert went to Spain to study Arabian mathematics at this time; later he became archbishop of Rheims, was subsequently appointed by the emperor to the see of Ravenna, and finally to the supreme pontificate at Rome. Arab travellers made their way all over the empire, and one of them, Ibrahim al-Tartushi, reported that oriental coins were in circulation at Mainz, and that Indian spices were on sale in the market there.

In the second half of the tenth century – or more precisely, around the year 1000 – European civilization began to take on some kind of shape, and there was a new air of stability, covering political relations as well as economic life. The theories of the Romantic period which allege that people at this time suffered terrors engendered by fear of the end of the world must be rejected. On the contrary, it was a time when the storms which had rocked the world were thought to be abating.

In Poland, Mieszko was baptized in 966 and in the year 1000 Otto III, who made a pilgrimage to the tomb of St Adalbert at Gniezno, granted the ancient title of 'friend and ally of the Roman people' to Boleslav the Bold. In 1025 Boleslav took the title of king, and his successor Mieszko II married the niece of the emperor. In Hungary prince Vajk, who took the name of Stephen (and was later canonized St Stephen), is supposed, as a boy, to have been baptized by St Adalbert. Otto III was his godfather and pope Sylvester II sent him a royal crown.

As recent excavations have shown, Polish agriculture and craftsmanship, which had started to make progress in the first half of the tenth century, underwent a rapid development at this time, and markets were established. In the second half of the century Polish currency made its appearance. Then urban life blossomed forth with the foundation and expansion of Poznań, Szczecin, Gdańsk, Wrocław, Opole and Łęczyca.

In Hungary, too, the barbarians from the steppe became civilized and the old Roman towns, which had long been abandoned, were reoccupied: Buda took the place of *Aquincum*, *Savaria* became Szombathely, and *Scarbantia* became Sopron, while Esztergom rose to the rank of metropolitan city.

In the kingdom of Bohemia, founded by Boleslav II in 995, Prague reached a striking level of development and an Arab traveller noted the importance of its market.

33 Bronze doors (mid-twelfth century) of the cathedral at Gniezno, the religious capital of medieval Poland. Eighteen bas-reliefs represent the life of St Adalbert of Prague, who died as a martyr in 997.

34 Ruins of the eleventh-century church at Sigtuna, one of the oldest and most important towns of medieval Sweden.

35 One of the earliest manors and fortified barns, built of wood, at Voss, Norway (thirteenth century).

36 Twelfth-century wooden church (*stavkirke*) at Torpo, Norway; shown here are the thirteenth-century Romanesque frescoes on the wooden vault in the centre of the present choir.

37 This door of the wooden church of Vågå, at Vågåmo, Norway, remains from an eleventh-century church retained in the seventeenth-century reconstruction.

In Scandinavia, the Danish king Harold Bluetooth was converted in 966, and the Norwegian king Olaf Trygvesson about 990. Otto I established a market at Bremen, as already noted, to provide a commercial centre for the new community of northern peoples, who were united by the union of what are called the five kingdoms under Cnut the Great (1014–35). The Scandinavians then turned their energies to opening up their own land: the primitive village, the *by*, was broken up into pioneer hamlets or 'torps'; it is estimated that from the ninth to the thirteenth century around 3,500 of these were established, 1,200 of them in Scania (Skåne). The first large town, Lund, was founded about the year 1000. Peaceful relations were established over a wide area; while English pilgrims reached Rome in large numbers, the last Anglo-Saxon kings, and Cnut himself, copied the titles of the Byzantine emperors in their charters: 'basileus Anglorum', 'totius Britanniae basileus', 'imperator a Christo' (from the 'Basileus ex Theo' of the Byzantines).

Byzantium was by no means inactive in eastern Europe, which was at this time in the process of being civilized. In 957 Olga, the princess of Kiev, went to Constantinople, and in 988 St Vladimir signed a treaty of friendship there – and was at the same time converted to Christianity. Otto III sent him an ambassador when he became 'friend of the Roman people' in 999. The Greek emperors made an effort to wear down the last invaders of the European frontiers of the empire, the Bulgars; they had their first successes in 972, and Bulgarian resistance finally came to an end under Basil II, the 'Bulgar-slayer', at the beginning of the eleventh century. There was thus a homogeneous political and cultural system stretching across the whole of Europe, through Germany, Poland, Hungary and Russia, and as far away as Byzantium and Turkestan. Raoul Glaber, the French chronicler of the middle of the eleventh century, gives evidence of it: at this time, he says (referring to the conversion of St Stephen around 1000), people began to go on pilgrimages by way of the land route across Hungary, because this had become safer than the sea route. Recent excavations conducted by Polish archaeologists at Opole in Silesia have revealed Arab coins, silks and other oriental fabrics, pearls from the east, Syrian and Rhenish glass, and Russian pottery, in a late tenth-century stratum. A chronicler tells us that when Otto III was received by Boleslav at Gniezno, two miles of the route along which the emperor passed were hung with baldaquins and samites, that is, precious silks from Baghdad and Syria.

It was therefore no accident that Otto the Great established his capital at Magdeburg, on the frontier of Saxony, and that he made it into a religious metropolis; he included the ancient Burg and the merchants' quarter within the walls, and built a new Jewish market in the town.

Nevertheless, it was not the land route across the Ottonian empire and its fringes which finally restored the great intercontinental link between east and west, but rather the rival sea route, and here Italy played an important part because of her geographical position. Although she had been almost equally strained by the raids and depredations of the Saracens, the Hungarians and occasionally also of the Northmen, Italy managed, in contrast to her neighbour France, to re-establish herself as a sea power. This was due in part to the soundness of her 'Roman' traditions, to her developed urban system and her network of roads which, on the whole, remained intact. It was due also to the survival of a class of merchants which had dwindled or disappeared in the course of the early Middle Ages elsewhere in the west. Above all, it was due to political circumstances; to the fact that at the two extremities of Italy maritime peoples found themselves strategically positioned where great political and economic powers came face to face. In the north, Venice, which remained in the Byzantine sphere of influence, provided an outlet to the sea and to the east for the Romano-Germanic empire. In the south, the ports of Apulia on the east coast and Campania and Calabria on the west were favourably situated as meeting-places for the Latin, Byzantine and Arab worlds.

*Venice*'s destiny as a sea power was finally ratified in the middle of the tenth century. When Otto I sent Liutfred, a rich merchant of Mainz, to Constantinople as his ambassador, it was from Venice that he set sail. The Doge's ban in 960 on the Venetians' taking letters and messages from the Lombards, Bavarians, Saxons and other Germanic peoples to Constantinople, reveals Venice's importance as an intermediary between the east, the plain of Lombardy and the regions on the other side of the Brenner Pass. Another piece of evidence, dating from 972, proves the existence of contacts with the 'infidels': at the request of the *Basileus*, who had thrown himself into the great Byzantine venture of winning back the Holy Land, the Doge prohibited the sale of arms and of wood for shipbuilding to the Saracens. In 992 Byzantium conferred a great favour on Venice, as a faithful 'subject' of the eastern empire, by granting the Venetians free access to Constantinople and a reduction in customs duty.

An official of the court of Pavia, writing at the beginning of the eleventh century but referring to the preceding period, emphasized the special character of the Venetian economy: the Venetians, he said, did not till, did not sow, did not plant vines; they were supplied with grain and wine from the ports of the Po. Venice was, in fact, the first city in the Middle Ages to live by trade alone. This in turn helped to give new life to the Po valley and to the market towns, such as Cremona, Piacenza and Pavia, scattered over it, which supplied her needs and received in exchange salt from her lagoons. There was a rapid river route by way of the Po: Liutprand reckoned that the journey from Pavia to Venice by boat, a distance of 250 miles by river and lagoon, took three days. Already the neighbouring regions, Venetia, Istria and Dalmatia, were turning towards the city that came to be called the 'queen of the Adriatic', and a little after the year 1000 the Doge added the title of duke of Dalmatia to his prerogatives.

In continental Italy the market of the northern capital, *Pavia*, was of great importance. It was dominated by Venice which supplied it with oriental silks and spices, though this trade was shared with the cities of southern Italy: Gaeta, Salerno and Amalfi. English merchants flocked to Pavia in large numbers to obtain embroidered fabrics and silks from Constantinople, which were copied in England under the name of 'opus anglicanum'. The market seems to have been admirably organized, with a system of currency, frontier customs-posts, and payments and dues made over to the royal officials who inspected it.

38 Silk fabric from Byzantium, ninth–tenth century.

*Milan*, too, was a fairly important market-town, and a charter of Otto I (952) gives us a picture of the 'public market'. Here we have the first evidence of a merchant class (*ordo negotiatorum*), which, together with the corporations of moneyers, may have survived from a very early period. An imperial charter of 968 speaks of the harbour at *Bergamo*, and the landing-stage for boats (*statio navium*) going to Venice, Comacchio and the Ferrara district. At *Brescia*, silk-culture made its appearance. The Arab al-Tartushi, accustomed to the bargaining of the middle-eastern souk, was surprised to see sales at fixed prices in the market at *Asti*, with price tickets attached to the goods. Finally *Rome*, the centre of pilgrimage, was naturally a centre of trade and exchange as well; at the end of the tenth century, prelates from the various parts of the Christian world were in the habit of going *ad limina*: many of them, like the abbots of Fleury-sur-Loire, must have taken back souvenirs for their churches. King Robert the Pious himself undertook the journey, and in the opposite direction Italian prelates loaded with presents visited their compatriot William of Volpiano, abbot of Saint-Bénigne of Dijon and Fécamp.

In southern Italy, *Gaeta* traded with Cairo from 973, and at this time merchants from *Salerno* visited Constantinople. *Naples* was praised by an Arab traveller in 977 for her fine fabrics. But according to the same traveller, Ibn-Hawqal, it was *Amalfi* which surpassed all other towns in its affluence and prosperity, and the monk Amatus of Monte Cassino called it 'a city rich in gold and cloth'. We know that the town was in regular communication with Constantinople: in 968 bishop Liutprand of Cremona, Otto the Great's ambassador to Nicephorus Phocas, saw that he was about to be deprived by Greek customs officers of some rich materials which he was taking back for his church, and protested vigorously for, he said, they were just the same as the fabrics 'the Venetian or Amalfi traders bring us'. The town's contacts with Cairo were sufficiently important for a pogrom to take place there in 996, as a reprisal for a disaster which befell the Arab fleet and which was blamed on the Byzantines: a hundred citizens of Amalfi, the only westerners mentioned in the texts, met their deaths, while the fonduk where they stored their goods was plundered. *Bari* was at this time the centre of Byzantine administration in southern Italy, and there were frequent contacts between its port and Constantinople; we know, for example, that Otto III's ambassadors landed there in 1001 while escorting the Greek princess he was to have married.

In short, all these southern towns were, together with Venice, outposts of the Byzantine economy. This accounts for the strong Byzantine influence on the Italian commercial and maritime institutions, and consequently on those of the whole western world. The contracts of *commenda*, *rogadia*, and *collegantia*, which came to regulate all the legal transactions of the Venetian merchants, as well as of Mediterranean Europe, are mentioned as early as 975, in an act by which a Doge's widow renounced the profits her husband had hoped to make out of his various business affairs; Greek prototypes for these contracts have been discovered, and they do not differ greatly from their Arab counterparts.

The *Tabulae amalphitanae* (of Amalfi) do no more than echo certain basic provisions of the 'maritime law of Rhodes' which was the foundation of maritime rights in the Christian Mediterranean. The 'lateen' or 'latine' (triangular) sail seems to have been derived from a sail which made its appearance in the Byzantine world in the ninth century. For their ships, the Italians followed types current in the Greek navy: the Italian galley took its name from the *galaia* (swordfish), and the *stolum* (flotilla) from *stolon*. Other words borrowed from Greek are those for hostelry (*xenodochium*), money-changers' table and money-changer (*trapeza*, *trapezista*), apothec or storehouse (*apotheca*), and policy (*apodixa*).

It is also worth noting the importance of words of Arab or Persian origin in the commercial and maritime vocabulary of Latin countries – though in many cases they did not make their appearance until much later. Some words which have also passed into English are: magazine (storehouse), bazaar, fondaco (fondego, fonda, fonduk, from Arabic *funduq*), arsenal, tariff, risk, cheque (Persian *shukuk*); weights and measures such as the cantar or quintal and the carat; names of fabrics such as cotton, muslin (from Mosul), organdie (from Urgench), damask, baldaquin (from Baghdad), gauze (from Gaza), taffeta, buckram, camlet, and so on; and other commodities such as alum, alcohol, sugar, rhubarb, artichoke, etc. Some authorities also attribute the first use of marine charts and navigation compasses to the east. The magnetic compass, known in China at the end of the eleventh century, appeared in Europe about 1190; up to the present, however, no connection has been established between the two, and some scholars are of the opinion that it was an independent European invention.

THE ECONOMIC ORGANIZATION OF THE BYZANTINE EAST

Whereas the reign of Justinian had encompassed the first golden age of Byzantium under the Macedonian dynasty, the tenth century marks the second. At this time Constantinople was, more than ever, the economic centre of the Mediterranean area. We gain a fairly detailed picture of its general organization from an important text, the *Book of the Prefect*, dating from the beginning of the tenth century (others date it from the middle of the century); it has been attributed to Leo VI. It appears that the economy was strictly controlled: each trade formed a corporation whose leaders were chosen by the 'eparch' or prefect. He inspected the shops, controlled purchasing, fixed prices, and pronounced sentence on those who contravened the regulations. The stocking, importation and export of goods were in the hands of the authorities. Entry into the corporations was subject to strict rules, and no one could engage in a trade which was the statutory province of another corporation. The members themselves saw to it that the regulations were observed, and remained loyal to one another: in most cases they acquired goods in common, brought them to the market and then their leaders divided them out in proportion to the capital invested by each man. Every morning, the leaders of the corporations reported to the prefect on the source and quality of the merchandise which had arrived, and subsequently the prices were fixed. The corn trade was virtually a state monopoly, both in the capital and in the ports of origin (such as Rodosto on the Black Sea), and the peasants were obliged to deliver their harvests to public agents who collected stocks in the state warehouses. This monopoly was the object of violent attacks by the great lay and ecclesiastical landowners, the *dunatoi*, who tried to put forward a liberal policy favourable to their own interests. At the same time they endeavoured to make a profit by selling off the assets of the small proprietors, or *penetés*.

The state reserved to itself the exploitation of the salt-marshes and mines, either administering them directly or on lease. The silk trade was subject to very strict control by the state at every stage, from the purchase of the raw silk, to spinning, weaving, the sale of silks, the manufacture and sale of silk clothing, and its export. Even where fabrics specially reserved for the *Basileus* himself were not concerned, silks were essential to the glamour and prestige of the empire, and the most valuable of them could not be exported.

Many foreigners went to Constantinople with their own merchandise, but there were severe restrictions on their entry, their place of residence, the length of their stay, the nature of their exports, and the taxes which they had to pay. We have already mentioned the presence of Venetians, Amalfians and other westerners in the capital. Syrians were also numerous, and at the end of the tenth century they had a mosque of their own; it was primarily through them and the Armenians that goods from the Middle and Far East reached the empire, while Russians and Khazars conducted transactions with the northern countries. Commercial treaties were made with several of these nations; apart from the treaty of 982 with Venice, we know of treaties made with Kiev in 907, 911 and 944, and with Aleppo in 969–70. This was one of the most important of its kind concluded so far during the Middle Ages: the *Basileus* and the emir divided up the customs duty of 10 per cent between them,

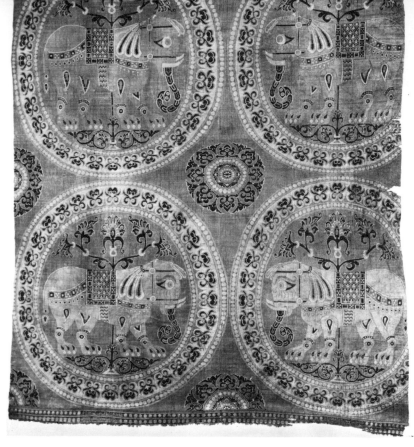

39 Byzantine silk shroud found in Charlemagne's tomb when it was opened in 1000 by Otto III.

according to the nature of the goods. Byzantine caravans making their way to Aleppo were announced to the emir's men; he had them escorted through his territory by his own guard, and was responsible for their safety.

Thessalonika, Cherson and Trebizond, and Antioch, were centres of great commercial activity, orientated respectively towards the Balkans, the Black Sea countries, and Syria. A silk industry was established in Greece, and we hear of a factory in the Peloponnese employing 3,000 workers.

The Byzantine fleet was at first the commercial and military equal of the Egyptian fleet in the Mediterranean and then surpassed it. As early as 921, the emperor Louis the Blind ratified, at the church of Arles in Provence, the Arlesians' right to collect tolls from Greeks and Jews at the town's harbour. In 924, after the destruction of the Arab fleet off Lemnos, the Moslem threat to

Byzantium diminished. In the second half of the century, the large islands of the eastern Mediterranean were reoccupied by the Greeks: Crete was retaken in 961 and Cyprus in 964. At this period a realignment of the two powers took place, when Nicephorus Phocas, John Tzimisces and Basil II resumed war on land, retaking Cilicia (965), northern Syria and Antioch (968–69), and Acre (975), and establishing a protectorate over Aleppo and Homs.

At the climax of her golden age, Byzantium stood guard over the great caravan routes bringing spices from the Far East and terminating at Aleppo and Antioch. The protectorate established over the Shahinshah's Armenia (whose capital Ani had its most brilliant period in the last third of the tenth century) and the liberation of the kingdoms of Georgia and Abkhazia (which also reached the peak of their development at the same time) resulted in Byzantine control of other routes from Central Asia, leading from India to Trebizond and the Black Sea. Finally, the close contacts cultivated with the Khazar khanate (on whose behalf the Byzantines built fortresses on the Volga and the Sea of Azov) brought the gateway to the routes from China via Turkestan under the control of the empire.

Constantinople was thus the principal centre of international trade at this time. Unprecedented luxury was displayed in the *Basileus'* palaces and churches, where gold and silver decorations, and ornaments of pearls and precious stones, were everywhere to be seen.

### THE ECONOMY OF THE ARAB STATES

In contrast with the Byzantine empire, which formed a homogeneous and centralized state surrounded by its satellites, the Moslem world was an agglomeration of nations of different races and cultures. It embraced principalities whose political interests were opposed to each other, and economic regions aligned in different groupings; in certain parts, heresies helped to drive a wedge between one area and another. Moreover, business was not confined to the Moslem Arabs. The Jews of Spain, the Gharb (Morocco) and Egypt traded in Europe and the Mediterranean region; the Near East and the Byzantine empire was the sphere of operations of a second group, the Melchites, Jacobites and Nestorians of Syria and Iraq; while the Zoroastrians of Iran looked to India and the countries of the Indian Ocean. Between them, these peoples controlled a sizeable proportion of big business.

In the central region of the empire, the economy was based almost exclusively on the gold dinar, while in its two wings, towards Iran in one direction and the Maghreb (the western Arab lands) in the other, the silver dirhem was predominant.

In Spain the Umayyad Caliphate finally became established in 929. In Egypt, the Fatimid schismatics gained power in 969 and the new dynasty extended its authority over the greater part of the Moslem Mediterranean. Even in the east the Caliph of Baghdad saw his power being whittled away at the hands of foreigners, while local dynasties established themselves at the fringes of his empire, on the frontiers of Turkish Asia, India, the Byzantine empire and the Arabian peninsula. The political disintegration accelerated still further in the course of the eleventh century, at the expense of the states which had been formed in the previous century: in Spain, North Africa and the Near East, the 'taifas' and the emirates were the Islamic counterpart of the duchies and the great feudal estates of post-Carolingian and post-Ottonian Christian Europe. But the main difference was that, in the Moslem world, each of these 'states' was established with a centre of wide-ranging influence as its nucleus, such as the Spanish ports (Almería, Valencia, Denia, etc.) or the caravan cities and great markets of North Africa, Syria and Central Asia: in an unstable political situation each of them retained a clear economic function. In fact, the whole complex was admirably constructed from the point of view of the economy, and men, goods and money circulated freely from the coasts of the Atlantic and the oases of the Sahara to the steppes of the Volga and Central Asia, and as far as East Africa and the north-eastern coasts of India.

Along with the Ottonian and Byzantine empires, the Arab world also enjoyed its period of greatest prosperity during the tenth century and the beginning of the eleventh. At this time the author of a treatise on 'The beauties of trade', Abu-al-Fadil, recommended merchants to engage in the profitable bulk trade in essential goods rather than in luxury articles, the problem being to buy cheaply in the places of production in order to sell dear in distant consumer-centres. Another author of the same period asserts that 100,000 camels (no doubt a grossly exaggerated figure) left Karamania every year with supplies of dates for the country areas of Iran.

Arab commerce extended over the whole of the then known world, and trade with China, Malaysia and India reached considerable proportions. The traditional route from the Indian Ocean towards the Mediterranean via the Gulf of Oman, the Persian Gulf, Mesopotamia and Syria developed to such a point that the customs-post of Siraf, on the Persian Gulf, brought in 253,000 gold dinars a year under al-Muktadir, and 316,000 in the second half of the tenth century. Business was so profitable that a merchant of Siraf was able to spend 30,000 gold dinars on decorating his house. But the Fatimids tried to develop another sea route, which had been used in ancient times, via the Yemen and the Red Sea. In consequence, Cairo and Alexandria built up a

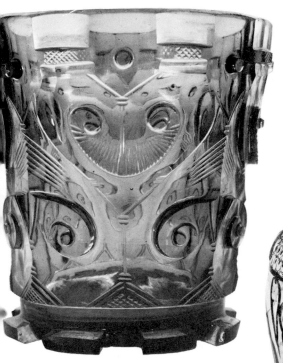

40 Fatimid rock crystal
beaker, *c.* 1000.

41 Mesopotamian lustre ware
of the tenth century.

42 Iranian cup of the ninth–
tenth century.

43 Al Medinat-al-Zahra, near Córdoba. Great hall of the palace of Abd-al-Rahman III (*c.* 947), during restoration. A great number of stucco fragments have already been put back into place, others await attention on the floor.

44 The Great Mosque of Córdoba. One of the doors of the west façade, corresponding to the enlargement carried out under Caliph Al-Hakam II (961–76), with sixteenth-century restoration.

45 The tower of gold (*Torre del oro*) at Seville, on the Guadalquivir port. This twelve-sided, crenellated tower, built *c.* 1220, is surmounted by a second tower and was formerly connected to the Alcazar by a wall.

thriving commercial life at this time, which was extremely profitable to the government since, as at Constantinople, it exercised strict control over the economy as a whole, and in particular over textiles, shipbuilding and trade; in the year 1050 there were 20,000 shops in Cairo.

The Arabs and Iranians advanced along the eastern coasts of Africa in search of slaves and wood for shipbuilding: vessels of tenth-century Persian design have recently been excavated in Tanzania, and fragments have also been found on the island of Pemba, to the north of Zanzibar.

The Maghreb was in a doubly favourable position since it had a dominating position on the Mediterranean and was also at the end of the Saharan trade routes; for once in its history it took advantage of this position to increase its wealth. Under the Zirids, Kairawan became a centre of international trade, while Sigilmassa in remote Tafilelt, which is just a heap of ruins today, was built as a desert metropolis to tap the gold brought by caravan from Mali and Ghana.

Moslem Spain at this period experienced its greatest prosperity. An undoubted improvement took place in agriculture, due to an irrigation system

which was admirably organized on the Syrian model, with dams, reservoirs, cisterns and chain-pumps (such as the great *noria* of Toledo described by al-Idrisi, which is reminiscent of the one at Hama). Canals were constructed from baked earth (*seguias*), and the waterways were regularly inspected, a practice which survived Moslem rule. Fruit and nut trees (figs, oranges, pomegranates, almonds) were cultivated in the *huertas*, while rice and sugar-cane were introduced in the Seville region; a great palm-grove was established at Elche; Spanish flax and saffron were exported all over the east. A silk industry was founded: 3,000 villages in the Jaén district, according to al-Himyari, and 600 in the Aljuparras, according to al-Idrisi, were devoted to silk-culture.

The Caliph had a monopoly in silk, kermes, pastel, madder and fuller's earth, and as a result of this his industries prospered. An industry for working leather in the eastern fashion was established at Córdoba, and damascened weapons were made at Toledo. Iron was mined in the Huelva region. During the time of al-Idrisi the mercury mines of Almadén employed 1,000 workers. The first paper factories in the west, founded at Játiva not far from Valencia, remained the most important in Europe until the fourteenth century.

46 Harvest, vintage and winepress; tenth-century Mozarabic illumination.

Urban development in Spain was striking at this time: Seville could stand comparison with Constantinople, by virtue of its manufacture of luxury goods and its harbour on the Guadalquivir. Málaga and Tarifa traded with Tangier, and Ceuta, Pechina and Almería with the east. Almería became the busiest port of the western Mediterranean, with its naval shipyards, and its factories making silk, and copper and iron utensils: at the time of al-Idrisi it contained 970 hostelries or fonduks. Córdoba, the administrative and religious centre, was the most populous town in the west with 21 suburbs, 113,000 houses, 900 hammams (baths), 50 hospitals and 80 schools. It was surrounded by the residences of princes and government officials: something in the region of 10,000 workmen must have been employed for ten years on the construction of one of these, Al Medinat Al-Zahra, three miles to the north-west of the city. It contained 4,313 columns: the ruins are still impressive today.

There was a steady flow of trade to the Christian states of the north, especially to the kingdom of León, across the barren no-man's-land separating them from the Spain of the Caliphs. According to many surviving tenth-century documents, their standard of living seems to have been distinctly superior to that of Christian Europe beyond the Pyrenees, and this was due to their southern connections.

Some of the Jewish merchants' letters found at the Genizah in Cairo, which are at present being studied and in the course of being published, illustrate very clearly the commercial contacts which were made right across the Moslem world, from Spain and Kairawan, via Egypt to Jeddah, the port of Mecca on the Red Sea, and India. Even more revealing is the *Book of roads and realms* by Ibn-Khurdadbeh, describing the routes from the far west to the far east used by Jewish merchants from the Maghreb, at a time which has generally been dated in the second half of the ninth century, but which seems to correspond much better to the situation in the middle of the tenth.

Four routes were used by these 'Radanite' merchants, two by sea and two by land:

(1) By ship from the Frankish kingdom, straight to Al-Farama on the Nile delta; by ship again to Al-Qulzum, near the present town of Suez; then via Al-Jar, the port of Medina, and Jeddah, the port of Mecca, to Sind, India and China.

(2) By ship from the Frankish kingdom, straight to Antioch, then overland to the Euphrates, and down river to Baghdad; then down the Tigris to Basrah; thence by ship again to Oman, Sind, India and China.

(3) From Spain or France to Morocco, and by way of Tangier and Ifriqya to Cairo; from this point, overland via Ramlah, Damascus, Kufa, Baghdad, Basrah; across Persia, Karamania, Sind, and India, finally reaching China.

(4) Starting from Byzantium, across the Slav countries, then the Khazar khanate; by ship across the Caspian, to Balkh and Transoxiana, before reaching Tughuzghur territory, and finally China.

From west to east the trade was in slaves, eunuchs, furs, swords, mastic and (from France) coral; from the east came spices (musk, aloes, camphor, cinnamon, etc.). Few documents give a sufficiently comprehensive picture of the great commercial movements which stirred the world at this time, but their existence is confirmed by travellers' tales like that of the Arab merchant al-Tartushi, who crossed Europe in 965.

The Jews played a vital role in linking the east with the west: St Adalbert, bishop of Prague, resigned his bishopric in 989 because he was unable to stop the trade in Christian slaves, which was in the hands of Jewish merchants; as late as 1009, the margrave of Misnia sold the families of his serfs to the Jews. Some were sent to Verdun, where, as in the early Middle Ages, they were made into eunuchs for the Spanish market; others were sent to Venice *en route* to the Maghreb and the Moslem east. The number of slaves of Slav origin was so large that in the west the word 'slav' and in Moslem Spain the word 'sakaliba' in the end came to have the exclusive meaning of 'slave'. At Córdoba in the middle of the tenth century these slaves, whether eunuchs or not, came to play a role in the personal service of the Caliph or as court officials comparable to that of the Mamelukes in Egypt.

The Jews seem to have taken over as the main commercial class from the Syrians who had held this position in the pre-medieval era. An imperial charter of 965 alludes to the existence of 'Jews and other merchants' at Magdeburg, which suggests that the Jews formed the greater part of the merchant class, and at Worms the bishop enlarged the walls to include the market, the mint and the Jewish quarter. In the Islamic world, a Jew was superintendent of customs at Córdoba, another was governor of Siraf, at the terminus on the Persian Gulf of the convoys from India and China; still others played important roles at the courts of Baghdad and Cairo. The Khazar people, on the Volga, were converted to Judaism; their territory was traversed by the international trade route bringing Caucasian gold and the silks of Turkestan to Constantinople.

Further evidence of the international economic community which existed at the time is found in a French text of the first half of the eleventh century, the *Life* of Gauzlin, abbot of Fleury. From it we learn that the abbot had copper sent from Spain to decorate the stalls of his abbey church; the work was carried out by an artist sent from Lombardy who was given the additional task of making a monumental choir in the Italian style. A marble and porphyry pavement was imported from Rome, where the abbot also obtained relics and silver objects. A large number of Arab carpets and silk fabrics from Spain were offered to the abbey by the Count of Gascony to adorn the church. The abbot recruited an artist from the Byzantine empire to decorate the sanctuary with a mosaic. Various other objects and manuscripts also found their way to him from England and Catalonia. His successor obtained many articles of silver-ware and tablets in 'Indian ivory' representing the Ascension, which must have been Alexandrine or Byzantine work. From this we gain some idea of the common civilization throughout the Mediterranean world, and the Frankish areas under its influence, during the second part of the tenth century and at the beginning of the eleventh.

# III  THE RISE OF THE CHRISTIAN WEST

France took longer than any other European country to recover. Since it was, so to speak, the promontory of Europe, it was buffeted by invasions from the two seas which washed its shores; it was ultimately laid waste by the raids of the horsemen from the continental steppes, and emerged from chaos only by slow degrees. With its towns ruined and its whole administrative framework shaken, France had to fall back first on agriculture: some kind of urban life reappeared only at the very end of the tenth century, and the towns did not start to thrive again to any extent until the end of the following century. There was a marked contrast here with Germany, where a trend towards urbanization developed as soon as the Hungarian invasion had ended. In spite of the length of France's seaboard, its economy was that of a continental country; economic life developed away from the coast, along the rivers which were the arteries for internal traffic. Ports like Marseilles and Bordeaux did not resume full activity until almost the middle of the twelfth century, when Italy had already begun its impressive commercial expansion in the Tyrrhenian Sea and the Adriatic.

Under the last Carolingians and the first Capetians, France almost unwittingly began, in response to the physical needs of its population, to adopt a policy of agricultural expansion. The Germans were above all merchants, operating along the great land and river routes; the Flemings were textile manufacturers; the Italians, sailors and merchants. But the French were primarily farmers. French industry and commerce had to start once more from scratch, and grain, wine and salt were the only goods in which there was large-scale trade. Consequently the continued improvement of the land represented a real increase in the wealth of the country; it formed the basis for the general economic growth which continued up to the end of the thirteenth century and the beginning of the fourteenth, and contributed to the development of western civilization.

In contrast with Germany, which had suffered less, and up to the twelfth century remained faithful to the old ways of the Carolingian period, the French countryside was slowly restructured during the tenth and eleventh centuries. The great estates had come through the troubles badly, and were now divided up. In the devastated areas it was often difficult to raise sufficient dues from the remaining tenants; and at the beginning of the tenth century the canons of Saint-Martin of Tours nostalgically compared the situation in certain of their estates to the situation which had existed before the wars. It was still more difficult to compel the dependants to carry out the heavy forced labour which they were bound to do on the manorial demesnes; the work tended to become lighter or was commuted to dues in kind or money. Because it was impossible to guarantee the cultivation of their own demesnes, the lords found it more profitable to divide them up among tenants who paid them rent, and later the tenants sublet them further. In Provence and the Rhône region, lands abandoned because of the continuing threat from the Saracens were reoccupied by those who wanted them, in return for payment of a *tasca*, that is, a division of the harvest between the landowner and the peasant. The same system developed in Languedoc. The necessity for bringing the land under cultivation again meant that all types of contract were found side by side, from an equal division of the produce to a levy of the ninth part. Sometimes the land itself was divided

47 One of the earliest bas-reliefs showing the Labours of the Months (early twelfth

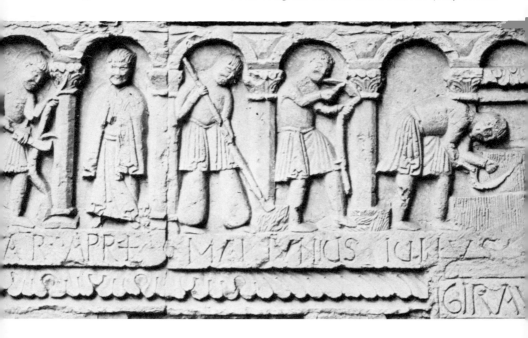

between the proprietor and the planter after it had been put under cultivation; in vineyards the usual custom was to make over half the vines to the tenant. All this led to the establishment of small private holdings, which are as characteristic of the classical Middle Ages as the great estate had been of the previous period.

The *villa* slowly gave way to the 'village'. The conditions of the people also became easier: the old Northmen had been uncompromising slave-owners, but in Normandy the price of renewed cultivation of the fields was a rapid disappearance of bond-service.

Migrations to uninhabited areas and newly cleared lands gradually brought about a weakening of the system of servitude. Besides, the serf of the classical Middle Ages was, even at this early date, quite different from the slave in the Roman or Carolingian period. At the beginning of the twelfth century, Louis VI relieved the serfs of the Persian abbeys of a number of their legal disabilities, and serfdom more or less came to an end at the beginning of the fourteenth century. The conditions of the villagers in northern and eastern France improved from the reign of Louis VI onwards as a result of the notable extension of civil liberties brought about by the charter of Lorris, and, later, by the charter of Beaumont.

century) on the tympanum of the old church of St Ursin at Bourges.

In the eleventh and twelfth centuries, extensive areas of virgin land were cleared in both France and England, and an astonishing increase in population took place. We cannot be sure which of these movements came first. Should we see the land-hunger of an expanding population, cramped in overcrowded areas, as the reason for the clearings, or did the increase in population result from better living standards among the groups which had settled in more spacious lands? At any rate, the two movements seem to be closely connected.

From the second half of the tenth century onwards, embankments were constructed along the rivers, and marshes were drained in Holland and Flanders, in the Saint-Omer region, and along the coasts of Poitou and Saintonge. The village lands were usually extended at the expense of waste and woodland; the limits of the forest were pushed back and the large woods broken up by the spread of land under cultivation. In Maine and the west generally, *bordages* or *borderies* were established: these were holdings which isolated peasants carved out for themselves from waste land, surrounding them with a hedge and a ditch, so as to prevent the communal herds from grazing over them. This was the start of the *bocage* typical of the French landscape. The 30,000 place-names of the present-day *départements* of Sarthe and Ille-et-Vilaine provide evidence of this type of settlement; their origins can be traced to the agrarian development of the eleventh to thirteenth centuries. Elsewhere 'newcomers' or 'foreigners' (*hospites, advenae, foranei*) were admitted to the manor, and joined forces with the original inhabitants to clear more land.

Country boroughs, which were at the same time markets and centres of agricultural activity, were founded in large numbers by the lords, especially in the west, between the middle of the eleventh century and the first third of the twelfth. According to region, they were called *sauvetés, villes neuves, abergements*, or *bâties*, and they were prepared to welcome peasant settlers, offering them advantageous terms. The lords even made use of entrepreneurs who recruited men, divided up pieces of land into lots, and built houses, on the understanding that they might keep part of the plot. Both lay and ecclesiastical landowners in Picardy and the Ile-de-France had recourse to this practice. From the middle of the twelfth century onwards, partnerships (*pariage*) grew up between lords, or between one lord, sometimes even the king, and an ecclesiastic establishment, to finance similar improvements in their properties; one of the partners provided the land, the other the capital, and they shared the rents between them.

Along with tillage, pastureland was laid down, resulting in a considerable increase of cattle in Normandy, to the north of Paris and in the west, since before this time stock had usually been run in the woods.

48 Cultivation of the land; late twelfth-century miniature.

49, 50 Different types of ploughing. Above, the Mediterranean swing-plough, with its ploughshare composed of an attached metal point, drawn by two beasts abreast.

In Dauphiné the hemp-fields spread, in Flanders the flax-fields and hop-fields and in Picardy the woad-fields. There was also remarkable development of viticulture in the marshes and gravelly regions of the Bordelais, and along the banks of the Lot, the Oise, the Seine, the Yonne and the Moselle; the wine-barrels could be sent by way of the rivers to the great agricultural markets of Bordeaux, Compiègne, Laon, Paris, Auxerre and Cologne.

Once the trend had started, it continued slowly from the middle or the second half of the tenth century. It became more pronounced at the end of the eleventh century, assumed national importance in the middle of the twelfth and slowed down only in the second half of the thirteenth, when most of the cultivable land had already been brought under the plough. The movement was of such proportions that certain historians have recently assigned one of the causes of the great agricultural crisis of the fourteenth century to the inexperience of these early settlers; it is suggested that out of lack of technical knowledge they had cultivated land which was unsuitable for working or which became exhausted too quickly, since at this time there were no fertilizers apart from animal dung, and this was unsuitable for improving fields which lay at any distance from the village.

Right, the plough of the northern countries, with mobile wheeled forecarriage coupler and mould-board, yoked to two beasts in a line.

At the same time some technical improvements also made their appearance which reduced the amount of labour required; a number of them had been known for some time, but had been applied only rarely before this date. Among them we may mention an extension of the practice of biennial or triennial rotation of crops, which was already followed in some ecclesiastical estates of the Carolingian period; the improvement of land by marling; and various methods of digging over fields and vineyards. Ploughs with metal ploughshares, or more often with wooden shares reinforced by metal, became less rare, although the virgin land can hardly have been cleared without the use of this heavy implement. It was provided with a fore-carriage, an asymmetric mould-board and two handles, and is illustrated in the iconography of France and England from the eleventh century, but apparently reached Germany and Italy only in the fourteenth. The use of the harrow became widespread. The shoulder-collar for the horse and the frontal yoke for the pair of oxen, allowing better use to be made of the beasts, were introduced, or became more common. Beginning with Normandy and Picardy, the horse was increasingly used for work in the fields, but superseded the ox only gradually, no doubt because of the high price of horses. Draught animals were now also commonly shod, and this presupposes that local sources of metal were utilized, and small smithies set up; the blacksmiths, or metal-workers (*fèvres*) as they were called, came to play a vital role in the countryside. Whereas life in the early Middle Ages had been based on the general use of wood, there was now a gradual transition towards another era when iron would play an increasing part, although it did not come to be really essential in rural life before the end of the thirteenth century.

In nearly all the manors, water-mills replaced the ancient hand-mills, or 'blood-mills' as they were luridly described. This development was connected with the extension of cereal cultivation, and it was made possible by the wealth of the lords whose resources had been increased by their growing revenue from rents; it also meant an improvement in the peasants' living conditions. But water-power was not only used to turn the mill-wheels for grinding corn. Great strides were made in the utilization of power: the continuous movement of the wheel was transformed by means of cam-shafts into reciprocal movement, so that a pounding motion could be achieved. In the last decade of the tenth century the hemp swingle (*battoir*) was introduced in Dauphiné, and in the eleventh and twelfth centuries it became widespread in the Alps and the Jura. In Provence, beaters (*paroirs* or *paradous*) were used for fulling linens and other cloths in the middle of the eleventh century, and they reached Languedoc at the beginning of the twelfth century. The fulling mill, which was independent of this southern technique, appeared in Normandy in the last decade of the eleventh century, and left its mark on the whole of northern France and England, where it made a great contribution to the remarkable development of the cloth industry. The tanning-mill, used for pounding the bark needed in the leather industry, appeared in the Ile-de-France and upper Normandy in the middle of the twelfth century; the whetting-mill, the iron-mill or tilt-hammer (*martinet*) which dates from the end of the twelfth century in Lorraine, and finally the hydraulic saw, all contributed to the development of the French countryside, especially in Normandy, northern France and Dauphiné.

Windmills first made their appearance on the coasts of Normandy, England, Ponthieu and Brittany in the last two decades of the twelfth century. This invention again spread very rapidly all over northern France and the south-west in the first half of the thirteenth century; and then, in the second half of the century, to Flanders, Holland and Germany.

When we compare the economic situation of mid-tenth-century France with that of the mid-twelfth century, the gulf between them is obvious. The land had been resettled, the marshes drained, and the rivers tamed; the forests

51 Joshua and Caleb fighting over a basket of grapes, decoration of a capital in Rheims cathedral.

had been thinned out, and in some places were on the way to being completely cleared; in the west, Champagne and the highlands of the south-west, new villages had been founded in the clearings; townships had been built more or less everywhere; isolated settlements were dotted over the Bocage and the fore-Alps; the abbeys had built granges throughout the 'waste land' and woodland; vast areas were covered with vineyards. Rented farms had replaced the manses subject to forced labour. The legal status of the 'villein' had been reformed, and at the same time, thanks to the consistent rise in agricultural prices, his diet had improved.

Markets were set up throughout the country and important fairs instituted in the towns and cities. Among these were the vital centres of the classical medieval economy – the fairs of Provins, founded at the very end of the tenth century, those of Torhout and Messines in Flanders, founded in the second half of the eleventh, and those of Troyes at the beginning of the twelfth. Meanwhile the Church tried to ensure the protection of the merchants by the 'Peace of God'.

Along with these developments, a monetary economy evolved. Historians have often drawn attention to the proliferation of mints under the feudal system as providing evidence not only of the lords' desire to make profits from minting, but also of the people's obvious need for currency which it was the mint's primary function to supply. During the eleventh century, and especially in the twelfth, certain coins began to circulate more widely than others. Thus broad monetary zones came into being, with coins of various origins as the dominant currency, such as the pennies (*deniers*) minted in Paris, Provins, Le Mans, Vienne, Toulouse (*tolzans*), Melgueil (*melgoriens*), Le Puy (*pougeois*), Besançon (*estevenans*), Rouergue (*raimondins*), etc. These coins circulated much more widely than was formerly supposed, and recent studies of the very important money-hoards found at Le Puy and Falaise, dating back to the eleventh century, provide evidence of this.

Under circumstances of which we still know little a network of roads was established: tracks connecting abbeys to their granges, villages to their mills, clearings to the villages, and castles or priories to each other. The administrative, judiciary and military centres, where the lords of the large fiefs installed their provosts or castellans, formed multiple junctions here, and the markets frequented by peasants from neighbouring areas also grew up. Routes were developed over much longer distances, across Burgundy and Cham-

52 The *camino francés* ('French route') by which pilgrims reached Compostella across northern Spain: ruins of a bridge over the Aragón river.

pagne, between Paris and the Alpine passes or the Saône valley, or across the Ile-de-France towards the market-towns of Artois and Flanders, whose economic importance was continually increasing. A new network of toll-houses was also established at this time, on both the roads and the rivers, as part of a system for protecting merchants and maintaining roads, bridges and ferries.

From the tenth century onwards, with the improvement in communications, pilgrimages became common, to Le Puy, Rocamadour, Mont-Saint-Michel, and many other regional or local shrines, as well as to Rome and Jerusalem. The first known pilgrim to St James of Compostella, the bishop of Le Puy, set off in 950, and in 961 the count of Rouergue and the archbishop of Rheims followed his example. Most of the roads were not constructed initially as pilgrim-routes, though this was the case with the 'highway' of St James, which rolled across Spain from the north to Compostella: it is clear, however, that the pilgrimages contributed to the improvement of the roads, and in particular led to the establishment of monastic hostelries which were placed at intervals along them and welcomed monks, pilgrims, merchants and other travellers.

The great expansion of the reformed Benedictine monasteries, which in the end established a real international community of monks, led to incessant

53 In the church of St Juan de Ortega, the tomb of the saint who, in the early twelfth century, constructed the pilgrims' road to Compostella across the Oca mountains.

travels by the abbots and their monks. The abbots of Cluny were always on the move, making their way untiringly from one abbey to another; St Mayeul, for example, made six journeys to Italy in the course of his abbacy (935–87).

For a long time the recovery made itself felt primarily in the rural areas: most of the towns remained no more than large villages, enclosed by walls which the inhabitants had restored as a protection against the invaders, and their populations could scarcely be distinguished from the surrounding peasants. The abbeys, built near the towns, were also confined within their walls, with their dependants and those who had sought refuge in them. This feature was responsible for the development of the twin towns so characteristic of medieval France, with their double nucleus of city and borough, as at Tours, Limoges, Arras, Autun, Rheims, etc.; sometimes they had multiple nuclei if there had been several abbeys giving birth to as many boroughs, as in Paris (Cité, Bourg Saint-Germain, Bourg Sainte-Geneviève, etc.), Metz (the city, and the *bourgs* across the Seille and the Moselle) or Toulouse. From the end of the period of the invasions, towns in Normandy and in Flanders, such as Dieppe, Falaise and Caen, Saint-Omer, Bruges, Ghent and Ypres, began to develop from the primitive villages or abbeys to which they owed their origin, but they started to take on recognizable shape only at the beginning of the eleventh century.

Urbanization began earlier in northern France and in the west of the German empire than in other regions. The river-route for small boats along the Scheldt and the Meuse doubtless helped to bring the countryside back to life, as well as the old Roman road leading from Cologne, the great metropolis of the Rhine, to the sea. This was also the region where the raids of the Northmen had come to an end earliest because of the stiff opposition of the leaders. Towns grew up round the *portus* and markets, which were essential to economic life, and the *castra*, which were indispensable to defence, and craftsmen and merchants gathered in them. The textile industry which had existed in this region in Carolingian times was revived: from the middle or the end of the eleventh century, wool-weavers flocked in from the surrounding countryside, while the merchants began to group themselves into guilds (corporative syndicates), or 'hanses', that is, associations which organized the flow of trade between cities. We have evidence of them in works like the *Conflictus ovis et lini*, a song in honour of Flemish cloth dating from the middle of the eleventh century.

Before they were incorporated into the towns, the *bourgs* (boroughs) or *faubourgs* (suburbs), where the artisans and merchants settled, were enclosed within their own fortifications. In many towns of both the north and the south there continued to be a distinction between the 'high' and 'low' town for a long time, as at Boulogne, Provins, or Nice; or between the city and the count's or viscount's town, as at Marseilles or Tarbes.

The 'burghers' formed one of the essential elements of medieval economic and social life and very soon they came to feel a corporate identity in the face of the authorities, especially the ecclesiastic ones, who continued to treat them as dependants, and refused them rights. Their *conjuratio* gave rise to the 'communes', the first of which was founded at Le Mans in 1039 but miscarried. The idea was revived at Huy in 1066, at Cambrai in 1076, at Beauvais in 1099, at Laon in 1112, at Valenciennes in 1114, and at Saint-Omer in 1127, but the commune movement, which was in effect a campaign for urban emancipation, gained momentum only in the second half of the twelfth century, coinciding with the industrial and commercial expansion of northern Europe.

THE RISE OF ENGLAND

The slow economic revival which has been described primarily in relation to France is even more strikingly illustrated by England; here the upward turn apparently started a little earlier, in the course of the tenth century, gaining momentum at a correspondingly earlier period, during the last quarter of the eleventh. In England, too, there seems to have been an extraordinary population explosion; specialists in this field estimate that between the *Domesday Book* of 1086 and the Great Plague of 1348, the population of England must have increased from about 1,100,000 inhabitants to nearly 3,700,000, and the earlier figure probably represents double the population of the middle of the tenth century.

As in France, forests were cleared and marshes drained, but on an even greater scale; in the time of St Dunstan the polders were made around Ramsey, Ely and Peterborough as a result of the efforts of the monks. The decrease in the number of pigs, which is revealed by a comparison of the *Domesday Book* surveys of 1066 and 1086, must be seen as the consequence of an increase in land under cultivation at the expense of woodland. Agricultural holdings and settlements multiplied. At the same time the numbers of serfs diminished and the status of the peasants tended to become levelled up in that of 'villeinage', while the manor★ extended its power over a growing number

★ *Translator's Note* The fact that the Norman clerks who compiled the *Domesday Book* surveys borrowed the French word *manoir* to describe English rural estates is perhaps confusing: though *manoir* simply meant 'homestead', the classical English 'manor' actually corresponds to the French *seigneurie*, which has thus been designated 'manorial' in previous and subsequent chapters.

of dependants by absorbing many of the smallholders. As in France, the spread of the water-mill (nearly 5,000 were counted over the country as a whole as early as 1086) and the constant rise in agricultural prices, which was particularly marked in the twelfth century, clearly entailed a better standard of living for the tenants.

Urban development in England was equally precocious. It apparently began in the time of Alfred the Great with the settlements formed by the Anglo-Saxons and Danes, or at any rate in the early tenth century when their successors won the land back. Under Edward the Confessor and Cnut the Great, England was ahead of the continent in this field, due to the vast economic and political association which had been established uniting the North Sea countries. As a result, the Anglo-Norman state on both sides of the Channel benefited, at the end of the eleventh century and beginning of the twelfth, from urban, commercial and industrial institutions superior to any found in France at this period. Even in the time of the Danes, Lincoln, London, and especially York had regained their prosperity: York, the Danish capital, doubled its area, and the author of the *Life of St Oswald*, in the second half of the

ANGLO-NORMAN
CATHEDRAL ARCHITECTURE

54 The church of Saint-Etienne, known as l'Abbaye aux Hommes, was built in Caen by William the Conqueror. The nave is eleventh century, the choir twelfth.

55 Peterborough cathedral: the nave is one of the most characteristic of Anglo-Norman Romanesque art (late twelfth century).

tenth century, held it to be a real economic metropolis. Abandoned towns of Roman origin, such as Chester, were reoccupied. Norwich had been a mere village at the end of the ninth century, but from 920 it possessed a mint and in 1087 had twenty-five churches; it became a bishopric in 1094.

At the time of the *Domesday Book*, the country had vast flocks of sheep; in certain areas there were woad plantations, and woad was also imported from the continent. One indication of the antiquity of the English cloth trade is that, in the twelfth century, the cloths of 'Nicole' (Lincoln) and 'estanforts' (cloths from Stamford) were to be found in every European market. English wool was the country's primary source of wealth: from the beginning of the eleventh century Tiel, Cologne and Bremen traded with England, and King Ethelred II granted privileges to the 'men of the Empire'. At the end of this century (according to Pirenne), or more probably at the beginning of the twelfth, the cloth-makers of Valenciennes went to England to buy wool. A little later, fifteen cloth towns of Flanders grouped themselves into a 'hanse' to trade with London and Winchester and at the fairs in the wool centres of St Ives.

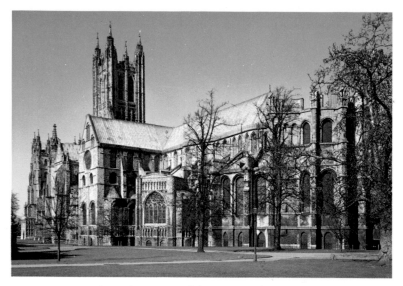

56 Canterbury: started in 1070 under archbishop Lanfranc of Bec. The choir was reconstructed by William of Sens beginning in 1175.

57 St Albans Abbey begun in 1077 by Paul of Caen (the architect of l'Abbaye aux Hommes); the choir is thirteenth century.

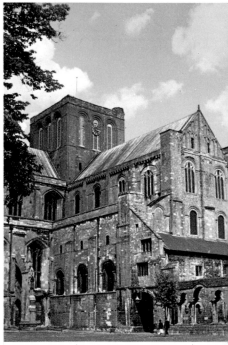

58 Winchester, started in 1079, has important Gothic alterations and additions.

59 Durham, begun in 1093 in the purest
Anglo–Norman style. The choir was rebuilt in the mid-thirteenth century.

These were the beginnings of the economic community of north-western Europe, which prospered in the following century, based on English wool and Franco-Flemish cloth. As early as 1130 a statute laid down the conditions upon which the 'Lorrains', that is, the people from the Meuse region, might introduce and sell their goods in London, and Cologne acquired its Guildhall, the parent of the future Hanseatic counting-house.

The Romanesque cathedrals and abbey churches, which are more 'monumental' than those of other regions, give evidence today of the wealth of the Anglo-Norman state during the last quarter of the eleventh century: within a quarter-century a start was made on the cathedrals which are numbered among the greatest religious buildings of the Middle Ages, Canterbury (1070), St Albans (1077), Winchester (1079), York (1080), Ely (1083), Worcester (1084), Durham (1093) and Norwich (1096).

THE CRUSADES

In the east, the splendour of the tenth century scarcely lasted, on an international scale, beyond the second or third decade of the eleventh century. While in the Christian west the trend towards agricultural revival and urban development continued and grew in strength, there were profound changes in the east and in the whole Mediterranean world, which affected first Islam, and then Byzantium. In the last third of the eleventh century their economic prosperity received a setback. The general stability of the east was upset by the attacks of uncivilized warriors, the Turks and the 'Frankish' knights. The Italian cities were the beneficiaries of these events: from the second quarter of the twelfth century their business activities increased rapidly, and the second half of the century saw the general rise of western economy.

In 1001 and 1011, Pisa was again plundered by the Arabs; in 1015 the Moslem fleet made its last attack in strength on the northern coasts of the Mediterranean. In the following year the fleets of Genoa and Pisa appeared for the first time in history and destroyed the Saracen flotilla off the coast of Sardinia. Pisa immediately began to lay siege to Corsica and Sardinia, which was a valuable asset because of its cereals, salt, metal, coral and slaves. In 1034 a Christian fleet intervened for the first time on the coast of North Africa when Pisa raided Bona.

The Normans, who had hitherto tended to form links with the Nordic world, and to look towards England, Ireland and the Baltic countries, now made war in the Mediterranean: they wreaked havoc in the Moslem lands, as their predecessors had caused chaos in the preceding centuries in the Christian west. The first Norman soldiers appeared in Apulia, near Bari, about 1017, and about 1020 Roger de Tosny rushed to Catalonia to relieve the Christians there. In 1038 a brother of St Olaf, king of Norway, fought side by side with one of the best Byzantine generals, George Maniaces, a Turanian Turk from Central Asia, when Byzantium decided to undertake the reconquest of Sicily from the Arabs: Byzantium followed the Romans in making frequent use of mercenaries. The Normans began to appropriate land and soon carved out a state for themselves at the expense of both Islam and the *Basileus*, taking Reggio and Calabria in 1060, Bari and Brindisi in 1070, Palermo in 1072, Amalfi in 1073, and Salerno in 1076. Robert Guiscard, who was already master of Malta, landed at Epirus and between 1081 and 1085 advanced as far as Macedonia and Thessaly. A new political power had risen in the heart of the Mediterranean; but it was left to the three great merchant cities of Pisa, Genoa and Venice to exploit the wealth of southern Italy, and in particular the inexhaustible grain of Sicily.

There was an even more important consequence of these events: Byzantium had been crippled by war and the disasters it had suffered in the east, and no longer had either the money or the fleet necessary to defend its Italian possessions. It had, therefore, to resort to loans, and to call upon the aid of the Venetian fleet. Venice was repaid for its fidelity by the Golden Bull of 1092, which gave it a privileged position in Constantinople and the whole of the empire; the Venetian colony established at Constantinople thus found itself gaining control of maritime trade in the empire.

In Spain, the Christian powers of the north launched out on the *Reconquista*, taking advantage of the conflicts between the Arab princes who had divided up the territories of the Caliphate between them. Adventurers from Aquitaine, Normandy and Burgundy enlisted in the service of the people of Aragon, Navarre and Castile. In 1063 the first Christian attack on Barbastro took place; in 1065 the Castilians reached the walls of Valencia; in 1085 Alphonso VI entered Toledo and occupied the greater part of 'New Castile'. The Almoravids (*Murabits*), a formidable people from the Moroccan desert, attempted in vain to rescue Spanish Islam. Something of a crusade was organized, culminating in the recapture of Valencia (1094) and Lisbon (1093). The Spanish economy, which was already much weakened, now disintegrated. The Christians concentrated on the daunting task of colonizing the interior, and recovering the whole peninsula: their conquest of the south was a mirror image of the German thrust towards the east, and was the result of a demographic expansion in the west similar to that which had resulted in these changes in Germany.

At the instigation of Pope Victor II in 1087, all the maritime cities of the Tyrrhenian Sea, Genoa and Pisa, Salerno and Amalfi, undertook a sea crusade; they gained possession of Mahdia on the Tunisian coast and demanded a crushing war tax of 100,000 gold dinars, as well as commercial privileges from the Zirid emir of Kairawan. The economic and maritime power of western Islam was well on the way to ruin: the Christian fleet dominated the Mediterranean, from Malta to Valencia; all the islands were in the hands of Christian powers – including even the Balearics for a short time at the beginning of the twelfth century. The Moslems could no longer obtain supplies of wood for building their ships; their exports, wool and leather, were in the hands of merchants from Pisa and Genoa, who set up trading colonies on the African coasts. The destruction of Sigilmassa at the beginning of the Almoravid conquest, and the consequent diversion to Egypt of part of the flow of gold which had previously crossed the Sahara on its way to North Africa, contributed further to the collapse of Islam in the west.

In the east the situation was even more catastrophic: the Patzinaks and Cumans managed to cut the trade-route from the Far East across the steppes of Central Asia. Under Togrul Beg, the Seljuk Turks, another people from the same steppes, invaded Khurasan and seized Iraq during the years 1038–40; they even entered Baghdad in 1055, and the Caliph recognized the victorious sultan as his temporal vicar. A little later they occupied Cappadocia, Armenia and Georgia, and Syria was plundered by the Turkish sultan Alp Arslan. As a result, Byzantium found itself cut off from its Asiatic hinterland at the very moment when its Italian possessions were falling away. The turmoil in Central Asia had the effect of making Egypt the unique terminus for Far Eastern trade, which from then on was confined to the Red Sea route. The emperor Romanus IV Diogenes, who had had the imperial crown forced on him by a military clique, suffered a total military disaster at Manzikert in 1071, the worst defeat that had ever befallen the Byzantine empire. In the greater part of Asia Minor its power collapsed. Here, too, Norman adventurers tried to establish a state. The Armenians were compelled to abandon their country of origin and retreated to a broad region around Sivas in the Taurus mountains, to Cilicia and to Antioch. The Turks settled in Nicaea, across the straits from Constantinople, as well as in Jerusalem.

Such was the situation when, on 27 November 1095, Pope Urban II launched the first Crusade. We need not concern ourselves here with its history, nor with that of the Latin states which were born from this tumultuous and bloody invasion of westerners spurred by their faith to liberate the holy places. We need only consider the economic consequences. From the point of view of the west the establishment of the kingdom of Jerusalem and the principality of Antioch was an event of the greatest importance, although its effects became apparent only a generation after the conquest. To orientals, it was only of secondary importance, since the occupation of the coastal strip had little direct impact on the Near Eastern economy.

The first point to be noted is that the Crusaders reached the Holy Land by a land route. Perhaps the west did not yet possess a fleet capable of transporting an army overseas and facing the Arab navy, which was still strong in the eastern Mediterranean. Besides, the maritime cities hardly seemed disposed to help the enterprise on its way: in spite of the privileges granted to it in the Byzantine empire, Venice had gained an important foothold among the Arabs and Turks in the markets of Alexandria, Antioch and Tripoli. Even on the eve of the Crusade, we know that one of its boats made the round trip between Venice, Constantinople and Antioch. The merchants of Bari traded with the same towns, and while returning from Antioch and Cilicia in 1087 its sailors seized the body of St Nicola of Myra and brought it back in triumph. Settlers from Amalfi were found in Turkish and Byzantine territory: a well-known Amalfi family, the Pantaleoni, had recently founded a hospital in Jerusalem which was later made famous by the St John Hospitallers, and at Constantinople they commissioned those magnificent bronze doors which now adorn the entrances of the main churches of southern Italy.

60 Bronze doors of Trani cathedral, cast at Constantinople in the eleventh century.

Pisa waited for three years after the departure of the Crusaders before sending them a relief fleet of 120 ships, during the siege of Jerusalem. Venice waited even longer to see how things might turn out, and it was only in 1100 that 200 ships were finally put at the disposal of Godfrey of Bouillon for the siege of Jaffa – no doubt because the *Basileus* could not have any ambitions in this region. Genoa committed itself to the venture somewhat earlier; but this was the work not of the city as a whole, but of a small nucleus of noble families. In July 1097 they sent ten galleys to assist Bohemund in his siege of Antioch: he granted them part of the town as a reward and then they returned home. Later Genoa saw a similar chance of fruitful plunder in Crusading expeditions as in its previous raids on the coasts of Spain and North Africa: when Caesarea was sacked in 1101, 15 per cent of the vast booty was reserved for Genoa's captains and officers, and the rest divided up between the 8,000 soldiers and sailors, who each received 48 gold dinars and two pounds of pepper.

In return for their co-operation, Genoa, Pisa and Venice, and after them Amalfi and Ancona, demanded quarters, warehouses, markets and churches in the principal towns, together with exceptional privileges, in both the commercial and the political spheres. The origins of the colonial empires of Genoa and Venice are to be found in these first concessions. They eventually became actual estates in the course of the twelfth century, administered by consuls sent from the metropolis; but for a long time they were merely ports of call or maritime bases. They enabled the merchant cities to put their economic interests in the Byzantine empire and their trade in Egypt on a firm footing, without involving them in any attempt at penetrating the interior. In particular Venice increased its pressure on the markets of Constantinople and Salonika, which played an important role in Balkan trade. By threatening to sack the Greek islands, Pisa extracted a promise from the emperor Alexius in 1112 to grant it the same privileges at Constantinople as those enjoyed by the Venetians.

The really decisive event took place in 1123, when Venice intervened for the first time with all its forces (15,000 men on 300 vessels, 120 of them large ships, commanded by the Doge in person): the Egyptian war fleet was intercepted and completely destroyed off Ascalon, while a great merchant convoy fell into Venetian hands. From this date the Moslem navy more or less disappeared from the eastern Mediterranean, as it had already disappeared from the west. Egypt was cut off from the rich forests of Cilicia. The Christian powers imposed an embargo on wood for building ships. Egypt thus became incapable of equipping a fleet of any size, and was forced to rely on the services of Christian ships.

In spite of wars and Crusades, citizens of various Italian cities set themselves up as traders at Alexandria and Damietta; some Pisans even managed to settle in Cairo. Venetian ships, among others, maintained the links with Constantinople, Acre or Tyre, and Alexandria, and this situation continued throughout the whole of the twelfth century in spite of stresses, strains and expulsions. During the last quarter of the twelfth century a Venetian businessman, Romano Mairano, kept up a profitable shuttle-service between Smyrna, Acre, Tyre, Alexandria and Bougie, taking political ups and downs in his stride. It was in Genoese ships that merchandise was carried between Morocco or Arab Spain and Egypt; they brought 'Saracen' wheat and barley to Alexandria, and even sent North African pilgrims on their way to Mecca (Ibn-Jobair in particular gives evidence of this). A record of legal proceedings in the archives of Savona gives details of all the movements of a vessel from that town between 1201 and 1204: it went twice from Ceuta to Alexandria, along the North African coast, calling at Oran, Bougie and Tunis, and it frequently made the round trip between Ceuta, Alexandria, and Marseilles or Savona.

The only restriction imposed on this traffic by the Christian authorities was an embargo on supplying the infidel with arms, war materials (wood for shipbuilding, oars, iron, pitch, etc.), and slaves; but the blockade does not seem to have been very effective since in 1154 Pisa undertook to deliver precisely those forbidden commodities to the sultan. As a matter of priority the western navies ensured that the bridgeheads taken by the Crusaders were supplied with food and arms. The provisions came mainly from Apulia, and thus contributed to the rise of agriculture in that region, which, together with Sicily, became the granary of the Mediterranean. The prosperity at this time of towns in Apulia such as Bari, Brindisi, Bitonto, Canosa, Siponto (near Manfredonia) and Trani, is indicated by the amazing number of Romanesque cathedrals in the region. The pockets of the Italian shipowners were lined by the transport of supplies and military reinforcements, pilgrims and Crusaders arriving late on the scene or returning home.

THE ECONOMIC RISE OF THE ITALIAN TOWNS

The first effect of the Crusade was thus a considerable increase in the size of the Italian fleets, and, as a result, an expansion of commercial activity. Throughout the century, the number of Italians at Constantinople continued to grow: when the notorious pogrom of the Latins took place in 1182, we know that families were massacred as well as priests and monks, and that 4,000 men were sold as slaves; the rest found refuge in 44 western galleys which happened to be in the harbour. All this illustrates the importance of the 'Latin' colony there.

61 Bird's-eye view of Venice; detail showing the Arsenale, from a woodcut by Jacopo de' Barbari, 1500.

le vergine.

S. piero ni castello.

.REGA.

From before the middle of the twelfth century, there was a tendency towards a division of trade on geographical lines. *Venice* entirely dominated the Adriatic; it ruined Ravenna and Pola, attempted to do the same to Zara, and allowed Ancona only a limited economic life; but it set its sights higher on monopolizing trade in the Byzantine empire, since its trade with the east was far more important than any other. Venetians were so numerous at Constantinople itself that 10,000 of them were imprisoned in 1171 as a reprisal ordered by the Emperor Manuel against the city of Venice. Later, in 1187, in compensation for the pogrom of 1182, the emperor Isaac Angelus confirmed the Venetians' former privileges and finally granted them unlimited freedom to trade in the empire, with total exemption from taxes. As a result, the Byzantine empire came under the economic control of the Venetians before the time of the first Crusade.

*Genoa* did not, indeed, neglect the area of the Holy Land and Egypt, but, being sympathetic to the Normans because of its Sicilian interests, it was scarcely in good odour at Byzantium; and it took no part in the second Crusade. Instead, Genoa succeeded in gaining control of the Ligurian coast, from Monaco to Portovenere, and this was finally recognized by Frederick Barbarossa in 1162. Genoa disputed with Pisa the sovereignty of Corsica and Sardinia, and took part in the crusade of Almería and the sack of Bougie, where it took over the customs dues in 1136. It contributed to the development of the Sicilian corn trade, visited the fairs of Saint-Gilles and the salt-works of Hyères. The Genoese claimed the exclusive right to trade on the coast of Tarragona, and the control of all maritime activity on the coasts of Languedoc and Provence. As early as 1109, Genoa demanded from Raimond of Saint-Gilles, in return for its assistance at the siege of Tripoli, that only Genoese ships should have the right of navigation between Saint-Gilles and the open sea. From 1150, the Genoese tried to prevent the merchants of Narbonne, Montpellier and Marseilles from trading by sea, and insisted that boats from Savona should load and unload at Genoa itself. In 1154, in a treaty with the Norman king of Sicily, it claimed a monopoly of trade in the kingdom for its sailors, and banned Provençal ships from entering Sicilian ports. At the beginning of the thirteenth century, Marseilles had some difficulty in resisting Genoese pressures aimed at preventing it from trading overseas. When the great Almohad empire was founded in the middle of the twelfth century by the 'Berber Charlemagne', Abd-el-Mumin, covering North Africa and Andalusia, Genoa took the opportunity of trading with all the North African ports. These included Tripoli, Gabès and Bougie, the centres of the wool and leather trades, Ceuta, the meeting-place of Africa and Spain, and Salé and

Safi (which were outlets for the rich corn lands of the Sous and the terminus of the routes used by merchants bringing gold from black Africa). Only in the first half of the thirteenth century did the Genoese economy gradually become oriented towards the eastern Mediterranean.

With half an eye on Alexandria, Constantinople and Syria, *Pisa* aimed at dominating the central Mediterranean: its attention was concentrated on the corn lands of the Maremma, Sardinia, Sicily and southern Italy, the iron of Elba and the Lucca district, and wool and leather from the North African ports (Bougie, Bône, Collo, Djidjelli). It therefore tried to deny Genoa any opportunity of expansion in the Tyrrhenian Sea, and a collision between these two commercial and maritime empires was inevitable. Rivalry between them was stirred up even further by the fact that they took different sides in the struggle between the partisans of the pope and the empire, the Guelfs and Ghibellines. This lasted for a century and a half, with fluctuations, until Pisa was completely defeated in the battle of Meloria in 1284: from then on it had to be content with a limited trade in Sicily and Sardinia, until it was finally driven out of Sardinia by the Catalans, and itself absorbed by Florence.

Together with the great maritime republics, the whole of Italy developed and expanded. The towns of the lower Po valley aligned themselves with Venice: from the second half of the twelfth century we see the emergence on

62, 63 Pisa: the metal chains which were extended across the port to prevent entry in times of danger. Right, the chain across the port, as shown in a thirteenth-century relief.

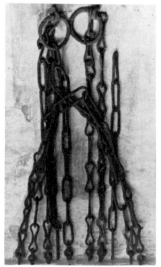

an economic level of what was to become much later (at the beginning of the fifteenth century), on the political level, the Venetian *terraferma*. Piacenza and Milan looked to Genoa, and the impressive expansion of the latter can hardly be accounted for without supposing that it had the backing of the bankers of Piacenza and Milanese manufacturers of textiles and metals. Pisa was supported by a remarkable rise in the economy of the Tuscan towns, first of all Lucca, and then Siena, Pistoia and Florence, although these cities had been in constant rivalry. The secondary ports of Liguria, in particular Savona, those of the Neapolitan region (Salerno and Gaeta), and of the Adriatic (Bari, Brindisi, Barletta, Ancona, Zara, Durazzo), expanded at the same time; Savona, however, had great difficulty in escaping from the clutches of Genoa, and the others from domination by Venice.

From the end of the eleventh century to the beginning of the thirteenth, there was a great advance in urban civilization from one end of Italy to the other. Such was its intensity that even antiquity offers no parallel. Taking advantage of anarchy in the feudal system and the imperial crisis, Milan even set up a republic in 1069; from about 1080, councils of notables, the 'consuls', made their appearance in all the large towns of the north and centre (Parma, Mantua, Piacenza, Asti, Lucca, Pisa, etc.) and the emperor was forced to promise to take the advice of the twelve elect of Pisa before naming his representative in Tuscany. The consulate quickly made its mark in Italy, and then spread to Provence and Languedoc.

Under the leadership of the merchants, the towns freed themselves from the feudal system and began to run their own affairs, minting money, fixing tolls and market-taxes and controlling the surrounding country, or *contado*. From now on, there were constant clashes with the emperor, who upheld the old order and was committed to the defence of imperial rights. There were also collisions with the pope; all too often the popes were concerned with protecting their own temporal interests, and those of the bishops, which were adversely affected by urban emancipation. This, in a nutshell, was the cause of the conflicts which tore Italy apart: Frederick Barbarossa, who from his accession in 1156 intended 'to restore the greatness of the Roman empire in all its former power and excellence', confided to his uncle, the chronicler Otto of Freising, the sorrow which he felt for the scandal of a country 'where young men of inferior rank and ordinary workmen engaged in the lowest mechanical trades' undertook the government of towns which flouted the supreme authority.

Notwithstanding the emperor's contempt for the councillor class of the Lombard communes, it is clear that the ruling circles in Italy were generally recruited from among the richest elements in the cities. At Genoa, from the beginning of the twelfth century, the councillors even belonged to families descended from branches of the viscount's house. Besides, in Genoa as well as in the other Lombard cities in the twelfth and thirteenth centuries, many merchant families possessed fiefs or allodial properties in the Apennines. No doubt others came from villages of the *contado*, and a few were descended from church *ministeriales* or from foreign merchants attracted by trade; but all of them, having made large fortunes in foreign trade, one after another promptly reinvested a good proportion of their profits in town houses, farms, and often also in manors and noble estates. This remained one of the characteristic features of the patriciate in Italy, where nobles became involved in trade and where, in spite of political conflicts, very little separated the nobility from the *populo grosso* except psychological obstacles and the weight of tradition.

## WESTERN TEXTILES IN INTERNATIONAL TRADE

In order to balance the imports of spices, cotton, silk and costly fabrics from the Orient, and leather, wool and gold from North Africa, a corresponding export trade had to be developed: sufficient revenue was not provided by chartering vessels to easterners or by the flow of western wood and provisions (corn, salt, oil, wine), and the large-scale trade in slaves had been halted after the conversion of the Slavs to Christianity. In the twelfth century the west found a solution to the problem in a remarkable expansion of its industrial production of wool, flax and hemp cloth, and metal products. In particular the textile industry, which had attained a high level of development in Frisia and Flanders from the early Middle Ages, acquired international importance in the twelfth century.

From the year 1000, imports of English wools supplemented the production of local wool: at this time Flemings, Normans, and merchants from Ponthieu and the Ile-de-France acquired market-toll privileges in London. Around 1100, guilds were established at Valenciennes and Saint-Omer for the purpose of importing wool, and in the middle of the twelfth century various local guilds amalgamated into the 'hanses' of Bruges and Ypres; these in turn were amalgamated into the 'Flemish hanse of London', which existed for the purpose of purchasing wool in London and the great fairs of England.

At the beginning of the twelfth century, three events happened almost simultaneously: the cloths of Ypres appeared at the market of Novgorod in Russia, the toll-house of Bapaume was organized to channel traffic between Flanders and the royal estate (merchants from Saint-Omer and Arras visited it in 1127), and the 'men of Arras and Flanders' were frequently seen at the fair of Saint-Martin at Provins (1137). Very soon, the southern regions and almost all the Mediterranean countries provided one of the main outlets for the textile industry, whether its products were brought to the southern markets by merchants from the north, or by Italian merchants visiting the areas of production or the intervening markets.

We have a good deal of evidence for the first procedure: for instance, in the oldest extant list of Genoese market-tolls, a record of 1128–29, which seems to refer to events before 1102 since the payments are provided for in a currency which went out of circulation at this date, it is said that the 'men from the other side of the mountains' brought bales of woollens (*torsellus lanius*) and canvases, or hemp cloths, to Genoa. In the registers of the Genoese notaries which have survived from the second half of the twelfth century, there are also many instances of merchants from the north and east of France who were frequent visitors at the market or themselves took stalls in order to sell Franco-Flemish cloths; this state of affairs continued until the first half of the thirteenth century.

64  Fairs: merchants at the fair of *Lendit* at Saint-Denis, near Paris.

65  Cloth: the stages of cloth-making, according to a stained-glass window.

In the opposite direction, the Italians frequented the fairs over the mountains from the end of the eleventh century: in 1074, Pope Gregory VII wrote to various French bishops condemning the king of France, who had permitted Italian merchants visiting the fairs 'of France' to be robbed; no doubt the *Lendit* and Compiègne fairs are meant since at this time the word 'France' referred to Ile-de-France. In 1127, at the time of the assassination of the count of Flanders, there were 'Lombards' at the fair of Ypres. But in the last quarter of the twelfth century an event of the greatest importance occurred when Italians appeared at the fairs of Champagne. These very soon became the centre of international trade in the west: here the merchants of the large Italian market towns bought the French and Flemish fabrics, which quickly became established as the chief export from the west to Mediterranean lands, and it was here that all financial settlements were made. The fairs of Champagne, together with the expansion of the Franco-Flemish cloth industry and the Italian banking system, were the most powerful agents of the rise of western economy during the Middle Ages.

Right to left, top to bottom: weaving, dyeing, carding and cleaning off.

66 Banking: the counting-house of an Italian banker in the fifteenth century.

# IV   THE MEDIEVAL WEST AT THE PEAK OF ITS PROSPERITY

The origins of the fairs of Champagne go back to the twelfth century, but they open a distinct new era in medieval economic history, and reach their peak during the course of the thirteenth; they may therefore be treated as a characteristic feature of the classical medieval period at its height.

In Champagne there were a number of fairs whose origins, like those of the local market, are in all probability to be sought in the early Middle Ages. The agricultural development of the region and its increasing population helped to make it an active centre of trade between town and country at the beginning of the twelfth century. In the middle of the century, cloth merchants and mercers came to it from Arras, Picardy, Flanders, Paris and the Ile-de-France. The fairs held at Troyes, Provins, Bar-sur-Aube and Lagny were especially favoured by the policy of the counts of Champagne and Brie, Thibaut 'the Great' and Henry 'the Liberal'. Merchants who flocked to them were placed under the guardianship of the count, who was prepared to ensure that his protection, his 'safe-conduct', was respected, if need be by force. A network of roads was set up, and the necessary buildings erected, contributing to the prosperity of the fairs. From 1169 onwards, the increase in receipts at the toll-house of Bapaume testifies to an expansion in trade between Flanders and the regions to the south of it.

In 1174, at the height of the Lombard league crisis, Milanese merchants made their first appearance at the fairs of Champagne: in this year Frederick Barbarossa crossed the Alps again to crush the communes of Lombardy, and at the walls of Alessandria came up against their determined resistance, which gained its reward at Legnano. Rather than wait for the men from across the mountains to come to them, the Milanese themselves (and, as we have seen, Italians had already been visiting the trans-Alpine fairs for a good number of years) journeyed to the fairs of Champagne, where merchants from Arras and Flanders brought their products, and where the fabrics of Champagne and Rheims, one of the most common exports to the Orient, could be bought. The pattern was set: the merchants of Piacenza and Asti (who supplied the Genoese market) and the Luccans (who at the time dominated the Tuscan

67 Portico around a church at Bar-sur-Aube, in which fairs took place.

economy) took the road to Champagne in turn, and we know that in 1175 merchants from Limoges, Rouen, Rheims and Paris also met there.

Very soon, as early as 1180, the fairs took on their final shape. They were established in four towns, and made up a series of six fairs, staggered over the year: at Lagny on 'New Year's Morrow', at Bar in the middle of Lent, then on to the May fair of Provins at Ascension, on to Troyes for the 'warm fair' of St John, to Provins again for the St Ayoul fair on Holy Cross Day in September, and finally back to Troyes for the 'cold fair' or the St Remy fair (Remigius) on All Souls' Day. The fairs took on a definite rhythm: to begin with, there was a week during which merchandise was exempt from taxes; then there was the cloth fair, then the leather fair and the *avoirs de poids* (goods sold by weight: wax, cotton, spices, etc.); finally came the concluding stage when debts incurred during the fair were settled. The complete cycle lasted from fifteen days to two full months for each fair.

The extraordinary success of the fairs of Champagne had many consequences, the most important of which were a fantastic rise in the cloth industry of north-western Europe and the appearance of an economy based on credit.

The merchants of Arras were the first to gain a foothold for their textiles in the south. The neighbouring towns, Hesdin, Montreuil-sur-mer, Saint-Omer, Abbeville, followed suit, as well as those of the valleys of the Scheldt: Valenciennes, Maubeuge, Cambrai, Tournai. A few years later, the products of Flemish industry predominated, with Ypres in the forefront, and behind her Bruges, Douai, Lille, Dixmude and Ghent. Before the end of the twelfth century, the industrial zone spread to Amiens, Beauvais, Paris, Saint-Denis and Château-Landon. In the same year (1180) the cloths 'of France and Flanders' appear in the price-list of the fair of Poitiers and in the records of the

Genoese notaries; at about the same date, they were sold at the fair of Saint-Gilles in Gard.

The fairs of Champagne were the chief source of the fine northern cloths which passed into the hands of Italian merchants: they were subsequently found in the majority of the markets of northern Italy and Tuscany, and they were taken in ever-increasing quantities to Sicily and 'overseas', by which was meant 'Romania', Syria and Egypt. In the second quarter of the thirteenth century, there was no shop which did not stock a few pieces for sale to people of every social class, for there were cloths of all kinds and at all prices. They made an important contribution to the rise of Italian industry, for soon raw cloth began to be imported by Florence, and prepared and dyed by her manufacturers, who belonged to the famous corporation called *L'Arte di Calimala*, the richest in the city.

In order to pay for their purchases at fairs, the Italians brought as much merchandise to them as possible, obtained from every Mediterranean country. One important commodity was alum, indispensable at this time as a caustic agent in the preparation of cloth, which was produced by Egypt in the twelfth and thirteenth centuries, before Genoa started drawing on the inexhaustible reserves of the coasts of Asia Minor (Ephesus and Phocaea); they also brought plants used for dyeing (kermes, lac, woad, brazil-wood, etc.); leathers, spices, and above all pepper. Consequently the fairs of Champagne helped to drum up international trade in the Mediterranean world.

Before the middle of the thirteenth century, they were attended by merchants from the whole of western Europe, and not just by those of northern France and Italy. Merchants came from the German empire, especially from Cologne, which was at this time the focus of the Rhenish economy, Lübeck, which was beginning to play a leading role in the German Hanse on the Baltic, and the great cloth-centre of St Gall. Other merchants from the south, from Lérida, Barcelona, Toulouse and Montauban, travelled on the great highway which was established over the length of France from north to south across the Massif Central. Whole suburbs were built to accommodate them, notably at Provins and Troyes, where stone market-halls were built for the sale of their products. As they travelled in caravans, they most often lodged with their animals and servants in hostels resembling oriental caravanserais, while after about 1280 the richest merchants were provided with private mansions.

Collective organizations were set up among merchants from the same geographic area, in order to facilitate negotiations with the public authorities. They were in fact 'hanses', like the association 'of the seventeen towns': this was a group of all the traders from the cloth towns of the north, numbering about forty, who had common economic interests; there was no political or linguistic discrimination, for some of the towns belonged to the kingdom, others to the empire, and there was even one English town among their number; some were French-speaking, others spoke Flemish. Similarly, all the Italians assembled as a 'nation' – although they belonged to towns which were politically at variance and often hostile to each other – and this fact perhaps helped to give birth to the idea of nationhood. At the head of this association was a 'governor' or 'captain' (*capitaneus*), elected by the representatives of all the cities taking part in the fairs, and each individual town also had its own interests looked after by one or two consuls. Finally, the southern French constituted a third group; the 'captain of the Provençaux' (in fact the people of Languedoc) was generally nominated by Montpellier, the most active town in the region.

The importance of the business done there would perhaps not have been sufficient in itself to make the fairs of Champagne the great international crossroads of western economy for a century and a half, if the market had not been provided with a completely novel organization which guaranteed its success. The merchants who came to the fairs were not only protected by the 'market safe-conduct' (*conduit des foires*) granted by the count of Champagne; he also arranged for them to be placed under the protection of the duke of Burgundy while passing through the Duchy, and subsequently he secured for them the vitally important protection of the king, when in the time of Philip Augustus the largest western kingdom once again became capable of extending its authority throughout its territories.

More significantly, contracts made at the fairs (or, as the saying went, 'sur le corps des foires' – *supra corpus nundinarum*) were valid everywhere, without dispute or delay. The security which this brought was of great benefit to the merchants: until then, they had had to rely largely on the authority of the lords which could hardly be exercised beyond the territories directly under their jurisdiction; now, at one stroke, a contract could be executed at Florence, for instance, between a Florentine merchant and his creditor from Bruges, without regard to the boundaries of manors or the frontiers of states. This advance was achieved by various stages. First of all, officials were created to superintend the rules and regulations at the fairs; later they made use of their personal seals to guarantee contracts; and finally, in the second quarter of the thirteenth century, they were provided with a jurisdictional seal. All contracts made at the fair and drawn up by the notaries were entered in the appropriate registers, and a special jurisdiction was set up.

In case of complaint by a creditor against a debtor the affair was investigated by the 'Court of the Fairs'; if the debtor refused to recognize the court, a report was sent to a political or jurisdictional authority which he did accept, requiring it to proceed against the offender. If he lost the case, a mandate was given to the authority to seize the defaulter's goods, to be set against the money owing. If he refused or resorted to delaying tactics, the officials had the right to pronounce the 'interdict of the fairs' against the town or state of the 'fugitive debtor' or defaulter. This was a sort of lay excommunication banning all the debtor's compatriots from the fairs. If necessary, a 'reprisal' followed (as in Italy), in which his countrymen's goods were seized up to the value of the unpaid debt, plus legal costs and damages and the accrued interest. Few cities were in a position to permit the fairs to be closed to their merchants, since they had become essential to their economy. There are examples of interdicts from the middle of the thirteenth century; they became more numerous at the end of the century and at the beginning of the fourteenth, when the threat lost its effect, since by this time the fairs had ceased to be the sole intermediaries between the towns. At all events, the fairs of Champagne brought undisputed benefits, since by their legal organization they contributed to the development of the rudiments of commercial law on an international level.

The rise of Champagne as a busy industrial region was primarily due to the fairs. From the middle of the thirteenth century, the cloths of Châlons and Provins vied with the products of the Flemish industry in the Italian market-towns, and at the end of the century they outrivalled them: Rheims linen was renowned for its quality as far away as the Orient, while other cloths 'from Champagne', manufactured at Troyes, Vitry and Epinal, formed an important part of a good many cargoes. The urban development to which the industrialization of the region gave rise led to intensive cultivation of what had formerly been only waste and woodland, while on the plateaux the Cistercian abbeys and the Templars increased their flocks of sheep to supply the workshops with raw materials.

It should also be emphasized that the entire road system of France at this time was organized to facilitate communications between Paris, the fairs of Champagne, the producer-towns of the north, and the foreign markets. From the north a complex network led to Paris via Bapaume and Crépy-en-Valois, and to Champagne via Rheims. There were also routes across Burgundy: one passed over the Franche-Comté and the Jura, by the Col de Jougne, and led to Lausanne and the Simplon or the Great St Bernard; another followed the Saône by way of Chalon (where very busy cloth-fairs were established at the end of the thirteenth century) and continued via Mâcon and Lyons. From

68 The road of Mont-Genèvre, one of the great Alpine routes between Dauphiné and Piedmont.

69 An example of great public works in the Middle Ages: the aqueduct of Spoleto, 220 yards long and over 80 yards in height, was the work of Matteo Gattaponi (c. 1362–70). A medieval road passed over this bridge, access to which was guarded by a stronghold.

there, the road forked, going across Bresse and Bugey to the Lake of Geneva, or else across the Savoy, via Pont-de-Beauvoisin and Chambéry, then across the Alps at the Mont-Cenis pass, while yet another route continued down the Rhône either via Avignon or Arles to Marseilles, or via Nîmes to Aiguesmortes or Montpellier.

The lord who held the passes which these routes for English wool and French cloth had to cross decided their policy in relation to them. The house of Savoy aimed at absolute control of the Alpine roads and tried to direct the merchants along ways which it decided they should follow. The Dauphins set themselves up against their cousins of Savoy. The ruling families of Chalon and of Salins in the Comté supported their own interests, and there were imperial pressures for the establishment of toll-houses and staple houses along the routes. There was economic warfare between roads, and between towns, which resulted in the construction of new routes, new bridges and new passes, and led to a lowering of toll-tariffs. International trade could only benefit from this; small market-towns grew up and the countryside through which the roads passed became rich. Pressures were exercised by the merchants who did not hesitate to adopt the route which seemed to them most economical or safe. They formed a kind of users' syndicate, indulged in collective bargaining with the authorities controlling the routes, and forced them to make improvements in the roads and to reduce their tariffs. As a result of their demands, a new road was opened side by side with the ancient road at the Mont-Cenis pass, and,

70 Aiguesmortes, the port founded by St Louis, was the main import centre of medieval France facing the Mediterranean.

further to the east, the St Gothard was put in order for the first time round about 1225.

Marseilles, which had so much difficulty in throwing off Genoese hegemony at the beginning of the thirteenth century, gained a new lease of life when the Tuscan companies began to use its harbour for loading the French cloths bound for Pisa or Porto Pisano, or Motrone, the short-lived port of Lucca. In the middle of the century the town, which had launched out into trade with the Orient in the wake of the Italians, found itself engaged in a big way in the trade in textiles which was essential to balance the spice trade.

From the day when St Louis, as a result of the altered political situation, found himself with direct access to the Mediterranean, he conceived the idea of creating his own export harbour out of the town of Aiguesmortes (which was incidentally very badly situated). It had been built by the Genoese, and it was from here that St Louis himself set out for the Crusade. The whole commercial policy of the monarchy for half a century was directed towards making it the obligatory outlet for national trade, and linking it with the fairs of Champagne. Italian merchants had to unload their goods there and to store them nearby in Nîmes, which was intended to rival Montpellier, then in Catalan territory. This economic warfare continued until Philip VI won Montpellier back.

Philip the Fair's policy was to gain control of this great international route from one end to the other: until this time it had passed through the territory of the empire along the Rhône. He also had his eyes on the business which the route would generate and on the resulting benefits to the regions through which it passed: having established a customs system at the frontiers and restricted the points of entry to a small number of passes, the king's agents insisted that the merchants should travel by the 'king's highway', across the Massif Central where the monarchy enforced its power jointly with the ecclesiastical authorities (by means of a series of *pariages*). The road went to Brioude, Le Puy, Alès and Nîmes via Nevers, Saint-Pourçain, Riom, Montferrand, while another branch went via Saint-Flour and Mende (or Marvejols) to Millau and Lodève and from there to Montpellier or Narbonne. The whole economy of central France was enriched by it in one way or another, and the vineyards of Saint-Pourçain, the mints, and the factories making cutlery and ironmongery were among the concerns to feel its benefits; of particular importance was the growth of intensive sheep-rearing in this region, which until then had been somewhat underdeveloped.

The wools of the Midi and central France served a new cloth-making area, whose products were reserved almost exclusively for export. Narbonne was revived in this way, to compensate for the loss of its harbour which became

71 Carcassonne, fortress city of Languedoc, has preserved its walls (Roman, Visigothic and thirteenth-century), which make it one of the most typical medieval cities.

silted up at this time, and from about 1300 all the towns and a large number of boroughs in the region also took up the manufacture of woollen textiles. About 1320, the seneschalship of Carcassonne alone contained more than fifty localities which prided themselves on being 'cloth-manufacturing', such as Lodève, Clermont l'Hérault, Béziers, Saint-Pons, Saint-Félix, Caunes, etc. The 'village cloths' flooded the Mediterranean markets in Spain as well as the east, while the textile industry expanded, reaching the neighbouring Roussillon, and then Catalonia.

### TRADE IN THE NORTH SEA, THE BALTIC AND GERMANY

The fairs of Champagne and the Mediterranean markets, although essential to the cloth industry of the Franco-Flemish countries, were not the only trading media used by them from the middle of the thirteenth century onwards: the position of Bruges, at the focus of all the major commercial currents of the time, promoted an expansion of the textile industry in neighbouring areas. There were also fairs in Flanders, dating from the eleventh century, which

72 Bruges: the Cloth Hall was begun in 1248. The belfry symbolizes city privileges; its square base dates from 1282 to 1296, the central part from 1395, and the octagonal top from 1482.

underwent a considerable expansion in the course of the thirteenth century, while others were held in Brabant, at Antwerp, Malines and Bergen-op-Zoom; they were attended by Italians and Germans, and were at the centre of a two-way commercial traffic.

The first of these streams flowed towards the Rhine and Meuse regions, in particular Cologne, where Rhenish wine was collected for transportation to the Low Countries, and Lorraine. From these areas the merchandise was redistributed by other routes, to Westphalia or to Basle and southern Germany, while a third route led over the Simplon or the St Gothard to Milan or Venice. These great communication routes were among the most important of classical medieval Europe.

The other stream was perhaps even more important. It linked Flanders and England, with the result that the economies of these two countries were for a long time complementary. The Flemish industry was partially dependent upon supplies of English wool, especially from the Cistercian monasteries, and, in return, Flanders sent large quantities of cloth across the Channel. The great

119

fairs of St Ives, St Giles at Winchester and St Botolph at Boston made their fortune out of this trade; it provided business for the English ports and supplied the king with a large part of his revenue by means of a heavy taxation (especially after 1266). The growth in demand stimulated an expansion of wool production, which accelerated in the second half of the thirteenth century and at the beginning of the fourteenth; it had a serious effect on the English countryside, where the clearing of waste land ceased and a good deal of cultivated land was converted back again into pasture. But there was a simultaneous and compensatory shift of the English wool industry from the traditional cloth towns towards the countryside, thanks to the systematic utilization of water power and the establishment of fulling-mills on waterfalls and rivers.

Finally, the monarchy for the first time devised a genuine economic policy and a new customs system, although this was done primarily for financial reasons. A system of export licences, associated with personal safe-conducts for the merchants, and levies of 'reasonable' taxes were substituted by the king for free trade, which had given many merchants of the Meuse, Flanders, the Rhineland, Brabant and Picardy direct access to England. As a result, we have evidence that in 1273 nearly 33,000 sacks of wool were exported, which at 166 kg a sack would mean about 5,500 tons. The interest of the Crown in this trade was such that the monarchy granted a series of 'establicemens' to foreign merchants. The statute *De mercatoribus* (1283) laid down a new procedure for the settlement of commercial debts. A 'ley merchant', distinct from common law, applied to all transactions. The Statute of Winchester (1285) expressly guaranteed the security of the roads; and finally, in 1303, the famous *Carta mercatoria* put the seal on the privileged position of the foreign merchants and protected them against paying exorbitant taxes. But it was mainly Italians and Germans who profited from the new commercial climate, since the Flemings, who had already stopped taking their products to the Mediterranean markets, began to adopt an increasingly passive attitude towards their sources of supply; they were now content to receive at Bruges or Antwerp wools brought to them by English, Italian, and especially Hanseatic merchants.

Apart from his efforts at organizing the Cornish lead and tin trade and the leather trade, Edward I decided to establish the English wool 'Staple' on the continent, thus finally bringing to an end a long period of uncertain economic policy, which had been dictated by internal struggles. The new system applied uniformly to all merchants, English as well as foreign, and gave the monarchy complete control of exports: as a result of the efforts of the king's agents, wool and fleeces were brought under central control and compulsorily channelled by the exporters, under royal protection, towards a 'staple' town where the products were retained by traders or overseers appointed by the king. In 1313, the king fixed the wool staple at Bruges, a measure which was of great importance for Anglo-Flemish relations and the economies of the two countries. Later, the staple spread to other towns, both in England itself ('home staple') and on the continent (notably Antwerp, Dordrecht, Middelburg, and finally, in the middle of the fourteenth century, to Calais). Meanwhile exports of wool had grown even further: in 1305 they rose to more than 50,000 sacks, or 8,300 tons, an increase of a third in the course of a generation.

Together with the fairs of Champagne, the rise of the Franco–Flemish cloth industry, and the English wool staple, the development of the German Hanse was one of the chief events of economic history during the classical Middle Ages in the west: it was to the northern countries what the commercial activity of the Italian republics was to the Mediterranean world.

About 1150 the town of Lübeck was founded, at the confluence of two rivers not far from the Baltic, and at the narrowest point of the isthmus of Holstein, across which trade between the Baltic and the North Sea traditionally flowed. Everything was carefully thought out to ensure the commercial future of the town; in Westphalia and as far away as Flanders and Holland there had been publicity to attract immigrants, while the duke of Saxony, Henry the Lion, informed the Russian and Scandinavian merchants of the event. The inhabitants of Lübeck were exempt from tolls throughout the duchy of Saxony, and the town received special privileges, the 'Lübeck rights', which were subsequently extended to many other towns of the Baltic region.

The purpose of the foundation was to enable German merchants to share in the profits made by the Gotland islanders from trade with Russia, and consequently Lübeck immediately became involved in the trade of the Gotlanders. In 1161 the association of 'merchants of the empire frequenting Gotland' was founded, the archetype of the future Hanse. To enable them to trade more easily, the Germans wanted to settle in Gotland, and before the end of the century the town of Visby was founded to accommodate them. From then on Lübeck and Visby, Dortmund and Soest acted in conjunction. In 1189, the Russian prince Yaroslav made a commercial treaty with Gotland, and a little later the Germans and Gotlanders acquired a 'counter' of their own in Novgorod, the famous Peterhof. The records of this establishment for the middle of the thirteenth century tell of ships and merchants coming from Gotland, assembling at the mouth of the Neva on the island of Kronstadt, and then being guided by Russian pilots up the Neva and across Lake Ladoga; after transhipment to clear the Volchov rapids, they reached Novgorod, a town of which we know a great deal thanks to recent Russian excavations.

The fur trade was the chief *raison d'être* of the journey, with honey and wax as subsidiaries, and perhaps also silver. As in the Mediterranean world, the cloths of Flanders were the medium of exchange; we also know that, from 1130, cloths from Ypres were sold at the Novgorod market. In 1201, according to the Chronicle of Nestor, German merchants also came for the first time by a land route, via the Dvina. Soon Germans reached the market of Pskov, at the lower end of Lake Peïpus, and those of Polotsk and Smolensk, and they tried to convert and colonize the Estonians and Livonians. Reval (Tallinn) was founded in 1201, then Dorpat (Tartu), and, in 1230, two hundred German merchants established themselves at Riga along with the Scandinavian settlers. These new towns, as well as Narva, helped to open up trade with the Baltic countries and Russia; in 1229, the prince of Smolensk, in his own name and in that of the princes of Polotsk and Vitebsk, defined the respective rights of the German and Russian merchants.

To keep pace with this economic development, new towns were founded all along the Baltic shore, notably Rostock (1200), Wismar (1228), Stralsund (1234), Stettin (Szczecin) and Elbing (Elblag: 1237), Danzig (Gdańsk: 1238), Greifswald (1238), and Königsberg (Kaliningrad: 1255). The region between the Elbe and the Oder (Mecklenburg, Pomerania, Prussia and even Poland) was systematically colonized, and towns were founded in Baltic and Slav territory to develop the agriculture and commerce of this vast area: Berlin (1230), Thorn (Toruń: 1233), Frankfurt-on-the-Oder (1253), Breslau (Wrocław) and Cracow (1257). These towns received the privileges of Lübeck and of Magdeburg. The demographic expansion which had caused intensive internal colonization in France and England, and which had given rise to the establishment of Italian merchant colonies in every eastern market-town, was also the reason for the massive German expansion, both in the field of agriculture and urban development, towards the east. Its results can be seen in the foundation of several hundred burgs (boroughs) across Westphalia, Saxony, Brandenburg and Pomerania, and the systematic conquest of Prussia by the Teutonic Order.

The German expansion was also directed towards southern Sweden, penetrating first to Kalmar, and then on to central Sweden where, in about 1251, the Germans founded Stockholm, which for a long time remained a mixed German-Swedish town. In the second half of the thirteenth century, Thuringian miners started to work the copper mines of Falun, which became the most important in Europe, and, a little later, the iron mines of Dalecarlia. In Scania, German merchants aimed at dominating the great international herring fairs, and they claimed the exclusive right to trade there after forbidding the

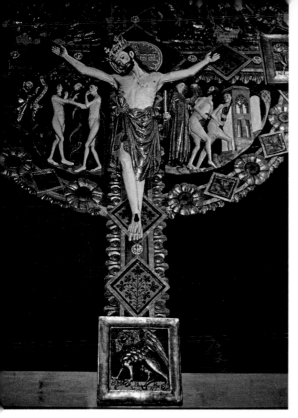

73 The island of Gotland was the centre of German economic expansion in the Baltic. This polychrome crucifix of the fourteenth century is in a Gotland church.

74 Courtroom of the town hall in Lüneburg, whose salt-mines and finance were the background of Lübeck's economic growth.

75 Medieval salt storehouses in Lübeck.

English, Frisians and Flemings access to the Baltic. Since they had the salt-mines of Lüneburg (near Lübeck) at their disposal, they eventually monopolized the trade in salt herring, which was a staple element in medieval diet. When the Hanseatic counter at Bergen, on the Norwegian coast, became one of their main centres, in the middle of the thirteenth century, they gained a monopoly in fish-salting.

Within half a century an economic power of considerable importance had thus established itself in northern Europe. The primitive community of the 'merchants of Gotland' was progressively replaced by a number of urban leagues: the league of Wendish towns, controlled by Lübeck and supported by the towns of Pomerania; the league of Saxon towns, controlled by Brunswick, to which Hamburg and Bremen gave their allegiance; a league of Westphalian towns, centred on Dortmund; and in the second rank the league of Livonian and Prussian towns, controlled by the Teutonic Order. At the end of the thirteenth century the various leagues combined together into one vast 'German Hanse', which, while acting on behalf of essentially economic

76 Toruń: ruined castle of the Teutonic Knights, built 1234–70.

77 Bergen, centre of Hanseatic trade in Norway. These Hanseatic wooden houses on the quay have burnt down and been rebuilt several times in their original style.

interests, became one of the most important political forces of Europe, although it took on its final form only in the course of the fourteenth century.

Just as the fairs of Champagne had made use of a purely economic weapon, the interdict, so the Hanseatics found an equally effective means of pressure in the boycott. In 1277, for example, as a reprisal against the Russians, they decided to compel all merchants, on pain of death and confiscation of their goods, to stop visiting Novgorod. In the same way, they transferred their business headquarters to Aardenburg in 1280, so as to bring pressure to bear on the people of Bruges who were encroaching on their rights; they agreed to return to Bruges only when the town agreed to confirm and extend their privileges. In 1284, they blockaded Bergen in order to apply pressure to the king of Norway; all deliveries of provisions were prohibited and they stationed ships to prevent the blockade from being broken. The famine was so serious that the king had to concede them absolute freedom to trade with exemption from all taxes. With a growing population in areas with a poor soil and an embargo on English grain, Norway had become purely a land of fishermen and had lapsed into complete dependence on imports of Hanseatic wheat.

The Hanseatic towns led the west in their fleet, consisting of ships of a special type, the *kogge* (which was adopted by the Mediterranean peoples under the name *coca*). It progressively monopolized communications between England and lands of the north, as well as the Low Countries. In 1273, the Hanseatics carried scarcely more than 4 per cent of the exports of English wool; from 1303, their share of the tonnage at Boston was more than 33 per cent, and in 1310–11, 54 per cent. Their privileges in England and Flanders continued to multiply. The return cargoes from Bruges consisted mainly of cloth – hence its vital importance for the Flemish economy – together with spices, but they also imported salt foods from the north and especially barrels and kegs of herrings, Prussian and Polish wheat, beer from Hamburg, wax and honey, and metals from Scandinavia and central Europe, via the Vistula and the Oder. They had also acquired something of a monopoly of furs from the east at a time when the fashion for them was spreading all over the west, and even to the Mediterranean countries. In 1311, the town of Pskov alone offered no fewer than 50,000 ermine skins, sables, etc., for sale to German merchants and in 1336 there were 160 Hanseatic traders at the Peterhof in Novogorod.

ATLANTIC TRADE

During the thirteenth century, and especially towards its close, trade along the Atlantic coast of Europe expanded considerably, supported by massive movements of goods; these consisted mainly of the wines of Poitou and Guienne, the traditional markets of which were found in England and the Low Countries; 'bay' salt from the coasts of Aunis, Saintonge, lower Poitou and the island of Noirmoutier; and the iron of Biscay.

*Wine*, more than anything else, contributed to forging the permanent economic and political links between England and her possessions in Guienne. From the second quarter of the thirteenth century the wines of Gascony found a wide market in England, and the king promoted their importation by granting generous privileges to the Gascon merchants. As a result there was a considerable expansion of viticulture in the whole Bordeaux region at the expense of other crops: the lowland areas, in the valley of the Garonne from Saint-Macaire to Bordeaux, were covered with vines; vineyards were planted in the Médoc; and, as a result of political changes, vines were even grown in

78 The treading of grapes; miniature from an early fourteenth-century English manuscript.

79 Delivering wine at the port of Paris; detail of a miniature from a fourteenth-century French manuscript.

the upland areas in the valleys leading to the Garonne. The wines of Cahors and Villeneuve-sur-Lot came from along the banks of the Lot, the wines of Moissac, Albi and Gaillac from along the Tarn, and the wine of Condom from along the Baïse. All actual production (except in the case of the wines of Bayonne) was concentrated in Bordeaux, the staple town, to which large fleets made their way to load up the casks twice a year, in autumn (from the end of September to mid-November) and in spring (for the Easter wine). The average annual tonnage from Bordeaux at the beginning of the fourteenth century was around 82,000 barrels, reaching a peak of nearly 103,000 in 1308–9 (the equivalent of about 850,000 hectolitres, or 18,700,000 gallons). At this time, wine represented 31 per cent of England's imports and 25 per cent of those of the Low Countries. It was one of the largest categories of trade known in the Middle Ages: the total freight figures are even higher than those of our own times, despite the incomparably less efficient methods of transport of those days. To this must be added a separate branch of the trade, which was also of considerable dimensions, in the wines of Aunis exported through La Rochelle, those of Poitou and the Loire region which went out through Nantes and the ports of lower Poitou, and those of the Adour through Bayonne.

There is little information available for this period on the *salt* trade on the Atlantic coasts, but its importance grew from the end of the thirteenth century, and it became indispensable to the salt foods of the north, such as fish, meat and butter.

The *iron* of Biscay provides the first example in medieval Europe, where until this time wood had been the basic material, of the exploitation of metal in appreciable quantities. There was an explosive rise in iron production in the last decades of the thirteenth century; it is estimated that an annual total of four or five thousand tons was exported through the ports of Biscay and Guipúzcoa, not counting the iron of Navarre, which was sent out through Bayonne. Once again, these exports were balanced by massive imports of French and Flemish cloth, especially from Tournai, Mauberge and Valenciennes, which quickly found their way to the Spanish markets.

The growth of this trade stimulated the rapid rise of a large and busy Atlantic fleet, which was, however, generally of only limited tonnage. Ships from England, La Rochelle, Brittany and the Basque country predominated until the arrival of the Hanseatics who, in the fourteenth century, attempted to monopolize the Atlantic bulk trade in wines, salt and iron.

At the end of the thirteenth century one of the crucial events of European history occurred in the waters of the Atlantic, when Genoese galleys made a direct maritime link between the Mediterranean and the North Sea by sailing

80 Cargo being unloaded at a fortified town; miniature from a late fourteenth-century French manuscript.

round Spain. Up until then, there had been two quite distinct economic sectors in Europe, two worlds which could be connected only with great difficulty by the extremely tedious land routes. The shortest, which was, however, little used, was the route between Bordeaux and Narbonne; the others ran between the Low Countries and Provence along the rivers (Scheldt or Meuse, Saône, Rhône); between Germany and the Adriatic; and between the Baltic and the Black Sea, along the great Russian rivers. There are indeed examples (which have been examined more or less thoroughly) of boats from the north reaching the Mediterranean at different periods, such as those of the marauding Vikings who plundered the Iberian peninsula, or those carrying reinforcements to Italy, or pilgrims to the east (and notably a Flemish ship which must have taken part in the Crusades), or the Basque vessels which intervened at the time of the *Reconquista*; but all these were exceptional. Only in 1278 were there, for the first time, regular voyages of Genoese galleys, loaded with merchandise. This usually consisted of alum bound for Flanders, an especially weighty commodity indispensable for dyeing the best cloth; Genoa eventually acquired a near-monopoly of it in the east. On the return trip, the galleys brought back good English wool, and as a result Florence, which up until then had been restricted to dyeing and finishing Franco-Flemish cloths delivered in a raw state, was able to develop an indigenous textile industry. Very soon, the Florentine cloths gained a very important foothold in all the Mediterranean markets.

For a generation, the link was somewhat precarious, and the Genoese boats, after delivering their alum to Flanders, or Moroccan grain and Spanish oil, wine and fruit to England, often returned to the Mediterranean in ballast. But from the beginning of the fourteenth century, important colonies of merchants from Genoa and Piacenza settled at Bruges and Antwerp, London and Southampton, and Mediterranean products regularly reached Bruges by sea, whence the Hanseatics distributed them throughout the Baltic.

Thus, after two centuries of separate development, the northern and southern economic sectors of Europe came to be linked. At the same time another land link was forged, when the Germans founded their famous 'Fondaco dei Tedeschi' at Venice – the great counting-house which was their window on the Mediterranean for two centuries.

The Iberian peninsula, the bridge between the two worlds of the Atlantic and the Mediterranean, became settled after the sacred union achieved at the battle of the Las Navas de Tolosa (1212) finally assured the future of Christianity in Spain. However, although the sailors of the northern coasts, from San Sebastián to Santander, became involved in an extensive Atlantic trade, Castile was primarily concerned with the completion of the *Reconquista* and with its own internal development: the conquest of Andalusia was driven forward to the straits of Gibraltar (1236–46), the foundation of the kingdom of Murcia followed in its wake (1266), and plans were made for taking Morocco. An agreement with Genoa opened up Seville to the Italian merchant republic, and enabled it to launch out on the great adventure of maritime trade with the North Sea countries.

Aragon, on the other hand, without in any way reducing the momentum of its internal development, especially in the Ebro valley, acquired a maritime and economic strength which had the effect of altering the balance of power in

81 The 'Fondaco dei Tedeschi', centre of German trade at Venice and for the Mediterranean as a whole. The façade on the Grand Canal was reconstructed 1505–8 in the Renaissance style and used to be decorated with frescoes by Giorgione (a few remnants can be seen at the Accademia). Today the building is the main post office of Venice.

82 Interior of the late fifteenth-century *Lonja de la Seda* (Silk Exchange) in Valencia, which was one of the centres of the international silk trade.

the Mediterranean. In 1227 James I the Conqueror proclaimed an 'Act of Navigation', giving a monopoly in his kingdom's trade to the ships of Barcelona. Subsequently he secured more elbow-room for Barcelona by taking the Balearics from the Moslems, between 1229 and 1235: these islands were the first stage on the journey towards the central and eastern Mediterranean, as well as being a necessary halting-place between the Christian coasts and Africa. In 1238 the greatest port on the east coast of Spain, Valencia, fell into his hands. When, by the treaty of Corbeil (1258), the king renounced his claim to the lands situated to the north of the Pyrenees, and restored the kingdom of Murcia to Castile in 1266, the state of Aragon found itself looking towards the sea. Barcelona's navy and trade were thus able to benefit from a support in terms of territory and human resources which the Italian republics lacked. Valencia, Palma, Montpellier, Collioure, and the secondary ports of the Catalan area (Tarragona, Tortosa, San Felíu, Blanes, Minorca), helped to more than double the potential of Barcelona, even though certain Crown lands were temporarily detached from it so as to form a separate realm granted in appanage. Majorca, too, remained economically linked with Barcelona; its commercial role, at the crossroads of the maritime routes of the western Mediterranean, was considerable, and its school of marine cartography, which it owed to its Jewish colony, rendered an inestimable service to navigation.

By means of his unremitting diplomacy, supported if necessary by military expeditions, the king did not rest until he had established his power over the kingdoms of Morocco, Tlemcen, Bougie and Tunis. The Arab rulers paid tribute to him, shared the proceeds of their customs duties with him, drew on the service of his fleet (which they paid for in gold) for the purpose of trading or making war, and finally enlisted Christian mercenaries in their forces. In spite of various strains and stresses, the Catalan penetration of Africa continued to gather strength; fifteen Catalan consulates and fonduks were established along the coast from Ceuta to Tunis, while groups of merchants advanced far into the interior.

Aragon was provisioned by Moroccan corn, and it was also carried by Catalan merchants to Kabylia which was ill-favoured agriculturally. Wools called 'merino' after the Marinid dynasty found their way to Catalonia, as well as the wax of Bougie, the exceptional quality of which resulted in its giving its name to the candles (bougies) which were made from it. Other imports were dates, skins and leathers, oil, coral, and alum from Bougie and Sigilmassa. It has been estimated that the exports brought annually by subjects of the Crown of Aragon, from the ports of call to the east of the 'beaches of Morocco' (that is, to the east of Safi) as far as Tripoli, must have risen between 1275 and 1330 to a

83 Detail from a Catalan world map, 1375.

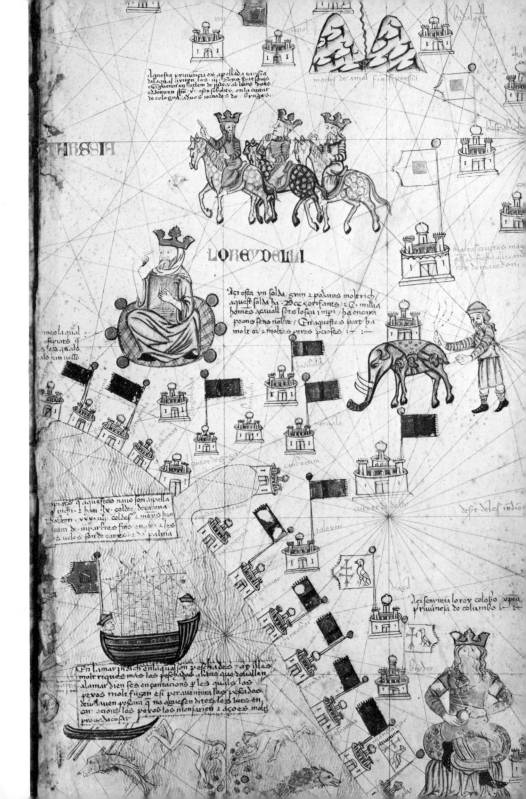

FISSHIA

aquesta prauincia es appellada tarssia
delaqual isqueren los iij. Reys fort sauis
elsquals uengueren an betleem de iuses alahon bona
eladoruren son y... son sebultz en la ciutat
de cologna. Adues iornades de bruges

LOREYDELLI

Aci esta un solda gran e poderos molt rich
aquest solda ha .Dcc. corsfants e CC. milia
homes acauall sots lo seu imperi ha encara
peong sens nobre. Et aquestes part ha
molt or e moltes peres precioses :

mes laqual
esenuars q
eles quals
alo han uestes

pres q aquestes naus son appella
da uichi e han lx. colks de cadena
e hobren xxviij. colks e mays han
cana de mjarbres fins en... ales
ucles son de cane... de palma

En lamar indich enlaqual son escludes e xij illes
molt riques mas los peschadors alba que trouallen
alamar bien se es encantacions e les quals los
reyes molt fugen esi peranenjura los peschadors
deu auen pesam q no aguessen dites los luns en
cantacions los reyes los menjarion e acons molt
proaducostar

mons de amol fin... perssia

malgat austus mas
... edificio allen...
rey de macedonia

desti del es indie

deis senyueia lo rey colobo una
prauincsa de columbo

value of something in the order of 400,000 or 500,000 gold dinars. This trade was balanced, once more, by exports of fabrics from Châlons and Ypres, Paris and Narbonne, and also a coarser type of cloth which formed the basis for an industry in Catalonia and Roussillon at the time; it developed rapidly and gave work to a considerable semi-rural population.

No doubt the monarchy wanted to go further. In the same way as James I and St Ferdinand had extended their lands in Spain by incorporating the territories claimed by each state, James II and Sancho IV agreed at Monteagudo in 1291 to divide the spoils of a prospective conquest of North Africa between them. The country to the west of the Moulouya was to be the Castilian zone; to the east, the kingdoms of Tlemcen, Bougie and Tunis were allotted to Aragon; and behind Tlemcen were strung out the caravan routes which brought ivory, incense, ostrich feathers and Bambouk gold along the long trails from black Africa via Sigilmassa. This trade was concentrated to a large extent in the hands of Jewish merchants, and it was certainly no accident that in 1247 James I gave his protection to Jewish families from Sigilmassa who had come to Majorca, as well as to all other Jews of the oasis, and that in 1274 he exempted the Jews of Tlemcen from the reprisals which had been decided on against those under the jurisdiction of the Abd-al-Wadits.

Aragon not only sought to attain those distant objectives in the interior of the African continent; it aimed at complete domination of the western Mediterranean and in so doing laid the foundations of the future Spanish empire in the Mediterranean. After the 'Sicilian Vespers' (1282), Sicily fell into the hands of Peter of Aragon. It was able to provide Catalonia with the corn without which Barcelona, surrounded as it was by poor soil, could not survive. The Catalan city of Trapani grew up at the eastern point of the island where trade routes connected North Africa with the kingdoms of Sicily, Aragon and Sardinia. Sardinia was seized from Pisa and Genoa in the second quarter of the fourteenth century; from then on, a whole fleet went to Sicily each year to carry off the rich produce of the country: lead and silver, corn, meat, cheese and salt, not to mention coral – the exchange currency of big business with the Arab world. The surplus Catalan population found living-space in Oristano, Iglesias, Cagliari, and on the western coast of Sicily.

Two years after taking Sicily, the Catalans had already managed to gain mastery of the Mediterranean, by taking Malta and Pantellaria from the Angevins, and Djerba and the Kerkennah islands from the Hafsids. They had thus gained a springboard for an expansion eastwards, for which Catalan mercenaries had prepared the way in Asia Minor and Greece: a merciless, century-long war with Genoa and the Angevins ensued.

The Catalans were newcomers to the political and economic arena of the Mediterranean: during the thirteenth century and the first half of the fourteenth, Genoa and Venice remained the two great commercial powers. By about 1230, the French and Provençal coasts had escaped from Genoese control, and Genoa also encountered difficulties in Africa due to the Catalan economic expansion in this area. Consequently it turned once more in a different direction, this time making a bid for the eastern Mediterranean. But it was met by the resolute hostility of Venice, which was prepared to defend its traditional positions tenaciously.

We often use the word 'Orient' as a term covering many contradictory and even hostile elements. The political situation, providing the context for commercial life, see-sawed unceasingly at the mercy of wars and conquests, estrangements and reconciliations; and the repercussions of events in Asia, far away or near at hand, had a significant impact. During the thirteenth century the following powers were strung out between the Bosphorus and Egypt (not counting the people living on the shores of the Black Sea): the Latin empire, the Greek territories, the Turkish sultanates, the kingdom of Lesser Armenia, and the Frankish principalities with their rival interests (Antioch, Tripoli, Acre), while the islands (Chios, Rhodes, Cyprus, Crete) kept a watch on the mainland and were a drain on its economy. Each of these territories had one particularly activity which offered the westerners great opportunities for trade, and consequently Genoa and Venice vied for supremacy over them. Others also came to do profitable business: in particular the Pisans, until they almost disappeared from the area after their sea power was crushed at Meloria (1284); the Catalans, who by contrast won a position of growing importance for themselves from this date; the merchants of Marseilles, whose trade reached its height in the second half of the thirteenth century; and to a decreasing extent the people of Narbonne, those of Montpellier, the sailors of Savona and Ancona, and especially, from the fourteenth century onwards, a few Dalmatians.

There is also a tendency to categorize as 'spices' all the extremely varied products of the east, which in fact consisted of a large number of heterogeneous wares: indeed this tendency is encouraged by many documents of the period. Some of these goods were products for the mass-market, such as alum, cotton, sugar, and most of the silks, originating in well-defined regions near the ports of call (which had often been established only for the purpose of handling them). Others were true spices, pepper, cloves, cinnamon, products used in

135

dyeing (like brazil-wood), and the very varied drugs of the medieval pharmacopoeia (liquorice, aloes, rhubarb, galingale, 'dragon's blood', etc.). A further category of bulk trade engaged a large number of vessels: corn was brought from the countries around the shores of the Black Sea to supply Constantinople, which would not have been able to survive without it; cereals from Asia Minor, wood from Cilicia for Egypt, which stood in great need of them; wines from the islands, wax, honey, furs, salt or dried fish; and the slaves who were essential to the army, the palaces and the rural economy of Egypt. Finally there were the products of high luxury: brocades, velvets and damask, cloth of gold, silk voiles, gold thread, Turkish and Persian carpets, pearls from the India Ocean, precious stones (rubies, turquoise, lapis lazuli, etc.).

Each of these products followed a special route, ending up at this or that market-town and bound for a particular destination. It is important to ascertain the governing factors for each type of product in order to understand the political or economic strategy of the individual western powers in trying to gain access to the product, and if possible to acquire a monopoly in it. Thus among the hundred or so seaports of any importance in the 'oriental' sector, Kilia and Mesembria (modern Nesebar) hardly ever handled anything but corn, Caffa (modern Feodosiya) and Tana were primarily slave markets, Phocaea and Ephesus dealt only in alum, Alanya exported only wood and carpets, silks and carpets were to be found in the small ports of the Armenian kingdom; cotton and sugar came in bulk from the Syrian coasts, flax could be obtained at Alexandria, mastic was a speciality of Chios, and wine made the wealth of Chios, Candia and Rhodes.

To take a concrete example of the specialization in trade, in 1275 a Genoese family, the Zaccarias, acquired a concession of the most important alum quarries, at Phocaea: these were one of the foundations of the economic power of Genoa, which retained them until 1458. This monopoly explains the start of the voyages to Flanders from 1278, the increased tonnage of the Genoese vessels used for transporting this commodity (which was particularly heavy), and no doubt also the expansion of the cloth industry in the west during the following years.

Another example is Venice's interest in the cotton trade, both in Asia Minor and in the plains of Antioch and northern Syria (Hama): each year a Venetian cotton fleet (*muda del cottone*) went to the ports of the region to load up with cotton. This led to a considerable expansion of fustian-weaving in Lombardy, and probably also in the towns of southern Germany which obtained their supplies at Venice from the 'Fondaco dei Tedeschi'; from the second half of the thirteenth century, cotton fabrics and mixtures of cotton and wool or

84 Commercial scene in Lesser Armenia; miniature from a fourteenth-century French manuscript.

cotton and linen, which had hitherto been quite unknown, began to compete vigorously with pure wool and linen.

In contrast with these products of the Near East, the 'spices' proper came for the most part from the Far East (China, Indonesia and India), and the extraordinarily long routes by which they made their way were many. There were maritime routes across the Indian Ocean, and then up the Persian Gulf or the Red Sea. There were routes partly by sea and partly by land, the merchandise starting out on its journey by sea, and then being sent across Iran or Mesopotamia. Finally there were routes which went overland all the way. These were also many and various, and they were connected to each other by link-paths. Some merchants made their way with pearls and gems via India and the Iranian plateau, others crossed the steppes of Central Asia and Turkestan along silk routes. If there was trouble in one of the regions on the long caravan trail, the itinerary was modified, and the merchants of the intervening places adopted another route for one or other stage of the journey. It is well known that the disturbances caused by the migrating nomads of the early Middle Ages had hardly subsided in the heart of Asia when the Seljuks, Mongols and Ottomans appeared on the scene; the very names of Genghis Khan and Tamburlaine are enough to evoke the widespread savagery of these wars.

137

At this period trade also tended to oscillate like a great pendulum sometimes towards the Black Sea and Constantinople, and sometimes towards Egypt and the Cairo market; the effects of this oscillation were considerable for history in general and the international economy in particular. In the same way, consignments were redistributed in intermediary cities (Delhi and Ghazni, Ormuz and Mecca, Baghdad, Damascus and Aleppo, Tabriz and Sivas, Urgench and Tana, to mention only those nearest the west) by various routes towards a number of places whose importance rose and fell according to the fluctuating political situation in the Mediterranean. Sometimes they were directed towards Damietta and Alexandria, or towards Acre, Tyre and Beirut; sometimes towards Antioch, Latakia and Ayas, at the base of the Gulf of Alexandretta; and sometimes towards Soldaia, Trebizond and Caffa, not to mention the large island bases which served as entrepôts (Famagusta, Rhodes and Candia).

This explains why the great western merchants specializing in the spice trade shifted their interest alternately from one geographic or economic sector to another. It was no accident that, during the last decade of the thirteenth century and first two of the fourteenth, Egypt was only rarely visited by westerners: clearly the pontifical interdict alone was insufficient to obstruct merchant enterprise, but at this time Egypt was to a large extent cut off from its contacts in Asia by its enemies the Mongols, and most of the caravans, taking advantage of the 'Mongol peace', preferred the slow but safe route through Central Asia, which came out on the Black Sea. Later on, Alexandria and Beirut regained all their former importance and once more became regular ports of call for the Venetians, Genoese and Catalans, while only tiny ripples of Asiatic trade still reached the Black Sea, until in the second half of the the fifteenth century Turkish Constantinople reassumed for a time her position as the spice metropolis.

The most serious conflict that arose between Venice and Genoa came about because both aimed to dominate the vast consumer-centre of Constantinople. While participating in the benefits of the spice trade and of international exchange, both of them tried to gain for themselves the profits which were to be obtained from supplying the imperial capital with corn and other food commodities, as well as the cloth and luxury products of the west. The opposition of the Greeks, the growing weakness of the emperors, the imperialist greed of the Italian merchants, were causes of the well-known events which followed: the fall of the Greek empire, the creation of the Latin empire, and its subsequent collapse.

From the end of the twelfth century, Venice already enjoyed a dominant
position in the empire: after the pogrom of 1182, Isaac Angelus confirmed its

85 The medieval citadel in the centre of Aleppo.

86 Marco Polo with natives gathering peppers in Malabar; miniature from a fourteenth-century French manuscript.

87 Venice, the Doge's Palace, capital showing the people of the world.

privileges and in 1199, in exchange for its political support, opened up the entire empire to Venice, from Adrianople to Macedonia, Bulgaria and Wallachia. The foundation of the Latin empire, in 1204, was only the culmination of a slow evolution, the Doge becoming 'master of a half and a quarter of the whole Empire', a formula which involved joint ownership of the empire. But it was easier to carry off and portion out vast booty collected in the fabulously rich Greek capital, than to maintain the government of an empire through a handful of inexperienced and unruly barons and greedy merchants. Venice did not have sufficient military power to take possession of the lands which it had been assigned: it had to renounce the continental territories, and confine itself to maintaining the maritime bases of Modon and Coron in the Peloponnese and the strongholds on the Dardanelles, and enfeoffing the islands (Corfu, Rhodes, Crete, the Archipelago, Euboea) to members of its patriciate and even to other Latins or Greeks. These 'vassals' took their ducal lordship seriously and the republic became militarily exhausted in establishing its authority over them.

88, 89 The fourth Crusade and the Latin occupation of Constantinople in 1204: mosaics from S. Giovanni, Ravenna.

But the most important result of the fourth Crusade was that the monopoly of the imperial economy became consolidated in the hands of the Venetians. Genoa and Pisa contested it keenly with Venice, competing over all the seas and stepping up their pressure in the Holy Land. Genoa in particular tried to outstrip its rival by competing commercially in Egypt, and when necessary by making a pretence of crusading (as for instance in the capture of Damietta in 1218; or the Franco-Genoese crusade of St Louis in 1249). Facing defeat in this area as a result of Venice's counter-move in concluding a treaty with the sultan in 1254, Genoa turned towards Byzantium, and by the treaty of Nymphaeum (1262) succeeded in re-establishing itself at Constantinople, at the time when the Greek emperor was making his comeback there.

Genoa subsequently founded its powerful colony of Pera, across the Golden Horn from Constantinople, made it the base for Genoese commercial activity in the east, and became engaged in the economic exploitation of the Black Sea area. Venice replied by making determined efforts to expel the Genoese from Acre and Tripoli, and obtained new privileges from the king of Armenia.

A little while after Genoa's return in force to Constantinople, the Tatar Khan of the Crimea had granted it a concession on the southern coast of the peninsula, on the site of ancient Theodosia. This town, Caffa, became the administrative centre of all the Genoese territories in the Black Sea, and with the support of Pera, capital poured in to finance operations in this region. Less than a quarter of a century after its foundation, Caffa had already eclipsed Soldaia, which the Arab traveller Ibn-Batutah nevertheless held to be one of the richest cities of the world, and the equal of Alexandria, Zaitun and Calicut. Caffa benefited from an exceptional combination of circumstances. Genoa had renewed its agreement with the reinstated *Basileus* (1262), and behind Genoa was all the economic potential of Europe at its peak. There was un-expected harmony between the *Basileus* and Egypt, which was authorized in 1263 to supply itself with slaves from the Crimea and southern Russia. Finally the Mongols and the Tatars were settled on the shores of the Black Sea, while behind them the silk and spice routes opened up across an Asia now at peace. As a result, Genoa was able to supply Constantinople with the corn, wax and fish which it needed; the Genoese carried Circassian, Valak, Tatar, Georgian and other slaves to Egypt, where they became the Mamelukes of Cairo; finally, Genoa itself pushed forward along the trails across Central Asia.

Caffa was indeed blown about by many contrary winds. At the beginning of the fourteenth century the town was even destroyed, and deserted for a few years: at this time big business, with its pendulum movement, was establishing bases at the Armenian port of Ayas, at Famagusta and even in Egypt. After the Egyptian offensive against the Mongols and the occupation of Lesser Armenia by Egyptian troops, the routes swung back again and in 1316 Caffa once more became for a generation the central market of Latin traders in slaves and spices. During this period, Venice concentrated similarly on its port of Tana, rebuilt at the mouth of the Don on the Sea of Azov. The disruption of Mongol Asia followed and between 1338 and 1345 the rupture of the great trans-asiatic link: the recession in Asian trade had repercussions in Caffa and Tana, and from then on they restricted themselves to regional trade, which continued, though dwindling, until the occupation of the area by the Turks in 1475.

The exaggerated importance attached by traditional history to the spice trade (properly so called) was certainly misconceived: it involved only a very small number of ships each year, and concerned a very restricted group of three cities, Venice, Genoa and Barcelona. The value of the cargoes was no doubt extremely high, but not very much higher than the cargoes of, for example, cloths from the west. But this limited trade was to a certain extent the motive force behind most of the other trade with the east.

90 Fourteenth-century fresco in the princely church (*Biserica domneasca*) of Curtea de Arges, built *c.* 1360 by Besarab the Great, who founded the principality of Wallachia at the crossroads of the Slav, Germanic, Byzantine and Turkish worlds.

91 The fourteenth-century church of St Peter and St Paul in the old town of Famagusta, Cyprus.

92 Rhodes, the fourteenth-century 'Auberge de la langue de France' in the street of the Knights.

It had perhaps a rather greater importance in political and social history, for it was a very specialized trade, concentrated in the hands of the biggest capitalists, who made enormous profits from it. The men who organized the official armed convoys were also the masters of the merchant republics, determining their policies and having a direct influence on peace and war, and hence on the general economy of the Mediterranean world. With a large amount of capital at their disposal, a technology in advance of that of other countries, and the best sources of information at their fingertips, they furthered their interests by speculating in goods and precious metals. They were, in fact, the pivot of the medieval economy.

THE WESTERNERS ON THE ASIATIC CONTINENT

The Arab countries had never allowed westerners to venture beyond Cairo or Baghdad on the routes to the Middle and Far East in search of pearls, spices and silk; they were too jealous of preserving the benefits of this profitable trade for their own merchants, and the Latins were hardly able to do more than carry on a coastal trade. Even during the era of the kingdoms of Jerusalem and Acre, there was no western penetration into the interior of the continent, nor beyond the Byzantine empire, so long as Byzantium itself controlled its own economic policy.

A different situation arose at the end of the thirteenth century and at the beginning of the fourteenth, when the Mongol peace reigned in the vast areas of Asia. We need not concern ourselves with the missionaries who spread to the furthest corners of the east, founding bishoprics throughout Iran, Turkestan, India and even China, where they installed an archbishop at Peking. They have as little to do with large-scale trade movements as ambassadors like Rubroek at the time of St Louis, or the 'Frankish' mercenaries in the service of all the 'infidel' armies, or adventurers of various kinds, such as the goldsmith and the French dressmaker who turned up at that time at the court of the Great Khan. Even Marco Polo, though he was brought up by a father and an uncle who were merchants, is not of direct interest for economic history, since he found his way into the Mongol ruling class, passed a large part of his life in the Far Eastern courts, and only returned home at a mature age to live the life of a Venetian patrician.

It is much more important for us to note that it was the pioneers of western trade themselves who forced open the doors of large-scale international commerce, and then pressed forward along all the routes to foreign lands.

From Ayas, the port of Lesser Armenia, or from Trebizond or some other port on the Black Sea, it was easy to get to the towns towards which the road

93 Ruins of the ancient fortress of Ayas, Lesser Armenia, bridgehead of western trade in Asia at the turn of the thirteenth century.

system of Asia Minor converged, Konia, Sivas, Erzerum, and especially Tabriz in Azerbaijan, where Venetians, Genoese and Piacenzians settled before 1264. From Tabriz, which was the hub of the great trade-routes, it was possible to reach the port of Ormuz on the Persian Gulf and continue by the sea route to India, the land of pearls and gems, and to China, or to take the land route leading across Iran via Yezd, and Ghazni, and over the Kabul passes to India.

The Florentine Pegolotti notes a completely different route in his great manual for merchants. He gives the following details of the stages and conditions of the journey: from Caffa or Tana the routes led to Astrakhan on the Volga, to Sarai and Urgench; then, striding over deserts and steppes, frozen plateaux and fiery wastes, via the Pamir and the Gobi desert, it reached Kaanbaligh (that is, Peking) after a journey of 284 days, making use in turn of horses, camels, ox-carts and boats. We know from another source that a different route led from Urgench straight to the south, subsequently rejoining the previous route towards Ghazni and India.

Indeed, one must not exaggerate either the quantity of goods transported by this route or the number of Latin merchants who had the courage to endure such privations. No doubt few reached the great Chinese emporium of Zaitun (Tsinkiang), one of the most active markets of the Far Eastern world, opposite Formosa, where it appears that the Christians had a fonduk. We know from a reliable source that some penetrated as far as Delhi, but the majority in fact stopped at Tabriz, which seems to have been the great crossroads of the Asiatic

145

routes, as is also shown by the many influences to which Persian art was subject at this time. At any rate, the silk of China made its appearance on the Genoese market in 1257, that is, from the time that the king of Lesser Armenia submitted to the Great Khan and it became possible to open up a route through a land which was at peace all the way from China to Ayas on the Mediterranean, by way of Tabriz.

This epoch is thus one of the rare periods of world history when, following unparalleled massacres, peace reigned over whole continents and when both men and merchandise moved freely from one end of the then-known world to the other. Giovanni di Monte Corvino settled in Peking, Marco Polo put himself at the service of the Great Khan, becoming his ambassador and provincial governor; Ibn-Batutah, starting from Tangier, journeyed all over Africa, the Near East, India and China; the emperor of Mali, Kankan Musa, was able to go on a pilgrimage to Mecca with a company of 15,000 men and preceded by 500 slaves, each one carrying a gold nugget weighing six pounds; finally the Vivaldi brothers from Genoa, setting sail one fine day in 1291, dreamt of reaching India by sailing round the African continent, but disappeared off the coasts of tropical Africa, which was still unexplored.

It was a momentous period for medieval civilization, when the furs of Smolensk and the dried whale of Greenland reached Bruges in Hanseatic ships, when the cloths of Flanders were exchanged in Africa for Guinean gold, and the linens of Rheims were bartered for the silk of China in the heart of Asia. But suddenly, round about 1340–50, this world founded on a peacetime economy was utterly ruined.

EXCHANGE, BANKING AND CREDIT

From the end of the twelfth century, in certain Italian cities and notably at Genoa, money-changers accepted deposits repayable on demand, transferred payments by order of their clients, and granted them advances on current accounts. From the last years of the century, these money-changers arranged settlements, not only between their own clients, but between clients of different 'banks'. These technicians of credit and exchange belonged most often to the cities of the interior, and especially to Piacenza and the towns of Tuscany, notably Pistoia, Siena, Lucca and Florence. In the process of making themselves into genuine bankers, they started up the great 'companies' which brought wealth to their towns of origin and were one of the motive forces behind big business in the thirteenth century.

The rise of banking practices was connected to a certain extent with the development of trade with the east, especially 'Romania'. The crusade of St

Louis, in particular, necessitated regular outlays on military pay (a new phenomenon), and subsequently on ransoms, and this clearly played an important role in leading the merchant money-changers to arrange massive transfers of coins to the Holy Land; in exchange they received credits in the form of mandates on the royal treasury.

The position held from this time on by the fairs of Champagne, whose commercial role we have already considered, was perhaps still more important in the financial field. Money-changers and bankers followed the merchants, for at that time the financial settlement of every transaction was an inevitably delicate question: the merchants avoided carrying coins as far as possible, and they had to operate by setting off one transaction against another. From before the middle of the thirteenth century, the fairs thus became a vast international clearing-house, and here again Piacenzians and Tuscans held the foremost position. Other money-changers came from Rome, Viterbo and Orvieto, Cologne, Toulouse, Cahors and Figeac. The traders from the last two towns played such an important role in the money market that those suspected *a priori* of usury finally came to be called 'Cahorsins'.

In previous periods it could certainly be maintained that monetary matters were secondary. The circulation of specie was mainly local or regional; barter and settlements in kind predominated in the markets; the delivery of produce in kind prevailed in rural areas; credit was rare and mostly took the form of a contract of mortgage, which the churches were prepared to countenance in exceptional circumstance (such as departure on a crusade). Whatever the business, however, capital was extremely limited.

Suddenly, in a generation at most, currency and credit became vital over a large part of the west, and associations of capitalists grew up. They established a network of agents and correspondents between their towns of origin, the fairs of Champagne and certain large centres of trade. It became possible for a merchant to transfer a sum from one place to another. The papacy gathered together the funds which its collectors sent in from the various Christian areas. Prelates attending the Curia, students studying in a distant university, and ecclesiastics who obtained benefices abroad, received the funds due to them through the agency of specialist bankers. Wholesale purchases were always arranged on account, at one or several fairs. In the merchant world, credit reigned supreme – almost too unrestrictedly, for there was not yet enough experience of its techniques, and the overdrafts were often considerable. There had only to be unexpected political tensions or a temporary recession for a chain reaction to bring bankruptcy to a whole series of firms, among them those which were apparently most stable.

94 Money-changers, detail of a stained-glass window in the cathedral of Chartres.

95 Money-changer and his clerk, illustrating the activity of a 'publican' in one of the frescoes by Niccolò Gerini of the Life of St Matthew, in a chapel of S. Francesco, Prato (1395).

96 Genoese bankers; miniature from a late fourteenth-century manuscript.

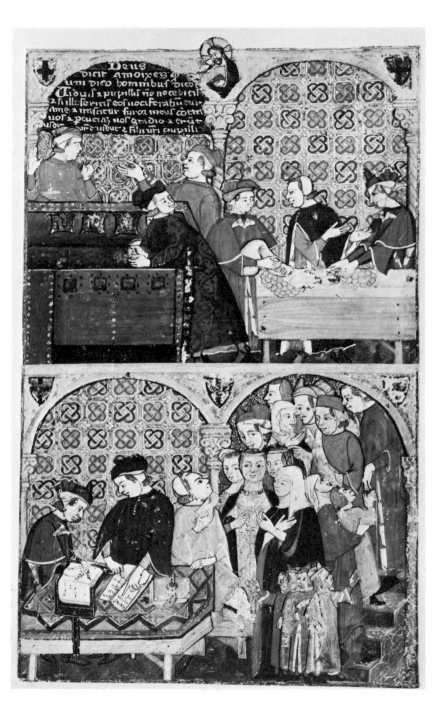

For a long time, the great majority of transactions were both drawn up and settled at the fairs of Champagne. Then, in the second half of the thirteenth century, the commercial role of the fairs apparently became weaker, while their financial character was strengthened. They now became the centre for settling transactions made in other places. Deals made in Champagne benefited from the jurisdictional privileges attaching to contracts made according to the statutes of the fairs, and businessmen obtained the liquid funds which they needed there. Accordingly, Italian merchants went directly to the centres of cloth manufacture, in Flanders for example, and made their purchases at the fairs there, but attended those of Champagne in order to settle their debts. Complex transactions were arranged: for instance, at Genoa in 1257 the Luccans bought Chinese silk which had been imported via Ayas in Lesser Armenia, promising payment at the fairs of Champagne through the offices of bankers from Piacenza; thus Genoa was able to obtain on the spot the funds necessary for purchasing Flemish cloths, which balanced its lucrative trade with the east.

Merchants tended increasingly to neglect the itinerant fairs; they were content to send their agents while they themselves made Paris their headquarters. That city, which from this time became the capital of the French kingdom and the main consumer-centre of the west, was conveniently situated for deals in the luxury trade and for money transactions. While Paris effectively absorbed merchant business, the fairs of Champagne changed their character and became a place of reference for the rates of exchange.

Aside from firms specializing in exchange, the largest commercial associations also conducted banking and credit transactions on their own account and on behalf of their clients. These took the form of companies formed by a varying number of associates, who often belonged to the same family or to a class of people allied by blood and political and economic interests, and each of whom contributed a share of the capital. The head of the company directed it from his headquarters in Italy, where he usually held an important position in the administration of the city-state; his associates and his agents or employees acted on his instructions and kept him regularly informed of the progress of affairs and of the changing situation. Deposits of money, made either by private individuals placing liquid assets, or by associates reinvesting part of their profits, were added to pure stock, and they converted the residue into considerable amounts of real estate, which formed a contingent reserve for the company in case of financial difficulties.

The second half of the thirteenth century saw a great flowering of these
companies, who put their enormous resources and their financial experience

at the service of sovereigns and princes. At this period, which followed a very long phase of monetary restriction, money flowed freely to and from all the great men, who never had enough ready cash; with greater or lesser alacrity the banks put themselves at their disposal, made them loans, often of considerable amounts, arranging the interest and the repayments, and received from them, as security, concessions in the field of the collection of taxes, or customs duties, the administration of mints and, according to region, monopolies in the export trade in corn, salt, or wool, or duty-free export licences. Some of these financiers were brought into the councils of sovereigns, in England, Flanders, Dauphiné, etc., such as the 'Mouche et Biche' (Musciatto et Albizzo de' Franzesi) in France, under Philip the Fair.

In normal times speculation was most profitable, but it became risky at certain periods when the lord became threatening or the people came to hate the bankers, and it could even become dangerous in moments of crisis. Hence the spectacular failure of the Buonsignori of Siena in 1295, the collapse of most of the big companies of Siena, Lucca and Florence at the beginning of the fourteenth century, and in particular the bankruptcy of the three most important banks of the Middle Ages, the Florentine companies of the Bardi, the Peruzzi and the Acciajoli. They had triumphed in the first third of the fourteenth century thanks to their perfect organization; they collapsed as a result of lending an enormous unsecured sum to King Edward III of England on the eve of the Hundred Years' War, counting on a quick and profitable victory. On the evidence of the chronicler Giovanni Villani, who was one of their associates and their representative in Flanders, the Bardi and the Peruzzi had advanced no less than 1,365,000 gold florins to the king when payments were suspended, and they had also lent considerable sums to the pope, the king of France and many other important people. We are told that the English debt was worth a kingdom: in order to appreciate its size, we have only to realize that in the same period, king Philip VI brought Montpellier for 120,000 gold crowns from the deposed king of Majorca, and Dauphiné for 200,000 gold florins from the dauphin Humbert II; these two individuals were also ruinously in the debt of 'Lombard' creditors.

The large banking companies were similarly involved in international big business. They had at their disposal a vast network of counting-houses and correspondents. Apart from their establishments in France, Paris, London and Bruges, the Bardi had thirty branches in the busiest economic centres of Italy, Spain, North Africa and the Greek, Latin and Moslem Levant. The number of people directly employed by them exceeded 350, not including individual associates and minor companies for which they helped to provide financial backing. Their financial power even enabled them to conclude commercial treaties (favourable to their own interests) with monarchs.

As a result of their expertise, banking techniques and accounting made decisive progress. The rigid system of legal contracts was supplemented by privately signed documents, simple correspondence between merchants (which was facilitated by the institution of regular couriers linking the fairs of Champagne to the great Italian cities) and finally by account books. From the middle of the thirteenth century, the validity of payments by bank entry was recognized by statute; confidence was developed by accounts in which no erasure was permitted, and by cartularies and manifests. From the end of the thirteenth century or the beginning of the fourteenth, simple 'letters of payment', the direct ancestors of the bill of exchange, tended to be substituted for contracts of exchange drawn up by notaries. The account books changed in nature, and became extremely complicated. Finally, before the middle of the fourteenth century, 'double entry', one of the most important achievements of medieval civilization, made its appearance. The spread of this practice was, however, slow and uneven, varying according to the city or firm.

It was not only trade that existed on credit, and not only the states and higher nobility that found themselves unable to survive except by virtue of the loans granted by the Italian companies: it was just the same with bishops and abbeys, towns and the petty nobility, burghers and even peasants. This clientele, however, borrowed less from the banking companies than from the 'lending tables', the *casanes* kept by the 'Lombards', who lent money on the strength of a written or verbal pledge, and more often on the security of real estate, of crops which had still to be harvested, or of personal chattels. The Lombards tended to displace the Jews, who had progressively specialized in this activity but did not have at their disposal comparable assets in cash, available in various places. Moreover, the Jews in France, particularly from the time of St Louis, were persecuted many times before finally being expelled from the realm at the beginning of the fourteenth century.

Between 1240 and 1340, but especially in the period 1280–1300, small banking houses opened in each market and each seat of a provost or castellan, in an area which included Piedmont, Dauphiné, Savoy, the Comté, the Duchy of Burgundy, Champagne, Lorraine, the Rhineland, Brabant, Flanders, Artois, the Ile-de-France, and part of Normandy. They extended their empire over a radius of about ten miles. A map showing their distribution would correspond fairly well to that of the primary economic network of these regions. In the most important towns, there were as many as five or six, and still more in the towns where the fairs of Champagne were held. Most of them were managed by Italians, originating from a small number of mainly Piedmontese towns, such as Asti, Albe, or Chieri. The literature of the time echoes the hatred which was felt against the Lombards: '. . . the Lombard monster not only devours man and beast, but also mills, castles, woods and forests, he drinks the marshes and dries up the rivers.' Or again: 'They never bring a ducat with them, nothing but a sheet of paper in one hand and a pen in the other; with that, they fleece the townsmen and then lend them their own money.'

In successive campaigns, the political authorities, starting with the kings of France, tried to take severe measures against these 'usurers', who were arrested, plundered and expelled. But their presence was necessary, and the monarchy often contented itself with imposing large fines on them; Philip III in 1277, echoing the condemnation of usury by Pope Gregory IX, ordered their arrest, then allowed them to continue their activities, on condition that they paid a 'settlement' of 120,000 gold florins. His successors acted in much the same fashion.

Between 1340 and 1350, however, most of them finally disappeared, at the same time that the big commercial and banking companies were also beginning to collapse. This was the period of the great economic and financial crisis with which we shall deal later in more detail. In the whole of the west the economy, finance, and the currency plummeted. Perhaps one of the reasons should be sought in the elimination of an economic group which had shored up the whole monetary economy for a century; or, probably, in the general indebtedness to which the population had become accustomed over too long a period of easy credit facilities.

It should also not be forgotten that the companies were impelled by their financial interests to meddle in the conflicts which tore Italy apart, drawing their own towns, on whose politics they exercised a decisive influence, after them. Thus Florence was on the Guelf side because her great merchants were loyal to the pontifical treasury, and upheld the policy of the popes. They therefore advanced to Charles of Anjou, the champion of the papacy, funds to enable him to embark on the conquest of the kingdom of Naples. Their reward was a dominant and profitable position at the court and advantageous concessions in the corn treaty with Sicily. In the same fashion a century later the Florentine banker Niccolo Acciajoli became lord of Corinth, under Angevin suzerainty, and his son Nerio prince of the Morea.

The growth in the wealth of the Italians had many consequences in their country of origin. It caused the astounding rise of its urban culture, of which

153

97 Wine harvest; miniature
from a fifteenth-century
Italian manuscript.

towns like Siena or Florence still bear striking witness today. But it also led
to a transformation of Italian agriculture, which was organized on an industrial
basis by the heads of companies who invested in land and forced their way into
the ranks of the feudal nobility. The Falletti, who were the main force behind
the *casanes* of eastern France, carved out something of a principality for themselves in the Piedmontese vine-growing district, around their castles of Barolo
and Rocca-Falletti. The Scotti of Piacenza gathered the richest lands of the
Po area into their own hands; the Bardi of Florence and the Bandinelli of
Siena launched into the exploitation of the Chianti vineyards; and so on. The
Tolomei of Lucca developed copper mines; the 'Mouche et Biche' reinvested
the profits of their business in France in the construction of the Piazza del
Comune at Siena, and colonized enormous fiefs as a base from which they
challenged both Siena and Florence.

### AGRICULTURE AND FINANCE

The classical manorial estates tended in this period to become dismantled as
new clearings were made. In order to draw a better yield from their property,
owners did not hesitate to authorize settlements in the woods and wastes of
the manorial demesne. The demesnes became smaller or were whittled away;
forests were cleared bit by bit and put under cultivation, and some of them
disappeared altogether (for example, the forest of Mant in Brie, of Héric in
Britanny, and of Brotonne in Saintonge, among many others). The Cistercian
and Premonstratensian monastic foundations were particularly active in
encouraging clearings, from which they made large profits, but ancient abbeys
like Saint-Denis acted in much the same way. As a result there were conflicts,
both between the lords themselves, and between them and the village communities which enjoyed extensive traditional rights of common for firewood

98 The castle of Rocca-
Falletti, Serralunga d'Alba.

99 Aerial view of the Palazzo
Pubblico and the Piazza di
Campo, Siena.

or building-wood and for pasturing cattle. The whole of the thirteenth century is full of these conflicts; no doubt they were minor, but they formed a continual undercurrent, since something very important was at stake for the country people.

The lords also found it profitable to lease to the peasants plots of land in the demesne which they had previously cultivated by forced labour: consequently pieces of land which were classified as *corvées*, or, in Lorraine, *ansanges*, might be found under private ownership.

There were additional factors that contributed to the erosion and dismemberment of the great estates during the course of the twelfth century, such as alms-gifts to churches and abbeys, the endowment of chapter-houses in castle chapels, assignments of property for the maintenance of the incumbent of the parish church, and the enfeoffment of property or rights (many of which were quite simply usurped) to manorial agents (*ministeriales*) and church attorneys (*advocati*); still more divisions of land resulted from inheritances and marriage settlements.

In the Midi, so many manors were broken up that co-lordship (*co-seigneurie, condominium*) became common in Languedoc and Provence. Elsewhere the land was not divided up in this way, but the different rights were each assigned in different proportions. Thus in the Ile-de-France, Champagne or Picardy, we know that during the thirteenth century in one parish the lord possessed the whole of certain fields, while in others he was entitled to only a third of the 'seam', and in others again to a still smaller proportion; he had the right to half the eels caught in the mill fishpond, and a fifth of the revenue from the mill, while the tithe-rights were divided in varying proportions, according to whether large or small tithes were involved. Neighbouring lords, their younger sons, families related by marriage, the parish priest, neighbouring priories, and manorial agents, divided up the manorial rights between them. Examples can be multiplied *ad infinitum*. At the end of the thirteenth century, the manorial system had withered away more or less everywhere, at least in France.

The proliferation of 'nobles' in certain *castra* eventually resulted in the pauperization of this social class, particularly in the Midi, Provence and Dauphiné. Many Dauphiné nobles were not even able to keep a horse. In Savoy and the Champsaur, the decline became so pronounced that in the end many nobles only possessed rights over a single family of dependants, or even part of a family.

The great lords formed the habit of ceding hereditary revenues, for life or for a set period, to relations or vassals, burghers or servants; this led to a change in the character of the important baronies. The income of fiefs was made up of the inherited wealth of the great fiefs, receipts from provostships, and the income from fairs, toll-houses and salt-works. The concept of money, which was foreign to feudalism proper, became universally established.

Gradually, 'noble lands', fiefs and fortified houses were acquired in ever-increasing numbers by the recently ennobled agents of the king, and still more by non-nobles; the trend became so prevalent that the king of France had to counteract it by proclaiming the non-validity of such transactions and reserving to himself the right to authorize them. As a result stewards were appointed to collect the taxes on freehold fiefs, and very long lists survive of transfers of manorial lands to burghers or to peasants who had become wealthy. The same situation is found in England during this period, as well as in Provence and in Dauphiné.

Everything that has been said about the great estate and the manor applies equally to the manse and the holding. As we have already noted, there were signs even in the early Middle Ages that the manse, the traditional unit of cultivation and financial assessment, was being broken up. Overpopulation, the division of holdings between several families of tenants, and the growing tendency for tenants to purchase and cultivate plots of land outside the estate, all contributed to the decline of the system. From the end of the twelfth century, it became common practice for the lord to authorize a tenant to divide up his holding, on condition that he paid a transfer tax and eventually accounted for the dues collected from its various component parts. These transfers became more and more frequent, since the harvest of *lods et ventes*, *muages, plaids, trezains*, etc., brought great profit to the lord. Heirs also paid the lord a substantial estate duty (*relief* or *réacapte*) on their inheritances and the division of lands resulting from inheritances carried the disintegration of the estates still further, all the more because the peasants subsequently divided up each of the component parts, the *climats* or pieces of land, between them. At the end of the twentieth century, agrarian dismemberment was complete: it was by no means rare to see fields reduced to strips consisting of only a few furrows.

In each parish at this time, peasant fortunes were made and unmade: while poor peasants, the victims of agricultural distress, eventually became depressed into a proletariat and went to swell the ranks of vagrants or the urban populace, others took advantage of the depression to enlarge their 'inheritances', parcel by parcel. In the village of Axat in Aude, for which we have (unusually) a census of peasants (whose legal status was that of *homme de corps*, i.e. serf), the spread of fortunes in 1304 was so wide that though 55 per cent possessed less than 2 lb of goods, 1 per cent had a capital of 25 lb.

157

The *nouveaux-riches* burghers of neighbouring localities flocked in to buy up fields, vineyards and meadows. This practice was particularly common in Italy, but it was more or less universal throughout the west. In Brie, in the second half of the thirteenth century, a financier named Renier Accorre, in the service of the counts of Champagne, took advantage of the non-repayment of loans which he had made to the peasants and their lords to acquire a pretty sizeable group of estates.

The 'parcelling' of the countryside had an important result for the administration of the estates. It became impossible to maintain the fiction that rents were due from the holding as a whole: they had to be reassigned realistically to each parcel of land or each homestead. Instead of the former quit-rent system, the practice of 'terriers' arose during the course of the thirteenth century, in the Midi and eastern France: these were records of transactions by which each tenant acknowledged, in front of a notary, that he held from his lord the property listed, with such and such particulars and such and such sub-tenants, and details of the dues required from each.

During this period the character of rural life was completely transformed. Rents in cash tended to be substituted for rents in kind; casual and 'mutable' revenues became regular, fixed ('agreed') and paid in money, such as the *albergue*, the *queste*, the poll-tax, etc. The services required from individuals tended to become lighter, and their nature was blurred. In many areas they were commuted to cash payments; serfdom was associated with holding certain pieces of land or living in certain houses, classified as unfree.

In order to avoid the ancient mortmain on the serf's inheritance, it was sufficient to pay taxes in cash or merely to marry a woman who was free or from another estate. Communities even bought their freedom collectively, risking indebtedness for a longer or shorter period; they often evaded the grasp of the lord only to fall into the clutches of the Lombard or the rich burgher nearby.

New relationships grew up based on the circulation of money: if the cash-rent was not paid, the lord proceeded to reclaim the land; or if the peasant was short of money the lord could buy back the rented land of which he was the ultimate owner. In that case the lord had the right to make a new contract with a prospective tenant; he might impose new conditions on him, such as the payment of an additional rent (*surcens* or *croît de cens*), or else demand a half-share of the crops (*medietaria*, *métairie*), or adopt quite a different system of field-rent paid in kind (*campipars*). He might also decide to plant the arable land with vines – which brought in a better income – or to have it tilled by paid workers, and the system of paid agricultural labour, at least as a makeweight, apparently developed during this period. Finally, short-term leases of land for three, six, or nine years made their appearance, and became very common. As a result of economic evolution the lord had become a land-rentier.

An even more important contributory factor to the growth of a monetary economy was the practice of leasing houses in the urban centres. In the chief towns, feudal properties were divided into lots, under conditions of which we know very little: the 'proprietors', who paid the landlord a larger or smaller rent, built houses which they leased to tenants. Rich burghers were in this way able to own in town, apart from their town mansions, one or several houses which they let (with shops, butchers' stalls, 'vaults', cellars, stables, work-shops), sometimes even room by room. From the beginning of the thirteenth century, this practice became quite common in the Italian towns, the French towns, especially those of the Midi, and most of the new towns and *bastides* (fortified towns). To help with the construction of these new towns, the lords had to call in the neighbouring burghers, and these developments probably explain the changed investment policy of the burghers of Cahors and Figeac, when around the middle of the thirteenth century they turned away from international big business, and invested their capital in urban building in the south-west.

Since the townspeople had to be taxed according to their 'quality', the municipal authorities established 'registers', listing the rural and urban property of each and sometimes also the debts owing to them and other personal assets. It was no coincidence that this practice had made its appearance even by 1250 at Chieri and Pistoia, which were towns where personal wealth increased very early; the institution became general at the beginning of the following century.

Holdings, fields and houses represented capital for their owners: in the middle of the thirteenth century it became lawful to obtain a loan on which the interest was guaranteed by this capital, or, in other words, to assign the rents. In return for a sum of money, the proprietor paid each year in perpetuity (unless the sum was redeemed) a fixed rent in kind (grain or wine) or in cash, representing interest of the order of 5 to 10 per cent; the landlord received a regular tax in return for his consent to the transaction. In the course of the thirteenth century and especially towards its end, assigned rents became an important element in the wealth of all social classes. By means of such invest-ments the lords regained a large part of the profits from the land which they had had to forgo as a result of changing circumstances. Churches often resorted to this expedient. It was one of the burghers' favourite types of investment, and the majority of urban fortunes were made up from a large number of assigned rents: the patrician was more often than not a man of property.

There were, in addition, an infinite number of other ways of making capital yield a profit, and the Italians were apparently the pioneers in every type of investment. Associations were formed between sleeping partners and craftsmen or shopkeepers who carried on their trade with or without holding shares in the business, the profits being divided according to agreements made between them; the arrangement was often that each party took equal shares. There were contracts of *commenda*, by which a financial backer handed over merchandise, or a sum in cash, to a traveller who obtained a return on it in a prearranged commercial operation, on condition that he kept a quarter of the profits for himself. There was maritime exchange. There were contracts of cattle-lease or *soccida*, making beasts over to a peasant who took care of them on his own land; the increase in the herd and their produce was shared between the interested parties in varying proportions according to the contract. Rents were assigned from urban exchequers. Tolls, salt-taxes, duty on corn or salt, etc., were leased. Ecclesiastic tithes and manorial dues, even the total revenue of a given estate were put out to rent; the king of France himself leased out the offices of provost, castellan, or scrivener for a limited period or for life.

Finally, in certain areas there appeared true joint-stock companies, that is, groups of capitalists who pooled their personal wealth in cash, acquired shares in a collective enterprise, divided the proceeds in proportion to their investment and were free to transfer their share to their heirs or sell it. From the end of the twelfth century this practice was common in the shipping business; the charter shares, the *loca*, were usually divided into 'carats' (1/24) or 'half-carats' (1/48), which were freely negotiable. It was extended in the thirteenth century to the component parts of equipment under commission, and subsequently, at Genoa, to loans made to the militia ('column') and to the 'Mahones', which were syndicates formed in the first instance to recover debts in overseas countries and which in the end severely exploited the colonial provinces of the Republic. A similar method of financing operated in the case of large industrial concerns requiring a high concentration of capital, such as the mills of the Garonne which supplied the great city of Toulouse – or the salt-works of Franche-Comté, the most important 'factory' of the Middle Ages, with its pits, its boilers, its conduits for salt water, its enormous requirements for firewood, and its parking-yard accommodating a hundred carts. In the fourteenth century, associations of capitalists were formed specializing in marine insurance, which was a source of considerable profits since at this time the fantastic risks from privateering and piracy were at their height.

We cannot deal with any of these topics in detail here, nor with any of the types of contracts which, in both the Mediterranean, and the Hanseatic and Atlantic areas (but here often much later), regulated commercial, maritime and banking transactions, and united the merchants as a group. What has been said is sufficient to show the great importance of currency and credit in medieval economy during the thirteenth century and at the beginning of the fourteenth: by these new developments the whole foundation of the previous manorial economy and all the relationships among individuals were undermined. It is not too much to say that new forms of civilization grew up during this period because of the important place assigned to money; at a time when authority was measured in terms of power over man and when the wealth of estates depended on human productive forces, a type of society arose where fortunes were determined by the amount of available capital and the profits derived from it.

GOLD AND SILVER

This transformation would not have been possible but for a new monetary revolution of far-reaching significance.

During the early Middle Ages, silver pennies of poor weight, struck in a plethora of manorial mints, had circulated slowly and sluggishly. At the beginning of the twelfth century, larger monetary zones were formed in which certain types of coin predominated, an example being the *parisis* of the royal domains which, from the reign of Louis VI onwards, had an increasing circulation following in the wake of the king's expanding possessions. In the Plantagenet domains of the west, a coherent system was established, and in this area an Angevin penny was worth two Le Mans pence and four English *esterlins* ('sterlings'). After the conquest in 1204 of the continental fiefs belonging to the English kings, Philip Augustus retained this system, but substituted for the Angevin penny the penny of Tours, minted on the standard of the eight-ounce weight (*poids de marc*) of Tours (217·55 gm); he arranged a stable rate of exchange between the *tournois* and the *parisis* and the rate finally became fixed in 1226, at the ratio of 4 to 5. The royal administration adopted the *tournois*; its use was gradually extended to a large part of the realm and spread beyond it, while the *parisis* was no longer employed except by the Treasury as a coin of account. Within half a century, most of the baronial coins became restricted to limited regional or even local areas, except for the currency of Provins (*provinois*), which was linked to the system of the fairs of Champagne and was also connected with the *tournois*. Many were bought up by the king and they ceased to be minted. At the beginning of the fourteenth century,

Philip V even decided that the time had come to restore to the kingdom a single currency, minted solely by the king. He was enabled to do so only through a net increase of the stock of mintable silver metal and a much more rapid circulation of the currency; even if the measure was premature, it was none the less indicative of a strengthening of the power of the Crown and the renewal of state authority.

The penny was, however, unsuitable for the transaction of the merchants; with the development of industrial production, the extension of big business, and the incessant rise in agricultural prices, they had to carry larger and larger sums around with them. Twelve pence (*deniers*) made one shilling (*sou*), which was the unit of account, and 240 pence one pound (*livre*), the higher unit of account. The smallest transaction of any importance involved transporting voluminous sacks of coins, and handling a considerable number of pieces; in trade with the Orient, use was made of ingots of precious metal, which were assayed and weighed. Venice was the first to realize the advantage of a new silver coin of a heavier weight, made from a well-tried alloy, and guaranteed by the Republic's mark: this was launched at the moment when the fourth Crusade made large transfers of coins necessary. This was the 'large Venetian' or 'matapan', minted at the standard of 965/1000 and weighing about 33·64 grains (2·18 gm); the former 'small' penny was from then on reserved for minor everyday payments. A little before 1237 Florence followed Venice's example.

The decisive step was taken by St Louis, when, in 1266, he introduced the large silver *tournois*, equivalent to 12 *deniers* (or one *sou*). This piece was much more suitable for the new conditions of trade. (The *denier*, which was already much debased, became a coin of small change, without relation to its true value; its pure silver content diminished progressively to the point where it became a 'black coin', because of the alloys it contained.) All the European states followed this example in the last third of the thirteenth century.

The success attending the large-scale minting of this new coin of almost pure silver illustrates how the west was becoming rich at the expense of regions which settled their trade deficit in silver. It also illustrates the great expansion of silver mining which took place throughout the whole of Europe, from Sardinia to the Apennines and Rouergue, from the Harz mountains and Bohemia to Silesia and the Balkans – though our knowledge of both these matters is still slight.

The renewed minting of gold in the west had still more important consequences. From the eighth century onwards, the Carolingian empire and its economic dependencies, apart from some exceptions, had lived under a mono-metallic silver system. Only Sicily and Spain had used gold coins, due to their geographical position and trade links, and by virtue of their use of gold they were also connected to the Arab system. Gold was essential to trade of any importance with the countries of the eastern Mediterranean, where in Constantinople and Alexandria the currency was respectively the bezant or hyperper and the Saracen bezant or dinar. In order to trade with these areas, the Latins of the kingdom of Jerusalem resumed minting gold at a very early date. The raw material was obtained by means of a speculative arbitrage operated between Frankish and Arab Syria. Western silver, the proceeds of collections, prisoners' ransoms, freight charges for the transport of pilgrims and reinforcements in men and provisions, and cash for the purchase of spices, was shipped in bulk to the Holy Land, and absorbed by Arab Syria in exchange for its cotton and spices, its brocades and most of all its gold. The rate of exchange with gold must have been fairly profitable since in a few years there was a complete reversal of the situation, and the east suffered from a deficiency of gold. Syria (Damascus), emptied of its gold, finally minted only silver dirhems, and even Baghdad followed suit, while the Christian market-centres of Tyre, Antioch and Tripoli minted gold, which was indispensable for their trade with Egypt.

In 1231 Frederick II, upon his return from his great expedition to Jerusalem, negotiated a commercial treaty with the Hafsid sultan of Tunis, obtaining from him an annual tribute in gold in exchange for Sicilian corn; it was apparently paid in 'gold of Pagliola' (or Pactolus), that is to say, native gold (in powder or nugget form) which came along the Saharan trails from black Africa. In the same year (perhaps only coincidentally) he minted the first western gold coin, the 'augustal', which even in its design was symbolically reminiscent of the *solidus* of the Roman empire, at a standard of $20\frac{1}{2}$ carats of gold and $2\frac{5}{8}$ carats of silver, and weighing 81 grains (5·25 gm). Thus the west came into line with the gold system of the Mediterranean.

The decisive moment came in 1252, when, at the end of an economic crisis following the defeat of St Louis' crusade, Genoa and Florence simultaneously began to mint the *januino* and the gold florin respectively. The florin left its

100 The gold florin.

mark on the whole commercial world. It had a distinctive design (the Floren-tine *fleur de lys*), weighed 54·47 grains (3·53 gm) of pure gold, and was equiva-lent to the pound, which was at this time solely a unit of account.

Consequently from this time on, there were three types of coins in circula-tion in the west: the small ('black') penny, very much debased with copper, for minor payments; the large silver penny, usually worth twelve small pence (*deniers*) or one shilling (*sou*), for the majority of transactions; and finally, the gold florin, worth twenty shillings or one pound, for international big business and transactions involving large sums.

St Louis adopted this system for his kingdom, probably in 1257, his gold penny, or crown, being equal to ten *sous* (or half a *livre*). Henry III did the same in England; but because of an insufficient supply of gold, and still more because the English economy was still very weak, this measure found little favour, and very soon England was even obliged to give up minting gold. It was able to resume this successfully only under Edward III in 1344. Venice began to mint its famous ducat in 1248; together with the florin, this became one of the great international gold currencies of the later Middle Ages.

To be sure, the monetary problem was not solved with the issue of large silver and gold coins: the relation between the two metals, their 'regulation', as well as the variation of their respective market prices in proportion to the small pennies, continued to cause grave concern to bankers and rulers. From the end of the thirteenth century and for the whole of the following century, the coins came out of phase with the units of account and this complicated circumstances still further. But by their very existence they brought about a complete revolution in the former situation. A simple comparison of figures is enough to illustrate this: it is estimated that in the tenth century, at a time when the Lombard kingdom was relatively prosperous, about 23,000 silver pennies were minted each year in Pavia, the capital; then Villani asserted in 1336 that Florence struck between 350,000 and 400,000 gold florins per annum; and in France under Philip the Fair, the profits of the king alone on the coins of the realm reached as much as 475,000 *livres* in 1298.

THE MINTING OF GOLD, AND THE EAST-WEST TRADE BALANCE

If the return to gold is an obvious sign of the economic expansion of the west, the manner in which it took place and the underlying reasons for it are not easy to analyze. Production of precious metal in Europe was fairly insigni-ficant, and the treasure-hoards which were put to account (a practice which began first in Scandinavia and reconquered Spain) were certainly of very little importance. Gold was, then, inevitably imported. Doubtless part of it was brought in by the Crusaders after the pillage of Constantinople, but this can be disregarded because of its exceptional character and because it involved particular pieces of religious goldware which, together with the relics, took their place in the churches of the west. Another more regular flow of gold imports came directly from eastern Europe (Silesia, Transylvania, and perhaps the Ural region), reaching Bruges and Venice by way of Cracow and Breslau; its effects were felt primarily from the second or third decade of the fourteenth century onwards. Gold also reached the European circuit as a result of the trade surplus of the Castilians, the Catalans, the Sicilians and the Genoese with the ports of North Africa, from Safi to Tripoli; this was mostly in the form of powder, grains or nuggets, originating in black Africa, but apparently the supply of gold only in the Spanish peninsula was influenced by this source in any decisive manner.

The larger part of the gold came from elsewhere, that is, probably from Egypt and the Byzantine empire. These two regions had nearly always remained faithful to a mono-metallic (gold) system, and the flow of gold to the west can only be explained on the hypothesis that there was an international arbitrage between gold and silver, or a western trade surplus with the east.

Some historians have strongly denied the existence of a western trade surplus. It would seem, however, that some time after the middle of the twelfth century and before the middle of the thirteenth, or perhaps more precisely at the beginning of that century, the trade balance swung in favour of the west. At that time – and this point must be emphasized – the easterners became fundamentally passive in their trade, in the sense that oriental merchants ventured no longer to the west, and all trade (even between the Arab countries of the Mediterranean) passed into the hands of Latin merchants, who clung like leeches to the borders of the eastern states.

The west sent to the east infinitely more than it received in return: the bales of beautiful Franco-Flemish or Flemish cloth cost far more, weight for weight, than packs of pepper, and they were exported in far greater numbers. In exchange for the primary raw materials imported from the east (alum, cotton, flax, wool), the west sent more expensive manufactured products (spun cotton, woollen cloth, metallurgical products). Even ivory did not make up for the chests of coral exported from Marseilles, Barcelona and Naples.

The main cause of this economic upheaval on a world scale was the industrial expansion of the kingdom of France, the Low Countries, the west of the German empire, and northern and central Italy to begin with, and then, a little later, of England, and southern Germany: this development was itself the result of the agricultural and demographic expansion in these regions. The industrial explosion gave the west, and especially France and the Italian towns, an extremely favourable external trade; it was the reason for the uninterrupted flow of gold and silver which entered the kingdom of France, whose wealth may still be seen today in the marvellous buildings of Gothic art. At the time of Philip the Fair, the amount of business done by the Italian firms (the traditional middlemen) at the fairs of Champagne and Nîmes may be estimated as being worth £3,000,000 (including exchange). In 1322–25, at a time of relative crisis, the average value of the goods which passed through the customs-posts of the kingdom amounted to some £2,000,000 to £3,000,000, and most of it was in Italian hands. It has been established that a little after the middle of the fourteenth century, at a time of economic stagnation, most of the ships docking at Aiguesmortes loaded up with goods which were definitely of greater value than those which they discharged.

The Italians enjoyed a near-monopoly of trade and finance, which gave them the considerable profits of commission. They gained at all stages: they bought the raw materials in their place of origin, carried them to the place of manufacture, and then bought back the finished products, in order to sell them in the consumer-centres, all stages being accompanied by the profits of transport, exchange, banking and credit. But it should not be forgotten that Italian industry also exported considerable amounts of fustian, haberdashery, the iron and steel products of Lombardy, the silks of Lucca, and the cloths of Florence. In 1339 Florence alone produced 70,000–80,000 pieces of cloth, worth 1,200,000 gold florins, in her 200 textile workshops, and twenty companies reckoned to finish 10,000 pieces from across the mountains each year, worth 360,000 florins; thirty years earlier, Villani tells us, there were 300 workshops, producing 100,000 pieces a year. As in France, the greater part of the production was for export.

Thus, whereas previously the west had paid in gold for her purchases of oriental spices, the thousand-year-old trend was reversed, and the east now sent the gold she had hoarded for so long to the west.

There was also an international arbitrage in precious metals, which was dominated by the Italians at the time by reason of their omnipresence and their expertise. In this field a combination of circumstances led to the growth of imbalance:

1. At the very moment when the trade balance of the eastern countries with the west was deteriorating and the deficiency had to be paid for in precious metal, the Mongol conquest occurred, cutting Egypt off from some of her sources of gold on the slopes of the Caucasus and in Armenia, while the route

101, 102 Fourteenth-century brocades from Lucca and Venice.

103 Order for velvet and brocade from the Order Book of Francesco di Marco Datini of Prato, 1 November 1408.

from the Indus was also disrupted. The disturbances caused by the brutal conquests of the new sultan of Mali, Sundiata, from 1230 to 1255 were even more
momentous; his battles with the Mossi, and in 1240 the total destruction of
Ghana, the ancient gold centre, brought with it a loosening of the traditional
links between Egypt and the black African countries that produced the gold.
The gold dinar clearly declined; a silver coinage appeared around 1230–35,
and it could not fail to attract western silver.

2. For similar reasons (a deficit trading position with the Latins and the
establishment of Mongol settlements along their frontiers), the Greek empire
of Nicaea, and subsequently Constantinople, experienced first the deterioration
and then the collapse of the Byzantine gold hyperper; in half a century its pure
gold content fell from 20 to 5 carats.

3. In order to trade with Mongol Asia, which accepted only silver in ingot
or coin, the westerners required silver; consequently they sold their goods for
Byzantine gold at Constantinople and Pera (hence its role as a centre of international exchange), and arranged the arbitrage of this gold against the silver
that was current in the Black Sea countries. Gold was thus grossly under-
valued, and passed to the west, which needed it in order to mint the new
florins, crowns, *januini* and ducats. Marco Polo tells us that in some parts of
Asia, the ratio between the two metals was 1 to 5 or 6 and we know that in
Europe at this time it was 1 to 10 or 12.

4. The inflation of the price of gold in the west caused by the demands of big
business and the mints led to a fall in the relative value of silver; this involved
speculation on the fall, and a massive stream of silver flowed from all the
Christian countries to the 'land of the Saracens', who overvalued it: they
absorbed the silver in hundreds of tons, since they needed it to trade with Asia
and for their own mints.

104 Venetian ducat, thirteenth century.

An entire literature bears witness to the damage caused by the relative abundance of gold in the west. It is reproached with being useless for the everyday life of the people. The 'bad regulation of coinage', as it was called at the time provoked a crisis with many repercussions, against which the authorities were powerless. The scarcity of silver, draining towards the east, led to a further debasement of coins with copper; the small pennies, the black coins, continued to deteriorate, while speculators melted them down to extract from them the minute amount of silver they did contain, in order to send it overseas. This poor coinage inevitably became inflated, and at the same time there were continual complaints about the lack of the raw material.

The industrial and agricultural growth of the west had been too sudden, too vigorous, and too prolonged, in a world which was very badly equipped intellectually and politically to face up to such problems. The rise in production had been overwhelming, at a time when the available stocks of money were still minimal. Precious metals were clearly mined in insufficient quantities; the westward movement first of silver, and then of African and oriental gold in increasing quantities, and the incessant speculation on currency, did not lead to an increase in the number of monetary denominations corresponding to the development of productivity and actual needs. The western world was in process of being completely reorganized, and in spite of the increasing wealth of a very large part of the population – who became rich but at the same time fell into debt – stability came to depend on credit in all social classes.

A serious crisis of overproduction occurred; at the same time sudden fluctuations took place on the exchange market and the precious metals market following events in Asia, which brought monetary upheavals in their train and caused the ruin of banking companies; wars of a new type broke out between states which were now more powerful, requiring currency in hitherto unknown quantities, at a time when the new structures of these states in any case demanded greater financial resources: consequently a crisis of exceptional gravity was brought on in all the western countries.

At the beginning of the fourteenth century, disturbing signs appeared one by one. Then, a little before the middle of the century the countries which had previously been the most prosperous entered into a long period of depression. The crisis gathered further momentum by reason of the competition from areas which up to then had been underdeveloped or not developed at all, and it marks the beginning of the period which is usually called the Late Middle Ages.

# V  THE LATE MIDDLE AGES

In the course of the classical Middle Ages, the countries of the west had reached a high level of development, due to their unprecedented population explosion, the extension of land under cultivation, and the spread of industrialization which was continually expanding into new fields. By about the year 1300 the towns were at the height of their prosperity and the density of population in the countryside, at any rate in France, was comparable to, if not greater than, that of the present day. Western merchants fitted out increasing numbers of ships, with an ever higher tonnage, since the seas had been cleared of their Moslem competitors; they were masters of the commercial and financial markets of the Mediterranean world, and they pushed on to the limits of the then-known world. After a break of half a millennium, the renewed minting of gold symbolized the achievement of two centuries of continuous progress, to which the whole of the interdependent west had contributed.

It is much more difficult to define the later Middle Ages, for the economic solidarity which had marked the preceding era was for a long time lacking.

In the first period, from the beginning or second quarter of the fourteenth century until the second quarter or the middle of the fifteenth, a series of disasters occurred which led the economy and society through many crises towards the forms which they assumed in modern times. Historians have tended to make varying judgments about this period according to the regions which they have studied; for in spite of much recent research, the mass of surviving documents has still not been worked over to the point where it is possible to draw general conclusions. The contrasts between the various regions of Europe were accentuated still more by the consequences of prolonged wars, catastrophic epidemics and monetary crises.

From 1420, 1450 or 1470 – according to region – after the areas which had been devastated in the previous century had been rehabilitated and with the consolidation of the gains made in other zones, a new European harmony came about, with a rapid expansion in men, technology, capital, products and trade. This period of general ferment, which opened during the Quattrocento and continued during the 'Renaissance' until about 1560, paved the way for classical Europe.

The later Middle Ages have often been described as 'dark ages', following the golden age of the classical Middle Ages and preceding the dawn of the Renaissance; or as a bloody period, since it opened with the massacres of the lords and the magnates in western Flanders, continued with the 'great desolation' of the countryside and towns of France at the time of the Hundred Years' War, and concluded with the exploits of the 'Ecorcheurs'. Within a century a demographic decline and disastrous plagues caused the European population to fall to perhaps a third of its 1300 level. There were deadly famines, causing villages to be abandoned by the thousand, many of them permanently, from Castile to Prussia, and from the Scottish borders to the Greek peninsula. Cultivated land, which had been won from waste and woodland by centuries of effort, reverted to fallow and pasture. The Bordeaux vineyards exported only a tenth of their early-fourteenth-century production. The countryside was continually overrun by bands of adventurers, who ruined

105 Rioters pillaging a house; miniature from a late fourteenth-century French manuscript.

the farms and plundered the houses, forcing the inhabitants to seek refuge in the boroughs and towns. There were sudden peasant risings sparked off by distress, an unmistakable stiffening of the exploitation of the peasants by the lords and a continual fall in agricultural prices. Industries declined or disappeared, commercial horizons in the east were lowered, trading or banking companies failed, the currency was debased and monetary stocks exhausted. Finally excessive taxation crushed burghers and villeins alike in the interests of war and the luxury of courts. It would be easy to add many further touches to this picture confirming the economic relapse and complete depression of the European west.

Yet this impression of recession, which is given by every study of the territories in the forefront of the advance during the preceding era, must be modified when events are viewed in the long term. All regions did not undergo the same calamities simultaneously, and, in between the periods of desolation, there were commendable efforts more or less everywhere to put matters to rights.

On a European scale, the picture looks quite different: economic development continued in the regions which had been least affected by the previous advance. Consequently the perspective changes according to whether one looks towards the west or the north, the centre or the east of the continent. The fourteenth century and the beginning of the fifteenth undoubtedly mark the zenith of the Germanic Hanse. At the same time the Scandinavian countries, Bohemia, Poland and Hungary, not to mention Portugal, entered the group of economically significant countries. Furthermore, it should be emphasized that the places where the economic currents of northern and southern Europe met – Venice, Bruges, Geneva and Frankfurt – reached their peak at this time.

VENICE
AND ITS FLEET

106 St Marks and the Doge's Palace; detail of miniature from a late fifteenth-century manuscript.

107, 108 Port scenes; details of Carpaccio's paintings of the legend of St Ursula. The artist has given a Venetian background to scenes which are supposed to have taken place in an English port (c. 1493).

Venice had to undergo terrible setbacks, the worst example being the war of Chioggia, but its Doge Mocenigo was justly proud of getting his city's economy in balance again in 1423. At this time the Venetian fleet included 3,000 boats for coastal trade, with a displacement of from 6 to 120 tons and manned by 17,000 sailors; 300 long-distance merchant ships, manned by 8,000 men; 45 galleys, manned by 11,000 sailors and soldiers; and there were 3,000 caulkers and 3,000 carpenters in the naval shipyards. Imports and exports each rose to ten million gold ducats, with four million gold ducats' profit going to the Venetians handling the trade; the cloths brought by the Florentines alone for distribution by Venice in the Mediterranean basin amounted to 16,000 pieces. The *Zecca* minted 1,200,000 gold ducats annually, and silver coins to a value of 800,000 ducats, with 15 per cent of the coins intended for large-scale international trade. The public debt had been brought down from ten to six million gold ducats. The annual returns of the budget rose to 1,614,000 ducats, of which 28 per cent came from the mainland states and 23 per cent from overseas possessions. More than ever before, the 'Fondaco dei Tedeschi' was the empire's window on to the Mediterranean; central Europe and the Balkans found themselves linked to the economy of the state which was Queen of the Adriatic.

Although Bruges had also had to suffer passing crises (when its role was taken over by Antwerp and Middelburg), it nevertheless remained by and large the point of contact between the Hanseatics and western countries, and the bridge between England and the continent; the Italians either made Bruges the headquarters of their principal banks, or else established branches there, and the Portuguese and Spaniards made it the centre of their far-flung business interests.

The fairs of Geneva had succeeded those of Champagne as the meeting-place for French, German and Italian merchants, and those of Frankfurt, at the crossroads of the commercial routes from southern, Rhenish and Hanseatic Germany, had become the most important economic centre of the empire.

The range of divergent aspects in this very complex period cannot, therefore, be overemphasized. The documents invite us to infer that there were profound changes in the way industries were set up, in the distribution of agricultural crops and animal husbandry across the whole of Europe, and in the commercial or financial function of many places. There was keen competition between different areas and towns: the dynamism of some caused their sudden rise, while other traditional centres became ossified, and this, quite as much as disasters generally linked with the actions of war, brought about their eclipse and decline, or even led to their disappearance.

174

109 Scene of a Hanse port, possibly Lübeck, 1497.

110 The bishop of Paris blessing the *Lendit* fair (*cf*. ill. 64); miniature from a French manuscript, 1395–1426.

111 A panoramic view of the port of Antwerp in 1515.

112 Aerial view of Nördlingen, Bavaria.

The historian contemplating the economic evolution of this period has the impression that he is witnessing a relay-race, with the torch being taken over in turn by one town after another, and sometimes returning to its starting-point after two or three generations. If the fairs of Flanders began to decline, the merchants brought prosperity to those of Brabant, held at Antwerp, Malines and Bergen-op-Zoom. If those of Champagne were deserted, the merchants reassembled at Paris and at the *Lendit* or Compiègne fairs, or those of Chalon-sur-Saône. The leading role was taken over by the fairs of Geneva; then those of Frankfurt and Friedberg in turn won a dominant position, accompanied by the fairs of Nuremberg and Nördlingen; Geneva regained its supremacy only to face competition from Lyons; finally the great commercial market-place was established at Leipzig. Failure followed upon failure in Tuscany among the bankers of Pistoia and Siena, to the point where these towns lost practically all their importance on an international level; but a new generation made Florence an even more important centre of commercial life. The bank of Lucca collapsed, but its silks made an immediate recovery. The rich cloth-trade of Flanders suffered the consequences of the country's policy towards the king of France, went through a period of social disturbance and faced competition from Milanese and Florentine cloth-manufacturers; in its place, the cloth industry of Brabant developed briskly and became one of the most active of Europe: Brussels again took up the torch which was handed on by Ypres.

A kind of perpetual balancing mechanism came into operation on a continental scale. The Mediterranean and Rhenish vineyards regained what had been lost by those of Bordeaux and Poitou; the abandoned fields of England and those ravaged by war in the Ile-de-France and Picardy were replaced by the rye-lands of eastern Europe; Danish butter supplanted Normandy butter; Portuguese salt from Setúbal supplemented the deficiency in supplies from the Bay of Bourgneuf; the pastel of Lombardy eclipsed that of Tuscany. Marseilles was in complete decline, Aiguesmortes was silted up and Montpellier waned in importance, but Barcelona reached the height of its powers, Valencia developed and Lisbon took its place among the great maritime centres. Milan, bubbling with vitality, relegated Piacenza and the other Lombard cities to second place, and Avignon took on the mantle of Rome.

There was thus a continuing dynamism throughout Europe. If a long period of crisis nevertheless set in over a large part of the continent, this was due to a succession of disasters. Where these calamities became more or less unending, as in France, they brought with them an economic collapse from which the country had great difficulty in extricating itself; but it should be emphasized that every period of respite was utilized, and attempts were made to give the economy a temporary boost.

113 The bridge of Saint-Bénézet, across the Rhône at Avignon. It is now broken, and only four of the twenty-two original arches remain; in the centre is the Romanesque chapel of St Nicholas. In the foreground is a tower of the city walls.

114 The population lived under the obsession of war: a fortified mill at Blasimont, in Guyenne.

In place of the multiplicity of city-states and fiefs with limited boundaries, which had been inherited from the early Middle Ages, new states were established with augmented powers, whose economic and political imperialism was supported by increased fiscal resources and an enlarged military strength. The wars consequently became harsher, and more protracted than in the past, if not continuous; they shook the economy and society over very wide areas.

But in spite of general taxation, these states were not sufficiently mobilized to officer the whole of their forces efficiently or to remunerate them regularly: every war involved banditry by land and privateering by sea. Mercenaries and corsairs fell upon any prey within their reach – friend, foe, or neutral – requisitioning and pillaging by turns to get their pay or simply in order to live; they held towns and villages to ransom, on the pretext of saving them from destruction or guaranteeing them protection; in fact, *patis* ('pact') became something of a medieval synonym for the modern 'racket'. Behind the knightly feats of arms, celebrated by Froissart, and in the guise of wars of chivalry, war was waged primarily with bare hands, involving systematic pillage, the destruction of villages, and gratuitous cruelties. It often degenerated into highway robbery which was resorted to by adventurers – nobles, younger

179

sons or bastards of lordly families, and vagabonds all mixed up together: Gascons and Provençaux, Bretons and Navarrese, Brabantese and Catalans, English, Welsh, Germans, Hungarians, Italian *condottieri* and French *écorcheurs* all lived from war and what it promised. Only the towns were spared for the most part, but they were obliged to put their walls hastily in order and to maintain them at great expense, sometimes even to the point of complete financial ruin. Behind the razed suburbs, on the far side of the ditches and ramparts, the proletarian crowds who had found refuge there were repeatedly struck down by famine and epidemics.

The so-called Hundred Years' War in fact consisted of four separate sets of wars which drove the powers back and forward for a hundred and fifty years: there were Franco-English wars, Franco-Flemish, and then Franco-Burgundian hostilities, a duel between Aragon and Anjou, and a permanent struggle between the perpetually expanding Ottomans and their neighbours, who fell to them one by one.

On land the war between France and England was the main regulator of the whole of political and economic life in the greater part of the continent, after Philip the Fair had seized English Guienne in 1294. It came to an end only after the expulsion of the English from Normandy, Bordeaux and Gascony (1450–53). The series of Franco-Flemish conflicts were linked with it; they erupted into a civil war between Franco-Armagnacs and Anglo-Burgundians which continued until the peace of Arras (1435), only to be resumed in the reign of Louis XI. Extremely large areas were ruined by the English cavalcades swarming over the realm from one sea to the other. The great companies of Charles V and, later, the royal army of Charles VII who won the kingdom back took their toll. Serious damage was caused by the actions of the Armagnacs at the gates of Paris, and of guerrillas under the leadership of small garrisons adhering to one or other party, isolated in their strongholds; while the activities of peasant bands who had taken to the *maquis* from penury as much as in a spirit of national resistance, also contributed to the ruin.

Each region in turn suffered utter devastation; the areas where the opposing forces met, such as the Bordelais, Quercy, Périgord, Poitou, Maine, Normandy, Picardy, Ile-de-France, Brie, Sénonais and Nivernais, obviously suffered even more than the rest. But bands of warriors also ravaged Limousin and Velay, and other *routiers* (mercenaries) operated with Raymond of Turenne as far afield as central Provence. Punctuated by truces, hostilities broke out periodically in various areas throughout the kingdom: in 1337–40 (the period of the first campaigns), 1346–47 (Crécy and Calais), 1355–61 (Poitiers and its aftermath), 1369–75 (in areas in the west and the mid-west of France), 1410–20

(Armagnacs and Burgundians, Agincourt), 1435–40 and 1447–50 (the reconquest of the kingdom).

By sea, the war was scarcely less violent, for the Mediterranean was the closed arena of two fundamentally hostile powers: the Aragonese, who united the economic and maritime forces of Barcelona and Valencia and those of Majorca, Sicily and Sardinia under their command; and the Angevins of Naples and Marseilles, who aimed at dominating Italy, the islands, and Greece, if not the Orient. The conflict which started with the Sicilian Vespers in 1282 came to an end only with the entry of Alphonso VI into Naples in 1443. Local wars in Italy, the reconquest of the pontifical states at the time of the Avignon papacy and the Great Schism, the ambition of the Visconti of Milan, and the life-and-death struggle of Genoa and Venice during the war of Tenedos and Chioggia (1377–81) also bore within them the seeds of destruction. Privateering wars between navies became a permanent fact of life.

A more serious state of affairs developed in 1300 when the Ottomans began to involve themselves politically in Asia Minor, but their progress became particularly rapid at the time of Murad II. From 1357 they established themselves on the Straits of Gallipoli; they crushed the Serbs at Kossovo (1389), and asserted their dominion over the Balkans: Nicopolis, in 1396, and Varna, in 1444, marked further stages in the expansion which culminated in the fall of Constantinople in 1453. In Asia there was the bloody interlude of the conquests of Tamburlaine who, starting out from Transoxiana in 1365, extended his empire from the steppes of southern Russia to Damascus in the west and central India in the east.

The events in Asia undoubtedly gave rise to a contraction of the European commercial frontier. Following the disturbance in the states which succeeded the Mongol empire, the continent became closed to Latin merchants. After the fall of Acre in 1291 and Lesser Armenia at the beginning of the fourteenth century, the Egyptian recovery and subsequently the Ottoman success had the effect of restricting the initiatives of western merchants, who had to organize their activities in relation to their island bases of Cyprus, Chios and Crete: they were once more confined to coastal trade, and for much of the fourteenth century did not even find it possible to send the usual convoys to the eastern Mediterranean; they were suspended for a century. In 1315 Arab privateering began again in the western Mediterranean.

The advent of the Marinids, who from 1321 to 1347 extended their empire over the whole of Barbary, threw the Catalans and Castilians on the defensive. At the same time Egypt was recovering due to two factors, the links forged with the Mandingo empire, which was rich in gold, and a fresh expansion towards the countries of the Indian Ocean, India, Persia and east Africa. In the whole Mediterranean area, oriental and African, we are faced with the inescapable fact that the Christian powers were on the retreat, torn apart by their perpetual conflicts.

As well as the wars, the plague also determined the rhythm of men's lives at this period. Since the sixth century, epidemics had hardly extended beyond regional bounds, and their effects, even though aggravated by malnutrition, inadequate hygiene and the precariousness of the conditions of life, had remained limited. Only leprosy had been a permanent scourge since the Crusades had brought Europeans into contact with the populations of the east, where it was endemic; but it attacked individuals rather than groups, and at the beginning of the fourteenth century it seemed to be abating.

The plague arose in the west, at a time when the great population expansion, set in motion three centuries earlier, had met with a perceptible check; perhaps from the last years of the thirteenth century or the first years of the fourteenth the increase in the birth-rate was halted, for reasons which are very little understood. Around 1310–40, the date varying according to region, population figures became stabilized at a very high level of density. Documents afford various samples in Normandy, the Ile-de-France, Languedoc and Dauphiné, which reveal many cantons where the density at this time was higher than the maximum reached in the modern era, that is, in the mid-nineteenth century. It is not certain that there was an actual decline in the birth-rate before 1340, and I personally do not accept the existence of a real 'demographic crisis' from the first half of the fourteenth century. It seems much more likely that the decline was caused by excess population in the rural areas moving to the towns, in particular the economic metropolises. At this time a great expansion took place in cities like Paris, Avignon, Bruges, London, Lübeck, Florence, Milan, Genoa and Venice. This migration from the country to the towns would be sufficient to explain the fact that new clearings were exceptional from the second half of the thirteenth century; even the agricultural expansion of the Germans towards the east seems to have fallen off. Only on the fringes of Europe did agriculture continue to develop, in Flanders, central Sweden, the Slav countries, Portugal and no doubt also Castile.

Suddenly, in 1348, the dreaded plague made its appearance in the west. It seems to have started around 1341 among the Mongol tribes of Central Asia, taking the double form of a bubonic plague, carried by fleas and flea-bearing rats, and a pneumonic plague, which was even more terrifying since no remedy was found for it until modern times. The abundant contacts which, as we have noted, linked India with the Far East and the Arab world at the time, as well as

the Mongol peace, led to the unleashing of the pestilence from one en
Asia to the other. In 1346 it ravaged the Caucasus and reached the Tatars o
Golden Horde; they then besieged Tana, and Caffa, passing it on to the Gen
(as the story goes) by throwing plague-ridden corpses into the enemy city. The
Genoese and Venetians carried it with them: it gained a hold in Constantinople
and then jumped from island to island, to Cyprus (and from there to Egypt),
Sicily and Sardinia. The infection reached continental Italy in the first weeks of
1347 or the beginning of 1348, starting with the ports, Genoa, Venice and Pisa.
In the first half of the year, it went up the Rhône from Marseilles towards
Avignon, and from there to Paris and Catalonia; in the second half, North
Africa and Portugal, Syria and London were all attacked at the same time. In
1349 it crossed Germany, Flanders and northern England; in 1350, it penetrated into Scandinavia and in the two following years ran through Russia
from one end to the other.

A grievous scourge was let loose over the whole world, without respect to
frontiers or civilizations. It was certainly the most severe disaster which had
struck mankind in the historical era. From the very numerous studies which
have been devoted to it, we may conclude that at least a third of the population,
often a half, and sometimes two-thirds, disappeared in the towns and the
countryside during the six months which generally marked the height of the
epidemic. The situation was most grave in the ports: it is estimated that at
Genoa there were 40,000 deaths among a population of 65,000; Hamburg lost
two-thirds of its population and Bremen 70 per cent; at Bordeaux, fourteen
of the twenty canons of Saint-Seurin died. The eastern part of the Low
Countries, Bohemia, Poland and Hungary, however, do not seem to have
been greatly affected.

The most serious consequence was perhaps that, after striking so heavily,
the plague became endemic in the whole of Europe for at least a century and a
half. The 'Great Plague' was followed by an immediate and fantastic rush of
marriages and births, as if those who had been spared were unwilling to lose
any time in giving new life to the continent. For example, in the well-known
case of the borough of Givry – the only place for which a register of births,
marriages and deaths survives – the number of marriages went up from an
average of 26 per annum before the plague to 86 in 1349. But from 1360 to
1362 it struck again, this time particularly at the young people who had been
born since the first epidemic, since its survivors apparently had the advantage
of immunity. It broke out once more in 1374–76: it is estimated that England
lost 25 per cent of its population in 1350, 23 per cent in 1360, 13 per cent in
1369, 12 per cent in 1375.

115 With war, plague and
famine ever present, death was
constantly set before men's
eyes. The Campo Santo in
Pisa was dominated by the remarkable fresco attributed to
Francesco Traini, *The Triumph
of Death* (*c.* 1370), now in the
National Museum, Pisa. Here,
a detail the legend of the
Three Living and the Three
Dead.

Even apart from the general epidemics, the disease whirled about across Europe, drifting hither and thither, and striking where disaster had undermined the population's resistance. Combined with the catastrophic consequences of the wars, its effect was such that the west seemed incapable of regaining its equilibrium: its vitality sank from generation to generation. Barcelona was struck down eleven times between 1396 and 1437, and, at the depth of its distress, Paris was afflicted eight times between 1414 and 1439, with smallpox and influenza adding to the effects of the plague. J. C. Russell has attempted to draw up figures for the expectation of life in medieval England, and even if his figures are debatable, they undoubtedly give at least a general indication of the situation; the average length of life, which according to him must have been about 25 years in the last quarter of the thirteenth century, fell to 17 years between 1348 and 1375, and did not reach 32 years until the third quarter of the fifteenth century. A recent thesis on a canton in Savoy has shown that about 50 per cent of the names of heads of families disappeared from the registers of taxes after five years and that the average life expectancy from the time they appeared on the registers was 12 years. Another thesis, surveying Dauphiné, mandment by mandment (a unit corresponding roughly to the modern canton), has shown that this province, which escaped relatively lightly from the events of war, lost about 40 per cent of its population between 1339 and 1476, and in the Champsaur the figure reached 70 per cent. Only at the very end of the eighteenth century, if not during the nineteenth, was the population density of 1339 once again achieved in Dauphiné as a whole; in the reign of Louis XIV Grésivaudan had still regained only three-quarters of its pre-plague population. In Provence (not counting the *comté* of Nice), the 70,000 households which had existed before the plague had fallen to 30,000 in 1471.

Scholars have by no means finished studying and discussing the demographic, economic and social consequences of this frightful catastrophe, which came just at the time when Europe was suffering from the effects of other calamities, the war and the havoc which it wrought, famine, increased taxation, and the closing of foreign markets.

Its most immediate effect was to trigger off a transfer of the population from the regions which were least affected towards richer areas in need of more labour, from areas where the manorial system was most oppressive towards those where better social conditions prevailed, and from the mountains to the plains. The drift away from the countryside towards the towns which had already begun accelerated still further, since in the towns the enormous increase in the number of vacancies caused by the disease meant that there were rises in wages which the public authorities, still inexperienced in such matters, were powerless to stop.

The gap between agricultural prices and ever-rising industrial prices, which had already been pronounced for a generation, widened still further. Consequently the towns which were engaged in industrial activity in a small way fared badly. In Provence the small towns, which had been primarily agricultural markets, collapsed: Apt, Forcalquier, Manosque and Riez lost more than half their inhabitants, while the notaries' registers of Avignon show that a considerable number of the residents of this great city, and possibly the majority, were born outside it. The high Alpine valleys and the plateaux of the fore-Alps in Dauphiné and Provence were less affected by the epidemic itself, but at a later date, during the following century, they too became denuded of their inhabitants. The movement affected three-quarters of the population, which settled permanently in Avignon and along the Provençal and Ligurian coasts, bringing new life to these areas; formerly there had been only a seasonal migration to them – though it was significant.

Insecurity also led countrymen to flock to the towns especially in the Paris region. Here new districts took shape, in spite of the very heavy epidemics which periodically decimated the city, and the population rose from around 100,000 inhabitants at the beginning of the fourteenth century – a figure which seems probable in spite of recent criticism – to at least 300,000 in the course of the sixteenth. Unemployment and social disturbances compelled the craftsmen and labourers of the towns most affected by competition to migrate to other centres, such as the Flemish and Brabantese weavers who were attracted in large numbers to Italy, England and Germany. Consequently, there was an intense ferment of population at the time, and the reconstruction of the fifteenth century helped to accentuate the migratory trend still further, when the lords called the people who had been least affected by the crisis to manual labour, in order to put under cultivation again the areas which had been devastated and allowed to revert to fallow, waste or woodland.

The sudden fall in population caused by the Black Death in the Hanseatic towns again unleashed a powerful movement away from the countryside towards the towns, and from the west of the empire (including Wallonia) towards the east. As a result, in spite of fresh epidemics, the hundred or so commercial centres comprising the Hanse of the time were swollen with new population: Lübeck grew from about 15,000 inhabitants around 1300 to 25,000 in the fifteenth century; Hamburg, with a population of 5,000 around 1300, lost two-thirds of it during the plague, but it increased to 8,000 in 1375, and to 16,000 in the middle of the fifteenth century; Bremen grew from 12,000

187

before the plague to 17,000 about 1400; Danzig, from 2,000 about 1300, to 10,000 at the end of the fourteenth century and to 20,000 in the middle of the fifteenth. The fact that none of the four burgomasters of Hamburg in 1490 had been born in the town illustrates the trend away from the countryside. The marginal villages in particular were abandoned by the hundred, and the infusion of new blood goes a long way towards explaining the dynamism of the Hanseatic towns. In this they were distinguished from those of western Europe, where the precariousness of life in the surrounding countryside did not always enable the necessary population renewal to take place which would have stimulated the urban economy by means of immigration.

AGRICULTURAL CHANGES
IN THE FOURTEENTH AND FIFTEENTH CENTURIES

Most historians regard the decline of the country areas and the recession of cereal cultivation in western Europe as the dominant features of the period; the inevitable result was famine, which, like the epidemics and the wars, formed an essential part of the fabric of life at this period.

While the population continued to increase more or less continuously until the first half or perhaps the middle of the fourteenth century, there were no new clearings of land between 1250 and 1350, the date varying according to region; even before this period it seems that in England cereal fields had begun to give way to meadows. If there were bad harvests, famine was not far away. There had of course been many times of scarcity in the past, especially in the eleventh century, when the extension of cultivation could hardly keep pace with the population explosion. There had also been many difficult periods in the thirteenth century in Italy, due to its extensive urbanization: large cities had to rely for their supplies on the corn lands of Sicily, Apulia, or the Maremma, and the task of provisioning them had been one of the major preoccupations of Venice, surrounded by marshes, as well as of Genoa, which had its back to infertile mountain lands. But on the whole, people had been reasonably well fed during the thirteenth century, at least in the west; the Holy Land depended exclusively on supplies from overseas, and Kabylia would have gone hungry without corn from Oran. The fourteenth century and the greater part of the fifteenth were particularly blighted by terrible famines and price rises, owing to the scarcity of provisions and to speculation.

Not counting the innumerable local shortages, regional famines spread over vast areas of the continent from the first half of the fourteenth century. The first raged over the whole of Europe, from the Atlantic to the Baltic, and lasted for three years, from 1315 to 1317. The bad harvest of 1314 was followed by two years with so much rain that catastrophic floods occurred more or less everywhere. At Ypres, where the textile workers were crowded together in a restricted area, nearly 2,800 bodies – 10 per cent of the population – were collected from the streets in a half-year period of 1316. In England, the price of a measure of wheat rose from 5 to 40 shillings; and at Louvain, in seven months, from 5 to 16 livres.

Other crises occurred: that of 1346–50, paving the way for the plague and then adding to its misery; that of 1361–62, which again seems to have opened the door to a second epidemic; and that of 1374–75, which broke out in the Mediterranean region and whose effects were reinforced by the third plague which raged from 1375 to 1377.

116 Citizens of Florence feeding victims of the famine in Siena; miniature from a fourteenth-century manuscript.

Some contemporary historians who have studied these events have come to wonder whether the succession of poor harvests was not due to a climatic change on a world scale. There are some indications in favour of such a hypothesis: after a warmer period which saw the settlement of the Scandinavians in Greenland and perhaps in Labrador, the climate of the northern hemisphere became colder and more humid, a process which reached its peak between the beginning of the fourteenth century and the end of the fifteenth. The glaciers in Greenland advanced and contributed to the eventual disappearance of the population there. The whole of the Baltic was repeatedly frozen over and even the Gironde froze in 1363. There was a remarkable lowering of the tree-line, and glaciers in the Alps extended further down the mountain-side.

Other scholars have tried to establish a connection between the cosmic cycle of the ocean currents, which would have reached their maximum strength in 1433, and the freeing of the ice-packs which caused communications between Norway and Iceland to be interrupted by drifting icebergs. This has also been said to be the cause of the tides which submerged the low-lying coastal areas of the Low Countries and in particular the Zuider Zee. It has been pointed out, too, that the period under consideration corresponds to an inactive phase of Vesuvius, which was so calm between 1306 and 1500 that the soil was tilled right up to the brink of the cone; this may also be linked with one of the phases of bradyseism recorded at Pozzuoli. It must be recognized, however, that our knowledge of all these phenomena – some of which may well be contradictory – is exceedingly scanty, and that they certainly need further study.

There are other more traditional explanations: some historians think that the clearing of land during the preceding centuries had been too extensive and that cereals were grown in soils which were extremely unsuitable for the purpose. Soil which had previously carried only acid moorland and woodland would become quickly exhausted if it were not nourished by massive applications of manure. The marginal lands which the pioneers had won back were therefore condemned, and this accounts for the retrenchment of English agriculture before the crises of the fourteenth century. (These theories were defended in a lively and pertinent manner at the International Congress on Economic History at Munich in 1965.)

Without completely rejecting any of these attempted explanations, I should like to draw attention to a number of more specifically economic factors which may have been more directly decisive. Every landowner, every peasant, instinctively seeks above all else a type of cultivation which is likely to bring

117 Harvesting of cereals, from an Italian Book of Offices.

him most profit. A kind of balance therefore tends to be established, at a given moment, between agriculture and stock-raising, and, among the various types of cultivation, between those which are more and those which are less remunerative, notably, between cereals and specialized crops (vines, vegetables, fruit, plants used for dyeing, etc.). Only one impediment stood in the way of these changes, a fear of a shortage of cereals for making bread. But with the money gained from their other business interests, the landowners were from this time on in a position to store the sacks of grain or flour which they required for themselves and their households. The progress of commerce and particularly of maritime trade at the end of the thirteenth century and beginning of the fourteenth might also appear to be such as to ensure, if need be, all the necessities of the population. Genoa, with its *navi* (large cargo vessels), was able to transport all the corn exported from Sicily or the Black Sea to the most distant countries, and the fleet of Hanseatic *koggen* was quite ready to take over the transport of grain from Prussia and Poland. It is almost certain that these foreign cereals were sold at a lower price than the native corn, and no doubt their arrival in bulk made an important contribution to the general lowering of grain prices which has been noted in all the western European markets from about 1315.

There was, therefore, nothing to prevent western farmers from reducing their marginal fields with a poor yield (those that could not be relied upon to produce four-fold) and even lands with a better yield, in favour of more remunerative types of cultivation. From the thirteenth century onwards, monoculture was substituted in certain areas for the traditional polyculture: regions such as the Auxerre district and Aunis devoted themselves completely to viticulture, and from then depended exclusively on the outside world for their supply of cereals.

From this point of view, the abandonment of cereal cultivation in some regions, and especially in England, must be seen not as an economic disaster, but as the result of agricultural changes so radical that it would be equally appropriate to speak of an agricultural revolution in the fourteenth century as in the eighteenth.

Previously general polyculture was more or less universal, where each piece of land, even those least suitable for cereal cultivation, had to provide food for the village as best it could. Now a relatively specialized agriculture was substituted. The map of Europe became clearly demarcated into areas which were more or less exclusively devoted to cereal cultivation, others which were used for industrial plants and viticulture, and lastly regions where circumstances had contributed to denuding large areas of their inhabitants, and where stock raising developed, putting an end to arable farming.

We shall now consider these facts under three headings: the development of maritime trade in corn; the development of specialized crops; and the change-over from agriculture to stock-raising.

In the fourteenth century, even more than in the preceding century, cereals became a commodity in which there was a large-scale trade, both on the rivers (the Vistula, the Main, the Rhine, the Seine, the Loire, the Saône, the Rhône, the Po), and on the seas. The traffic perhaps occupied the greatest number of fleets, and the largest vessels.

In the Black Sea, exports of spices and slaves became rarer, but Genoese ships visited it in increasing numbers, and came away loaded to the gunwales with the corn which the Genoese, Greeks and Armenians drained from the interior, from Crimea and the Ukraine, from Thrace and Bulgaria, towards the ports of 'Gazaria' (Khazaria). These vessels were no longer confined to provisioning Constantinople but passed on in large numbers towards the western Mediterranean.

Venice also acquired supplies of Macedonian corn at Salonika, which was subsequently stored at Negroponte. It transformed Crete into a granary for its own use and that of Cyprus, which was from then on devoted primarily to sugar production. Anatolian corn also formed part of the traffic.

Apulia, with its two ports, Barletta and Manfredonia, which were used solely for loading corn, had become the organizing centre for cereals in the Mediterranean during the last quarter of the thirteenth century. When a particular area was suffering from shortage, the king opened his granaries to it, sometimes waiving customs duty, especially if this was in line with his political strategy.

Together with Calabria and Sicily, Apulia in any case reckoned to supply Florence, Venice and often Genoa with the bulk of their requirements. All the Florentine companies were concerned in this traffic, and we know that the three large companies of the Bardi, the Acciajoli and the Peruzzi exported 280,000 hl. (770,000 bushels) in 1309, 515,000 hl. (about 1,400,000 bushels) in 1311, and 320,000 hl. (980,000 bushels) in 1320; in 1329 the Acciajoli alone dealt in 340,000 hl. (more than 900,000 bushels).

Traditionally, Sicily (which was now in the hands of the Aragonese) played a similar role with its specialized ports, the *caricatori*; in 1340 they were, in order of their importance for handling corn, Agrigento, Sciacca, Licata, Eraclea, Termini, Palermo, Trapani, Marsala, Mazzara, Augusta, and others.

Ancona and the Marches were of much less importance, as well as Arles and lower Languedoc, but the Tuscan Maremma, with Corneto (Tarquinia) and Montalto, pushed its cereal production to its limits.

Sardinia, which was in the hands of the Catalans, became vital to them for their provisions: each year, in the middle of the fourteenth century, a fleet of 50 to 100 *navi*, or sometimes smaller boats, went to Cagliari (and others to Oristano) to take on corn and other available provisions; Sardinia exported up to 100,000 hl. (275,000 bushels) from Cagliari, bound principally for Barcelona and Majorca.

Orania, and Morocco itself, came to play a not inconsiderable role, especially in supplying Valencia, Majorca and even Kabylia. In 1317, at the height of the famine in England, a Genoese convoy was assembled to carry corn from Morocco to Sandwich; one of the largest Genoese ships of the time, loaded beyond the authorized limit, carried on this occasion about 8,500 hl. (24,000 bushels) of corn.

Finally, the Portuguese, who had just discovered Madeira, established large-scale cereal cultivation there, anticipating the sugar industry of the following century.

A colonial-type economy was thus established in the Mediterranean region on the initiative of the merchants: its aim was to exploit certain areas for the production of massive quantities of cereals intended for the industrial urban centres. Its consequence was that the rural masses in the south became reduced to a proletariat.

Along the Baltic coasts the situation was similar. The Hanseatic merchants maintained the flow of cereals, in particular rye, which was produced mainly by Prussia and Poland and sent to Norway, the British Isles and the Low Countries. The Netherlands fleet emulated the Hanseatics and did its best to compete directly at the centres where stocks were held; from the English side, 300 ships went to buy corn at Danzig in 1392.

The Hanseatic merchants more than once brought pressure to bear on their partners by withholding supplies. We have already mentioned their blockade of Bergen in 1284, as a result of which Norway became completely dependent upon Baltic grain. In 1359–60, at a time of great scarcity in Bruges, the Hanseatics decided to abandon the town, to boycott it, and to station ships in order to prevent grain smuggling. They did the same in 1436, transferring the headquarters of their business to Antwerp and causing famine in Flanders.

Unfortunately no figures are available for the corn trade during this period. We know only that in 1400 the granaries of the Teutonic Order at Danzig (Gdańsk) contained about 15,000 tons of rye, 6,000 of oats, 1,500 of barley and 800 of wheat, and at Toruń there were other granaries, some of which still survive.

In 1481, 1,100 ships from Danzig arrived in Holland, Zeeland and Friesland; they supplied only part of the provisions of this region, however, for (according to a note written by the shipowner Weinreich), when shipments were abruptly stopped in the autumn, there was a staggering rise in the price of rye, which went up from 48 to 80 florins in Zeeland.

At the very end of the fifteenth century, rye exports from the port of Danzig alone exceeded 20,000 tons, and we know that the excessive increase of cereal cultivation, which was pushed through by the lords with an eye to export, was one of the reasons for the gradual deterioration in the economic and legal status of the peasant classes, finally leading to their enslavement.

Thus in the fourteenth century, in the two sectors of Europe – Hanseatic and Mediterranean – vast areas were put under cereal cultivation; they flooded the western markets with their massive output, obtained from enslaved dependants. No other explanation is required for the fall in cereal prices in the countries of western Europe, and the transformation of their agricultural economy.

Wherever possible, specialized crops were grown which brought in a better return. The vine is the most obvious example, for it demanded much more advanced methods, there was no need to fallow, and the harvest, although much more uncertain than in the case of corn, was annual. Recent studies have shown that, in contrast with that of grain, the price of wine was maintained at a constant level: during the whole of the fourteenth century, its price rose only to keep pace with monetary devaluations and the increase in wages.

A change in taste led to a demand for the heavy and sweet wines of the south, such as those of Rhodes, Cyprus, Candia and Malvasia, or the 'Greek' wines of Naples. To exploit this market Genoa planted rich vineyards in the *cinque terre* along the coast, especially at Vernazze; when transplanted to Sardinia the stock produced the *vernaccia* and also the *grenache*. The Greek and Spanish wines reached England and the countries of the north.

Promoted by the dukes of Burgundy, wine-growing extended all over the slopes of Beaune and Nuits; the produce of this area was distributed in the Low Countries and in Paris. The counts of Burgundy and Savoy also developed their vineyards at Arbois, Poligny, Seyssel and Tresserves, and the pope those of Châteauneuf and Tain. The vineyards of Piedmont, Vaud, Valais and Neuchâtel were considerably enlarged. But it was the wines of Alsace and the Rhine in particular which won a leading position from the end of the thirteenth century. They were exploited by the merchants of Cologne, Duisburg and Frankfurt, being transported in fully loaded ships on the Rhine, towards Basle or to the Low Countries, as well as on the Danube; they went right across Germany to reach Lübeck, and they were to be found in all the market-towns of the empire. At Tiel an average of 12,000 hl. (264,000 gallons) a year passed along the Waal at the end of the fourteenth century, and at Dordrecht 33,000 hl. (726,000 gallons) in 1380. Around 1400 the duty on wine at Cologne corresponded to transactions of the order of 120,000 hl. (2,640,000 gallons). At Passau on the Danube, something like 100,000 hl. (2,200,000 gallons) of wine passed annually in the other direction. At the same date Colmar, which was only one of the regional centres of production, handled about 93,000 hl. (2,046,000 gallons). This may be compared with the average total of all the wines passing through Bordeaux, which fluctuated between 50,000 and 90,000 hl. (1,1000,000 and 1,980,000 gallons) throughout the Hundred Years' War, apart from a short period of prosperity at the time of the Black Prince between 1356 and 1369. The comparison aptly illustrates the new importance of the Rhenish vineyards, and it may be wondered how far their extension was a burden on the surrounding countryside, since we know that at this time many villages in the non-vine-growing areas were deserted.

195

118 Harvesting of grapes and wine-making; detail from a fresco, *c.* 1450, in Trento (left).

119 A fruit merchant; miniature from an Italian manuscript of 1492.

The vineyards, which were often in the hands of burghers, were planted in a circle round the great cities, especially Paris, Toulouse, Marseilles and Genoa, as well as Buda. Then market-gardens, the Parisian *marais* and the *hortillonages* of the northern French towns, were developed. The diet became more diversified, leading to an increase in the demand for herbs, green vegetables and fruits; the accounts of this period show purchases of plants, notably strawberry plants, as well as of vegetable seeds.

Fruit made its appearance on the tables of the rich. Orchards were planted, especially on the Ligurian coast: from the middle of the fourteenth century boatloads of oranges from San Remo were brought in to Aiguesmortes, while those of Portugal reached England and the court of Burgundy, together with lemons, figs, pomegranates, raisins from Spain and Greece, and almonds. Large consignments of walnuts and hazelnuts came from Provence and the Neapolitan region, while the almonds were made into *torrons* and *massepains* (marchpanes, or marzipan cakes).

Sugar-cane was planted in the warm regions, such as Cyprus, where it became widespread, Crete, Sicily, Andalusia and the Algarve; in the fifteenth century Portugal turned Madeira into a sugar island.

The introduction of the mulberry into Calabria led to large-scale production of silk in the region, and a parallel development took place in the Granada district.

Textile plants, flax and hemp, were planted over large areas, notable in Hainaut and the valley of the Lys, in the Neapolitan region, in Piedmont and

197

in Montferrato, round Alessandria and near Pinerolo. Even more significantly, corn was replaced over wide areas by plants used in dyeing. The Abruzzi abandoned corn in favour of saffron, and the market of Aquila became a meeting-place for German importers. During the fourteenth century woad was grown extensively in an area of about 1,000 square miles in Piedmont, between Alessandria, Acqui, Tortona, Voghera and Valenza. It was used in the industries of Milan, Verona, Venice and southern Germany, and also exported, by way of Savona and Genoa, to England and the Low Countries. In 1396 the London branch of the Borromei of Milan had 1,400 hl. (3,850 bushels) of woad in store, as well as 263 bales weighing 260 pounds each. A lawsuit relating to the estate of a great woad merchant tells us that the merchandise stored in his two warehouses in Pavia and Voghera in 1475 amounted to 330 tons. The tax concession on Lombard woad amounted to more than 20,000 gold florins in 1445.

This was not the only area where woad was cultivated. There were also extensive fields in Tuscany and Emilia; in 1377 Florence had 500,000 pounds of woad in reserve in its storehouse of Città di Castello, and 190,000 pounds in the town, a total of nearly 250 tons. Lauraguais and Albigeois were in the same line of trade with their 'pastel', which found its way to either the market of Toulouse, or the cloth towns of Languedoc, or La Rochelle, from where it was exported to England. This industry must have brought great prosperity to the region and to the city of Toulouse, which dominated it economically, at the end of the fifteenth and during the sixteenth century.

In consequence viticulture, market-gardening, and industrial crops, which supplied a remunerative industry, usurped the privileged place held by cereal crops in many regions since the early Middle Ages.

In the less well-endowed lands, where the extension of cash crops could not be considered, many lords and landowners boldly made a complete change-over from agriculture to stock-raising. Sometimes the change was attempted as soon as the first symptoms of the crisis in agricultural prices were felt in the west; elsewhere it had to wait until the marginal lands were abandoned. In fact, the desertion of farms and hamlets led to a complete transformation of the agrarian economy, the effects of which have on the whole continued up to the present day, giving the countryside a desolate appearance. Methods varied a good deal from region to region, but in every case they were geared to a scanty labour force and made impressive profits for the owners – who were more often than not large landowners or capitalists.

In France, in Sologne and in Brenne, in Bresse and in Dombes, the great lords (counts of Blois and lords of Thoire-Villars) and the abbeys played a leading part in the construction of artificial pools; they formed thousands of fish-ponds, which finally extended over nearly 40,000 ha. (nearly 100,000 acres) in these four regions. Dikes, sluices and drainage canals were built; they were stocked with fish, most often pike and carp (which had been imported from eastern Europe, probably in the thirteenth century). Every three years the ponds, from six to eighteen feet deep, were emptied: the bottom was ploughed up and yielded a rich harvest of oats for one season, while the fish was sent to supply the townsmen, who paid a very good price. In spite of the changes which have taken place since the eighteenth century, the landscape of these regions and their economy even today show the effects of this transformation which began at the very end of the thirteenth century, grew more marked in the course of the fourteenth, and reached its height in the fifteenth.

But by far the most important agricultural change which took place on a European scale in the fourteenth and fifteenth centuries was the enormous expansion of sheep-rearing; it developed at the expense of cereal crops, and was sparked off by the needs of the wool industry. It was even claimed that 'the sheep's foot changes sand into gold'. Until the beginning of the fourteenth century, English wool, which was considered best, had been the chief source of raw material for the Franco-Flemish wool business, and the English weaving industry was sacrificed in favour of exporting wool to the Low Countries. When the Italian textile trade developed, it made extensive use of wools of North Africa (Kabylia and the Maghreb), which were of mediocre quality; but Florence and Milan continued to take supplies of the English wool. At the end of the thirteenth century and the beginning of the fourteenth, it came to Italy either by the land route, starting from the staple town of Bruges, or by sea, as soon as Genoa had established a regular line of communication with Southampton and Sandwich.

England seems to have reacted at first by increasing the volume of her consignments, which reached 43,000 sacks (or about 7,000 tons) in 1353. Production of wool was increased at the expense of arable crops in the eastern counties (Norfolk, Suffolk, Yorkshire, Lincolnshire), whose ports (Hull and Ipswich) were responsible for shipments to Flanders; there is evidence of a striking fall in the population of these areas during this period. In the middle of the century, during the reign of Edward III, England launched out more vigorously into the manufacture of cloth, which had the effect of progressively reducing its exports of wool by two-thirds in the space of half a century, at the same time causing the ancient corn-fields in the Midlands (Oxfordshire, Leicestershire, Northamptonshire) to be converted into pasture. Taking advantage of the virtual desertion of the countryside, abbeys and lords allowed grass to grow over what

199

had formerly been fields, and the dead villages to fall into ruin. The historical problems posed by these 'lost villages' are among those in which British historians and archaelogists are most keenly interested.

Another change accompanied these developments: in order to feed the cattle during winter, the proportion of cereals in the remaining crops diminished in favour of leguminous crops, in particular vetches. The manor of Wistow, which belonged to the abbey of Ramsey, produced 16 per cent of leguminous crops in 1307, 36 per cent in 1340 and 44 per cent in 1379; similarly, the proportion of leguminous crops in the abbey of Leicester rose from 17 per cent in 1363 to 32 per cent in 1401. Consequently from this time on, in spite of a fall in population, England was largely dependent on the outside world, mainly the Hanseatics, for its supplies of wheat and rye.

In order to meet the merchants' growing demands, due to an expansion of the textile industries, and faced with a continued fall in supplies of English wool, the Italians and Flemings had to find new sources of supply. Spain, in particular, was transformed into a gigantic pastureland for sheep. The *merinos*, a breed with long, strong hair, no doubt originating from North Africa at the time of the Marinid dynasty, was introduced to Castile, and a new organization, the *Hermandad de la Mesta*, was formed to provide links between the breeders; its treasurer was the grand master of the order of Santiago. The breeders were dominated by the great lords and the rich monasteries, whose flocks rose to several tens of thousand head. The total number of sheep has been estimated at around 1,500,000 in 1350 and 2,700,000 in 1467. They flowed like living rivers over the *meseta* from north to south, over the plateaux of Castile, León, Logroño, Soria, Sigüenza, Teruel and Cuenca, towards Badajoz, Beja in the Portuguese Estremadura, and Andalusia or Murcia. The *Mesta* governed the entire life of the countryside, which from then on was regulated by its rhythm. As a result, in the later Middle Ages and the Renaissance Spain became largely dependent for its food supplies on Baltic and Mediterranean corn (from Sicily and Sardinia), and then, from the second half of the fifteenth century, after the economic recovery of France, on French corn which came down the Seine, the Loire and the Rhône and was shipped in bulk to Spanish ports.

Simultaneously, a similar development took place at the northern end of Apulia, in the Capitanata, on the 'Tavoliere di Puglia', a kind of treeless steppe between the Apennines and the Monte Gargano promontory. It had formerly been corn land which brought wealth to Manfredonia, the port constructed by king Manfred near Siponto expressly for the export of cereals. In the course of the fourteenth and fifteenth centuries, the country was emptied of its inhabitants, and thirty-four of the sixty-four parishes which existed in the first

120 The former cathedral of S. Maria Maggiore, all that remains of the abandoned village of Siponto, stands in the deserted countryside between Manfredonia and Foggia.

quarter of the fourteenth century disappeared subsequently without trace. From then on it formed winter pasture for the flocks of the Abruzzi, criss-crossed by tracks sixty paces wide (the *tratturi*), and gradually became stripped of its population. The system of *tratta* for cattle was finally organized in 1443 by the royal government: in 1460, there were already 1,500,000 sheep, and a century later the number rose to 5,500,000.

The same situation is again found in the coastal plain of Latium as far south as the kingdom of Naples, in the Roman Campagna, and on beyond Civita-vecchia; at the end of the fourteenth century and the beginning of the fifteenth another important zone of transhumance was established along the *via doganale*, owing to the destruction of villages in this area. Where there had formerly been dozens of villages and numerous small towns, now only flocks of sheep were to be seen and a poverty-stricken population, afflicted by malaria right up to the present era, because the drainage system was not maintained.

121 Sheep-shearing in France; detail from *Les Très Riches Heures* of the duc de Berry (left, above).

122 Sheep being loaded on to a ship, from a late fifteenth-century Flemish manuscript (left, below).

123 Sheep-shearing in England; miniature from a late fifteenth-century manuscript (right, above).

124 Bartering wheat for wool; drawing from a late fifteenth-century manuscript (right).

125 House in Gloucestershire of William Grevel, wool merchant.

Animal husbandry also became widely established in the lower Arno valley (perhaps from the end of the thirteenth century), in the Luccan Garfagnana, in central Sicily and in the Sardinian countryside which had been laid waste by the incessant insurrections of the indigenous peasants against their Catalan masters. The lords responded to every labour crisis by using still less local labour; every act of destruction meant the extension of pasture for cattle, and since a labour-force was not needed, more fields ran wild. *Latifondi* (extensive land estates) were formed in this way, their wealth based on the possession of bare land, suitable for extensive stock-raising, which was a good source of profit. These have been maintained right up to the present, with familiar social and economic consequences.

In Provence, the *terre gaste* which was used for raising cattle had presented virtually no problems until the end of the thirteenth century, and the inhabitants of the communities were accustomed to pasture their flocks there. A little before 1300 large-scale transhumance began between the winter pastures near Saint-Maximin and Brignoles, and the summer pastures in the 'alpe'. In the first half of the fourteenth century, the lords claimed the right to send large flocks freely into all lands where they possessed even minimum rights of co-lordship: tens of thousands of beasts invaded the pastures. The inhabitants reacted vigorously, resolving to make their ancient entitlement of up to 240 head of sheep per household respected. Consequently the 'mountains' became overloaded and there were frequent conflicts. Many inhabitants left the region, while others found relief in seasonal migration. The plague gave further impetus to this trend: the death-rate and migration towards the richer low-lying country eventually led to the rapid depletion of the mountains. Between the alps and the winter pastures, in countryside which was virtually empty, a seasonal rhythm was established: during the summer *nourriguiers* (capitalist stock-breeders from the low-lying country) sent flocks of several thousand head into the 'mountains' leased from the lords and the communities (both in mountainous and low-lying country), who used them for their own stock during the winter. In 1471 a survey revealed the existence of 50,000 head of sheep in the two provostships of Grasse and Saint-Paul de Vence, an average of 100 animals per household, and the community of Saintes-Maries de la Mer declared 30,000 sheep to the surveyors. Each year the *nourriguiers* even sent flocks, some of them numbering between 3,000 and 4,000 beasts, from Salon into the Mercantour and the Tinée valley, the Valbonnais, the Gapençais, the Champsaur and the Trièves district. Stock-raising brought a degree of prosperity to the remote, high valleys around Briançon, the Valpute (Vallouise), and the Queyras. The sheep fairs of Briançon and Bersezio were extremely busy, and in 1343 the syndics of the communities in the high mountains were able to buy back privileges from the Dauphin, for the enormous sum of 12,000 gold florins and a yearly rent of 4,000 florins.

The same situation existed in the Massif Central, where the peoples of the Causses, Aubrac and Margeride mountains lived according to the rhythm of transhumance, selling wool at Toulouse and at the fairs of Geneva, and cattle to the Provençal breeders and Marseilles butchers. Transhumance also developed in the French Pyrenees and in Aragon. In winter the flocks of the Aspe and Ossau valleys reached the forests and wastes on the outskirts of Dax; they overran the moors of Bigorre, settled in the viscounties of Marsan and Gavardan, and in the fifteenth century pushed on towards the north as far as Médoc and into Agenais.

Everywhere sheep (and goats), with their great need of space, settled on fallow ground and in areas which were deserted as a result of demographic depression, but they also contributed to stripping the poorest regions of their inhabitants and crops. On the other hand, they brought business to the fairs and riches to the stock-breeders, which included the nobility, even the higher nobility – king René himself had his herds of sheep – as well as the burgher-class which invested part of its fortune in *gasalhe* (cattle) contracts.

Cattle-raising has been studied less thoroughly than sheep-rearing, but it seems that the number of cattle also increased quite sharply. The accounts of slaughter-houses which have come down to us from this period indicate that consumption of beef and veal was relatively high. In upper Auvergne around Salers and Mauriac, in Rouergue, upper Dauphiné and Provence, in central Sicily and Sardinia, quite extensive herds were apparently formed. Many of them were pastured on the transhumance pattern, either with the sheep or by themselves, and in the Alps a system of summer pasture became the rule for horned cattle. In the first years of the fifteenth century, several hundred animals were kept for fattening right in the town of Digne, and one pro-prietor owned eighty. In a fiscal return for 1471 (which is no doubt under-stated) the inhabitants of Saintes-Maries de la Mer declared a herd of 1,000 head, and the small locality of Seranon, near Grasse, no less than 360 oxen for 41 households; Comps, near Draguignan, 280 for 38 households; Château-vieux, in the neighbourhood of Castellane, 104 for 5 households. At this time the number of horned beasts in the region was, according to the returns of their owners, three or four times higher than in 1956.

In the Scandinavian countries, which had become dependent on the Hanse for their grain supplies, and where a large part of the population, at least in Norway, was engaged in obtaining the fish necessary for their trade with the

Hanseatic merchants, the economy evolved towards bulk production of beef and butter. In Denmark, the cattle markets of Ribe, Kolding and Assens reached their peak in the fifteenth century: between 5,000 and 10,000 oxen and several thousand horses left each year for the south along the *okseveje* ('oxen ways').

The development of Norwegian, Swedish and Danish butter was of great significance, since in the course of the fourteenth century the diet of western Europe changed and butter was substituted for lard. This change was clearly connected with the decline of the large herds of pigs, following the clearing of the forests; they were replaced by the domestic pig reared on the farm, a system which was incapable of maintaining supplies of fats for the large towns.

Certain regions did, however, go in for pig-breeding on a large scale, either in large herds, which might reach several thousand head, as in the Jura and the forest of Haguenau, or in a proliferation of small herds of twenty to fifty animals, such as were found in the Bayonne hinterland and on the hillsides of Béarn.

Finally, horse-breeding made its appearance in certain areas, in Friesland and around Deventer, in Romagna, the Camargue and Béarn; they were also bred in studs, after the kings of France developed this system at the end of the thirteenth century for remounting their armies. Mule-breeding was also found in Poitou and Provence, especially in the areas around Brignoles and Salon. The specialized types of breeding of the period have hardly been studied at all, and we still know little about them.

The extension of stock-breeding had another consequence: the butchers or *mazeliers* were concerned not only with retailing slaughtered meat, but also with breeding and trading in beasts on the hoof, often on a considerable scale. This explains the sizeable fortunes which were amassed by butchers everywhere. For example, at Toulouse they were numbered among the richest citizens, wealthier even than the money-changers and the mercers. At Ghent, their corporation was the first to receive (in 1325) the privilege of hereditary recruitment. One need only recall the role and affluence of the butchers in Paris at the time of the Caboche revolt, and the attack on the patriciate in Lübeck by the butchers' trade in 1380.

One of the reasons for their wealth, at least in certain towns, was that the number of butchers' stalls or shops was restricted at an early date, when the consumption of meat was relatively low. In the fourteenth and fifteenth centuries, however, as a result of the considerable increase in livestock, meat played a greater part in the diet of all regions and all classes, if indeed it was not the chief ingredient.

126 Open market of medieval type at Pinzio, Portugal.

127 Covered market-place at La Côte-Saint-André in Dauphiné, a well-preserved example of numerous market-places of the fifteenth and sixteenth centuries which still exist in France.

This change, in conjunction with the increased consumption of vegetables and fruit, also enables us to understand better the decline of cereals. Compared with preceding generations, the place of cereals in the diet, whether in the form of bread, pancakes or dumplings, seems to have diminished everywhere in the later Middle Ages in the same way as bread has come to form a less important part of the diet in our own time.

With the crisis of depopulation as a background, the essential features of agriculture in the later Middle Ages may thus be seen as: bulk production of cereals in the 'colonial' lands of the Mediterranean and the Baltic, with Italian and German shipowners organizing their exportation; the fall of grain prices in the west; the abandonment of marginal lands and of numerous villages; specialization in cash crops; and a considerable extension of stock-raising.

A number of additional features of the period should also be noted. There was cultivation of millet and millet grass, which had gone on from early times. Rice was introduced in Italy and Spain and spread rapidly so that, together with lentils, it formed an appreciable proportion of the diet of sailors from the middle of the fourteenth century. Buckwheat spread more slowly from the Mongol countries via Russia, and was found from 1395 at Nuremberg and Antwerp (as *Buchweizen* or *boecweyden*). Crops were developed for cattle-feeding, namely sorghum (which seems to have spread from Italy) and vetch. Finally we have evidence that the consumption of wine increased in all social classes. There was also a heavy increase in the consumption of *cervoise*

128 Tavern scene; illumination from a late fourteenth-century Italian manuscript.

(a kind of beer), and then, after the adoption of a new technique based on the use of hops, of beers proper, notably from Hamburg, Bremen, the Low Countries and northern France. In the fifteenth century cider-drinking became widespread in Normandy.

It is fair, therefore, to say that the period of the later Middle Ages was a time of very radical changes in all spheres of agricultural life: only the havoc wrought by epidemics and the destructive effects of wars prevent us from observing and studying the evidence for this vital aspect of history as we should, in all its detail.

INDUSTRIAL CHANGES
IN THE FOURTEENTH AND FIFTEENTH CENTURIES

The Flemish cloth industry, together with that of northern France and Champagne, had made an important contribution to the economic expansion and prosperity of western Europe during the classical Middle Ages. First Milan and Florence, and then Narbonne and Languedoc, had co-operated in bringing about the remarkable development of cloth production which gave the west the exchange currency it needed for its relations with the Mediterranean countries. Some historians believe that the crisis in the Franco-Flemish industry at the beginning of the fourteenth century sounded the knell of the western economy, but this theory must be rejected. Ypres, Douai, Arras and

129 Home manufacture of wool; miniature taken from an early fifteenth-century French manuscript.

209

Châlons were not the only representatives of the medieval European textile industry, and there were few fields where so many changes occurred in the leadership of the group of industrial towns as well as in manufacturing techniques. The textile industry had been the main type of business during the whole of the Middle Ages, bringing prosperity to that town whose products proved themselves to be the best, the finest, and the most reliable; but reputations were made and unmade with nearly every fresh generation, and competition was always extremely keen. It is nonsense to speak of a decline of the cloth industry in the west during the later Middle Ages, when, as we have just seen, the enormous expansion of stock-raising put a quantity of wool at the disposal of the weavers which was three, four or five times greater than had been available at the time of the golden age of the Franco-Flemish industry.

Around 1320 the rich scarlets of Brabant outrivalled the fine Flemish cloths. The cloths of Brussels in particular were such a success commercially, that within a few years they became the cloths of courts and rich men, a state of affairs which continued for half a century: their price was higher than that of the most sumptuous cloths of gold. The cloths of Malines and Louvain met with almost equal success. But when the fashion changed in favour of the cloths of Normandy and England, Brussels – like Paris, Arras and Tournai – turned towards an even more profitable industry, that of tapestry, while secondary centres like Pierre or Vilvorde became known internationally for their utility cloths.

In Flanders itself, there was a change in the pattern of sales. When the Mediterranean markets became closed to its products as a result of the competition of the Italians, Ghent turned towards those of northern Europe, and the Flemish industry benefited from the economic expansion of the Hanseatic countries. Ypres, which was in decline, revived, defeating its rivals, Dixmude and Poperinge, but it received a setback in turn with the rise of the village cloth industries of the Lys: about 1360, Wervicq and Courtrai once more succeeded in selling Flemish cloth in every Mediterranean market-town. At the same time, the rural group of Langemark introduced its products into Spain in bulk.

Apart from 'rich' cloth, 'small cloth' or 'new cloth' found a growing market for reasons of fashion and economy. Even the great cloth towns like Brussels and Ypres adopted the new process in the end. A 'dry' cloth was developed in place of carded cloth and twill or serge; it was the same on the right and wrong side, and did not need to be fulled: examples were the fine woollens of Hondschoote, Gistel and Bruges, as well as those of Caen and England, which met with increasing success. These various cloths also catered for different needs,

130 Spinning and weaving; detail from a fresco by Pinturicchio, c. 1509. Note the frame of the loom, with pedals and counterweights.

for besides fabrics for clothing, there was also a demand for lining materials, furnishings, etc.

The important cloth centre of Paris was forced to abandon weaving for finishing and in particular dyeing, and Provins, which had at one time held a dominant position, completely disappeared from the textile manufacturing map; in the middle of the fourteenth century the exports of Beauvais formed the largest category at the port of Aiguesmortes. Bourges also had its hour of glory. At the end of the fourteenth century and the beginning of the fifteenth Normandy overshadowed every other cloth-producing province: Rouen and Louviers, and subsequently (and in particular) Montivilliers, had a commanding position everywhere, and a large number of secondary centres, particularly Saint-Lô, carried on a sizeable business. At the *Lendit* fairs the Normandy cloths were by far the most important.

It has also been established that new cloth-producing areas developed, such as Languedoc and Catalonia, many towns of Tuscany and Lombardy, Holland, and in particular a vast region comprising Rhenish and central Germany (Speyer and Mainz, Frankfurt and Friedberg, Limburg and Montabaur); cloths came, too, from Switzerland (Fribourg), and even Silesia and Poland.

But the most significant development was without any doubt the rise of the English cloth-trade, which expanded, especially in the Cotswolds, around Bristol, and even in London, among other regions. At the end of the fourteenth century England began to lay siege to the continental markets; in the following century it was dominant everywhere: at Toulouse in 1380, 80 per cent of the cloth sales were of Flemish or Brabantese products, but fifty years later English products accounted for the same proportion. The export figures which are provided by customs receipts bear this out: from 700 pieces of cloth in 1350, English exports rose to 9,500 pieces in 1360–61, 13,000 around 1370, 20,000 in 1382, 30,000 in 1390, 40,000 in 1392, and then from 50,000 in 1402 to 90,000 a century later. Exports of raw English wool fell correspondingly over the same period from 43,000 sacks to 10,000.

Leaving aside woollen cloths, we find a comparable expansion in the production of 'fustians', that is, heavy, strong cloths of mixed wool and cotton weave. In the thirteenth century Piacenza, Pavia, Verona and Bologna dominated the market and exported their products to most of Europe; in the fourteenth century the fustian manufacturers of Genoa and Cremona apparently held first place. Then Italy was supplanted in its traditional markets, as well as on its own soil, by the products of southern Germany; here, too, the cloth-trade was constantly expanding, notably at Ulm and at Augsburg. The Fuggers were by origin fustian manufacturers of Augsburg, who sold the products of the Tyrolean copper and silver mines at Venice in order to obtain in the Venice market the oriental cotton which they needed. So as to satisfy the requirements of its German customers, Venice devoted the major part of its activities in Syria and Cilicia to purchasing cotton. Cotton plantations were also established or expanded in North Africa, Spain and southern Italy.

In spite of sumptuary laws condemning luxury or attempting to prohibit it to certain social groups, fashion dictated the wearing of velvets and silks, sometimes decorated with gold or silver thread. This luxury cloth-trade was developed with a very high degree of success in the first half of the fourteenth century; it competed with the rich Franco-Flemish cloth, and, at the end of the century, with the scarlets of Brussels. But, apart from Cyprus, the east hardly contributed to the production of these brocades, damasks, samites and other silk goods. In spite of passing crises, the silk-manufacturers of Lucca continued to expand their production, while the 'mercers' of the town became suppliers of luxury merchandise (velvet, cloth of gold, jewels, silk purses embroidered and sewn with pearls, etc.) to the princely courts. In the lighter silks, Venice and Bologna competed with the Luccans, and then it was the turn of Milan and Genoa; finally, in the mid-fifteenth century, Florence made up for the decline of its woollen industry by manufacturing silk fabrics.

As the habit of wearing cotton or linen underclothes became accepted in all social classes, and with the spread of the use of house linen (sheets, table cloths and towels) and the appearance of light clothing (especially in *treillis* – a kind of canvas), linen industries grew up. The industries of Champagne (Rheims and Troyes) and Lorraine (Epinal) declined, but, as a result of the success of the fairs of Geneva and Frankfurt, production expanded considerably in the district of Constance and Saint-Gall, which was already famous in the thirteenth century for its 'German' linens. The fine linen cloths of Nivelles, and the linens of Flanders and Brabant, brought prosperity to many villages where weaving was complementary to agriculture; from the middle of the fifteenth century the villages of the Lys valley, around Courtrai, tended to surpass the others. Burgundy offered the greatest range of products, from thread, which was exported to every Mediterranean country, to the great ships' canvases which found a growing market due to the increase in the number of sailing craft; there were also the more or less fine linens of Chalon and Mâcon, as well as the coarser products of Bourg-en-Bresse, Bugey and the high Alpine valleys. At the end of the fourteenth century, the manufacture of canvas in Brittany and the neighbouring region of lower Normandy, and then, as a result of the rise of the Breton fleet, the fine linens of Vitré, brought work to regions which until then had known little industrial activity.

131 Tailor's workshop, miniature from a fourteenth-century north Italian manuscript.

132 The dyeing of cloth; miniature from a late fifteenth-century French manuscript (below).

133 Cloth being sold, at left, in a covered market; detail of a fifteenth-century miniature (right, above).

134 Cutting and sewing of cloth; detail from a late fifteenth-century French miniature (right, below).

To sum up this evolution briefly, there were widespread changes in the textile industries which to a large extent had been the basis for the prosperity of the western countries in the preceding centuries: new types of wool-weaving were developed, cotton-weaving spread and there was an expansion of flax- and hemp-weaving. Due to political factors, the whole of France, and in particular Flanders, was apparently a good deal worse off as a result of the change; but throughout Europe, fresh regions launched out into industrial production, and new cloth towns grew up whose activity was sometimes centred on a single product which had proved successful (such as the *cadis* – light woollen serge – of Perpignan). Frequently the manufacture of cloth shifted from the towns to the villages, especially in Flanders and in England, and over large areas it brought the peasant families rewards which made up for the fall in their profits from agriculture.

The increased use of cotton, and in particular the fashion of wearing the 'chemise', had another unexpected result, giving rise to another new industry in the west: the rag paper industry. We know that, following the example of the Arabs, Italy and Spain had begun to use rag paper for writing from before the middle of the twelfth century; but in France the practice did not reach the south of the country until the middle of the thirteenth century: it was not known in the north until the second half of this century; and only spread to England, the empire and the Low Countries in the first decades of the fourteenth.

The first factories were set up in Spain, at Játiva and Alcoy, in the kingdom of Valencia, where they formed a monopoly in the hands of Arab or Jewish craftsmen, protected by the kings of Aragon. More important on an inter-national level were the Italian workshops at Fabriano in the Marches, founded about 1260, and subsequently, in the last years of the thirteenth century, those of Parma and Bologna, which no doubt played a part in the increased pro-duction of university manuscripts and consequently contributed to the fame of the school of Bologna. Other factories were established in Tuscany (at Colle Val d'Elsa), at Treviso, and elsewhere. For a very long time, France was dependent on Italian and Spanish paper, but before the middle of the four-teenth century, the first French paper-mills were established simultaneously at Troyes, at Essonne (near Paris), in the Barrois, and in the Comtat Venaissin. Before the end of the century Nuremberg (the German fustian centre) became a centre of the paper industry.

The general acceptance of the use of paper, which was a relatively eco-nomical writing medium, was one of the chief events of the Middle Ages: at this time learning was making great strides, and the availability of writing materials also enabled more account-books, more detailed rent-books and more complete archives to be kept. As a result, it led to an improvement in the administration of agricultural estates and commercial companies, as well as in the organization of public authorities.

The salt industry, involving salt-marshes or mines, was one of the major fields of economic activity in the Mediterranean region from the second half of the thirteenth century, and from the middle of the fourteenth in the Atlantic sector. The increased consumption of salt is partly related to the change in diet which gave increasing prominence to meat and vegetables in place of cereal pancakes and dumplings. But it is connected in particular with the growth of stock-raising and fishing: enormous quantities of salt were needed to preserve meats and fish, cheese and butter; salt was needed for tanning skins; and it also came to be used to supplement the diet of cattle. The Alpine regions (upper Provence, Dauphiné, Savoy, the Swiss Alps) had no salt resources of their own and the climate of the North Sea and the Baltic was not very suitable for salt-marshes: the salt pans on the English coasts were threatened from the moment they faced competition from the southern salts.

135 Traditional salt-works at Trapani, Sicily.

Since the early Middle Ages, salt had been one of the bulk commodities, and its monopoly of Adriatic salt no doubt contributed to the rise of Venice. But salt did not really become one of the key factors in the international economy, one of the main items of taxation, and, because of the importance of the interests at stake, one of the significant factors in international diplomacy, until the later Middle Ages.

Where artisans and peasants had previously worked the coastal salt-marshes, capitalist enterprises now grew up, sometimes on a large scale, and the government claimed back its sovereign rights, which it had frequently abandoned until then to abbeys or lords. In the interior of the continent, mines, demanding new techniques and considerable capital, replaced the salt pits which still acted as a makeweight in Lorraine in the fourteenth century.

The quantities produced by the salt-marshes and salt-works were so high in the fourteenth and fifteenth centuries that salt may be considered, together with grain and wine, as one of the three most important commodities of international trade in terms of weight; perhaps its volume even puts it in first place among all transported goods in absolute figures. Since the traffic had to converge on localized centres of production, there was a heavy concentration of transport to and from these points. The salt-works of Salins and Lons-le-Saunier, those of Lorraine, of Lüneburg near Lübeck, of Salzburg, and Wieliczka near Cracow, required thousands of very heavy wagons, and salt routes had to be set up. From 6,000 to 10,000 wagons, each carrying about a ton of salt from the Salzkammergut, passed through Munich each year in the middle of the fifteenth century. In a good year the large sea-salt marshes were visited by whole fleets coming to the loading-places, often consisting of several hundred vessels: in the Mediterranean, after Pisa had been eliminated, Venice and Genoa, together with Barcelona, had large ships at their disposal which brought them a near-monopoly of the trade. The Hanseatics had an equally commanding position in the west. There were also fleets of little Majorcan and Sicilian boats in the Mediterranean, and boats from Brittany, Normandy, La Rochelle, England and Holland in the Atlantic. At Rouen, in 1477–78, a third of the ships coming in from the sea (163 out of 469) were loaded with salt; on the Seine, as on the Loire, a large percentage of the traffic consisted of salt-boats: out of 88 boats recorded in 1477–78 between Rouen and Paris, 77 were loaded with salt.

One of the main centres of production in the Mediterranean was the mouth of the Rhône, between the kingdom and Provence: the salt-works of Aigues-mortes and Peccais, acquired by Philip the Fair in 1290, and the salt-works of the Camargue at Saintes-Maries and La Vernède, which were organized by

Charles of Anjou. These two rulers came to an arrangement in 1301 to exploit the production of salt jointly: it was distributed along the Rhône by a busy fleet of small boats, heavily laden, which often carried up to 200 tons and sometimes more, and sailed in convoy. In 1398, the two princes of France and Provence formed a company called the *Tirage du Rhône* ('Rhône haulage'); the river route was duplicated by land routes via Avignon, Romans and Lyons. This Franco-Provençal group produced nearly 25,000 tons of salt annually, in more or less equal proportions. Provence also derived profits from the salt-works of Berre, which supplied central Provence and the Alpine regions by mule train, and from those of Toulon and Hyères, the entire output of which was often bought up by Genoa, for distribution in northern Italy. The output of Hyères reached an annual average of 8,000 to 15,000 tons, with peaks of 18,000 tons at the beginning of the fourteenth century and 35,000 in the second half of the century: in some years, Genoa sent 300 ships to carry away its share.

The salt-works of Sardinia were at first a prize in the contest between Pisa and Genoa, and later passed to the Aragonese; their production subsequently decreased from 4,500 tons in the middle of the fourteenth century because of constant disturbances in the island. In some months, twenty to thirty vessels entered the port of Cagliari, and very often five to nine boats would be found there simultaneously in process of being loaded.

The little island of Ibiza in the Balearics was considered to be *the* salt island, and Venetians sailing in the western Mediterranean had orders from the Republic to take on a load there whenever they were on their way back to their home port; they also called at the salt-works on the eastern coast of Spain, in the Valencia district. Venice did not forget that salt had helped to make its fortune, and this continued to be one of the principal commodities of its trade with Lombardy, Friuli and Balkan Europe. Venice reserved the best sites in the salt-marshes of Cyprus, Apulia and the lower Adriatic for itself.

The salt-works of Brittany supplied the greater part of the French market, directly via Nantes and the Loire valley and indirectly via Rouen and the Seine valley, meeting up with the salt of the Rhône in the Massif Central, the salt of the Comté in Charolais and Burgundy, and the salt of Lorraine in the Barrois. Brittany salt also supplied England and the Low Countries, carried by a considerable fleet of small boats from Brittany and lower Poitou. From the beginning of the fifteenth century, the Hanseatics went regularly to the Bay of Bourgneuf: more than 200 ships, of an increasing tonnage, assembled there each year, for the 'salt of the Bay' had become essential for salting Baltic fish. The 'trade of the Bay' was therefore, together with grain from the north, one of the main categories of Hanseatic business: of the 314 ships entering the port of Reval from 1427 to 1433, 105 came from the Bay of Bourgneuf, and the imports of salt originating in this region totalled around 5,000 tons a year. From the middle of the fifteenth century, however, the Portuguese salt-marshes of Setúbal and Alcácer do Sal created increasing competition until the salt of Brouage was finally developed. The salt of lower Poitou (Noirmoutier) and that of Guérande, north of the Loire estuary, where the workings were on a smaller scale, remained in the hands of Breton and English sailors, who operated a less long-distance trade.

Salt-mines had been known and exploited for a very long time, from the middle of the fourteenth century. As a result of technical and industrial management they became the first large modern industry, involving considerable interests. They required gangs of skilled workmen day and night, and armies of labourers to stoke the boilers, and to handle and transport the finished product. In the middle of the fifteenth century, the salt-works of Salins used no less than 11,000 tons of wood for an annual production of about 7,500 tons of salt. The whole economy of the region depended on the progress of these 'manufactories'.

In the classical Middle Ages, iron, which was still rare, remained virtually a luxury product, and most utensils were made of wood. Mines and forges were very scattered, still on a small scale, and their products hardly ever spread beyond regional, or even local, bounds. In the last decades of the thirteenth century, as we have already noted, the first large iron works were established, in Biscay and central Sweden. Many historians have spoken in terms of stagnation or recession with regard to the iron industry from the beginning of the fourteenth century until around 1460. The impression of recession is in fact illusory, though the disappearance of many peasant forges and the decline of the less favoured regions might well lend it some colour. The areas which did not have sea or river routes suitable for transporting the mineral or its products economically, and those which did not possess the water, wood or mineral resources necessary to supply the centralized and developed forges, went to the wall. It is rather as if one were to conclude from the closing down of a large number of individual enterprises during the Victorian era that the volume of industrial production diminished in the nineteenth century.

We have only indirect evidence of the development of Biscay and the Bilbao, Bermeo and San Sebastián region, in the links which they formed with Nantes and La Rochelle, and with England and the Low Countries; we know that iron always constituted an important, if not the main, part of the cargoes to these countries. The Hanseatic navy also played a part in transporting the increased output of the region.

After the great privileges granted by king Magnus Eriksson to Norberg in 1354, the Swedish industry was rationalized and extended. In the last quarter of the fourteenth century, exports to Lübeck and Danzig were tripled, though they were still modest, and they multiplied ten times in the following century.

About 1310–40 an important iron-producing region emerged, extending across Champagne, the Barrois, Lorraine and the Franco-Belgian Ardennes. The abbey of Clairvaux took an interest in it; a great Parisian burgher, Gentien Cocatrix, paid the debts of Saint-Rémy of Rheims – the enormous sum of 3,500 *livres* – in exchange for the right to work the iron mine belonging to the abbey in the forests of Othe for fifteen years. The count of Bar advanced capital to the burghers of Pont-à-Mousson to enable them to construct a new type of forge at Briey, worked by water power and with a capacity double that of the former system. At the same time, the count of Savoy, the Dauphin, the count of Vaud, and the king of Navarre became interested personally in the exploitation of the mines in their domains, and Philip the Fair had a series of forges built in the forests of the Black Mountain (in the southern part of the Massif Central). The mines of Allevard in Dauphiné were particularly busy at the time, and the toll-house accounts which have survived show us that their production was exported across the Alps.

The high Alpine valleys, from the Val d'Aosta to the Trentino, by way of the famous Val Camonica and the Val Trompia, were covered with mines and forges; the production of this region was the most important in Europe in the fourteenth century and supplied the industry of Bergamo, Brescia, Como, Milan and Venice. This zone extended to Cadore, Friuli and Carniola, which had links mainly with Venice, and part of their output also reached Switzerland and southern Germany. The celebrated weapons and armour which were manufactured at Milan and Brescia were largely made from Alpine iron, and Milanese mercery – horseshoes, nails, locks, keys, needles, etc. – spread across the peninsula as well as towards Avignon, Paris and Bruges.

Genoa took advantage of the eclipse of Pisa to get its hands on the iron of the island of Elba for a time, and in 1309 a bank was founded to finance the operation. Lucca developed its mines of Pietrasanta and established various arms factories, which went towards supplying its international trade throughout the fourteenth century.

At the same time, another metal-producing region came to the fore in central Europe, the area of the Upper Palatinate and of Styria, Carinthia and Carniola. It took first place in iron production among all the European centres and tended to attract the more important enterprises. The iron from these two sources contributed to the development of local markets and many small industrial centres in Bavaria and Austria, and helped to make the markets of Nuremberg and Augsburg the equal of those of Milan for weapons and iron-mongery; these goods reached Vienna via the Danube, and Bruges and the Low Countries through the fairs of Frankfurt or Cologne. The mining activity of this region partly explains both the economic expansion of southern Germany in the fifteenth century, and the fortunes of the Fuggers and the Habsburgs. But across Europe many other metal-producing regions saw their output increase, and the Hungarian iron of Slovakia, and the iron of Silesia and Little Poland, helped to supply Hanseatic big business via the Vistula or the Oder, by way of Toruń and Danzig, or Stettin. Although the traditional forges of the Forest of Dean, in the west of England, appeared to be on the decline – perhaps owing to lack of adequate fuel, the result of over-intensive exploitation through the centuries – other iron and steel centres developed in the north of the kingdom, around Sheffield and Durham, and in Lancashire. This source of supply was, however, still insufficient to cover England's total requirements, for at this time it was also importing iron from Spain, West-phalia and Sweden.

The fourteenth century might justly be called a century of iron, not so much because of the bloody wars which exhausted the west, but because, for the first time, the metal was used on an unprecedented scale compared with previous centuries, although the quantities involved seem extremely modest to modern eyes. The availability of plated and mail armour, arrows, spurs, and especially cannon, made war easier and at the same time infinitely more costly. Nor should we forget the proliferation of iron utensils and the general spread of the practice of shoeing animals.

136 Mining scene; detail from late fifteenth-century German manuscript.

The increase of iron production was made possible only by the use of new techniques: the drainage of galleries in the mines was improved and seems to have been perfected at the beginning of the fourteenth century in the Liège district; hydraulic bellows were used in the forges to speed up the smelting of the mineral from the first half of the same century; iron hammers or tilt-hammers spread, becoming very numerous in the whole Alpine region and eastern France at the same period; and finally the blast furnace made its appearance at the very end of the century, probably in the Liège region or on the banks of the Rhine.

Other extractive industries also developed. The use of coal as a fuel had been discovered at Liège in 1198, and it was very widely employed from the last years of the thirteenth century at Liège itself and in the lands of the abbey of Val Saint-Lambert, at Seraing and Marihaye. From then on *houille* (a local Liège term for coal) conditioned the entire life of the city; it occupied a considerable labour force, and the town was supplied with water drained from the galleries by means of a pumping system. In England, the coal of Newcastle made its entry into international big business.

The tin and lead mines in Devon and Cornwall, the lead and silver mines in Sardinia, and the copper and silver industry of Rammelsberg in the Harz mountains appeared to be stationary or in recession. The mines of Sweden (at Stora Kopparberg), and of Hungary (in Slovakia and Transylvania), however, provided an important source of supply, with their output going towards the Hanseatic countries as well as to Venice. The towns of southern Germany, especially Nuremberg, profited from the development of the Tyrolean mines, whose products were mainly directed towards Venice. Venice also attracted

137 Armourers at work; marginal illustration from a Flemish manuscript, *c.* 1400.

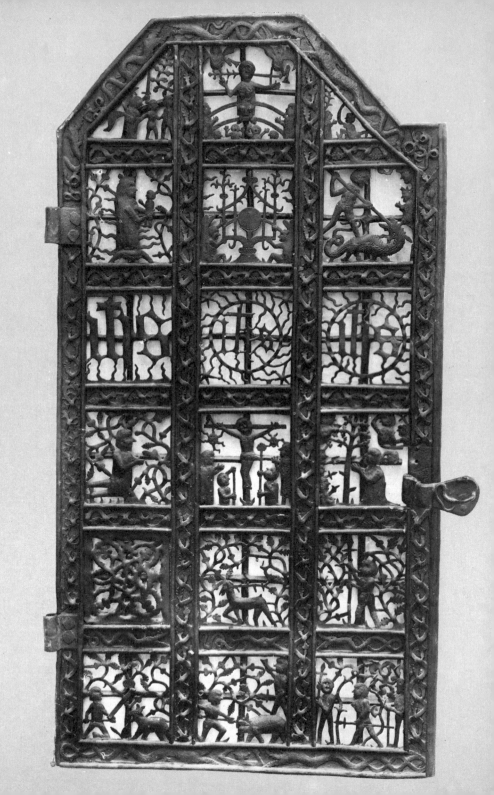

138 Tabernacle door from the Bürgerspitalskirche in Krems, Austria; example of wrought-iron work, c. 1470.

139 Iron armour; detail of an early sixteenth-century Italian fresco.

the output of the new mines of Bosnia and Serbia, and Venetian vessels carried copper with the Republic's die-stamp to Alexandria and Beirut, where it was popular in exchange for Venetian purchases in the east.

The shift of the great centres of the extractive industry towards central and south-eastern Europe should be emphasized; and there may be justification for seeing a relation between the end of the German agricultural expansion towards the eastern plains and the massive influx of Germanic miners into central Sweden, Slovakia, Silesia, the mountains of Bohemia and the Alpine valleys. At any rate the market-towns in these areas expanded, as did those in Tyrol and Transylvania, acting as centres for the products of the mines.

German technicians were constantly called to the fourteenth- and fifteenth-century courts, whenever there was a plan to develop mines and forges, in Sweden or in Italy, in Berry or in Forez – or anywhere else.

The Germans, and sometimes the north Italians, were also called upon to install and overhaul the complicated mechanisms of *clocks*. These were one of the most important acquisitions of medieval civilization; they came into use in the course of the fourteenth century, and had an immediate and resounding effect on the life of urban populations. The municipal clock appeared about 1330, and in less than half a century spread to all the urban areas in northern Italy, southern Germany, the Rhineland, the Low Countries, France, 225 especially Provence, and Catalonia. In England, the Salisbury cathedral clock, dating from before 1386, is a remarkable example of the clocks of this period: it has recently been restored and reinstalled, and still works. In spite of extreme financial difficulties, even modest municipalities had no hesitation in taxing themselves heavily in order to build a clock-tower, install the expensive mechanism and face frequent repairs. They were provided with a set of bells, and from 1351, at Orvieto, with automatic chimes ringing out the hours. From then on clocks marked the beginning and end of the working-day in the workshops, and released lay people from the tyranny of the canonical hours which sounded from the belfries of churches: it was the first step towards equal hours, which were to be substituted for the unequal hours (inherited from the Romans) whose length varied according to the seasons.

140 Various types of timekeepers; miniature from a Flemish manuscript, c. 1450.

## SOCIAL CHANGES AND THE CLASS WAR

The later Middle Ages is a period of violent contrasts, and this is particularly true in the social sphere, where there were profound differences between the various orders. A clear distinction existed between the economic organization of the countryside and that of the towns, where hierarchies of privilege and fortune made deep divisions between the classes. During the whole period, social conflicts and class warfare continued to grow.

The 'adversity of the times' weighed especially heavily on the country areas. Poverty was widespread among the peasants: their harvests were destroyed in the granaries and their casks emptied in the cellars. They were often driven to seek refuge, without resources, in the neighbouring towns; many were reduced to beggary and some of them forced into a life of crime. Certain of the better-off peasants, however, as well as some of the lords' farmers, were able to profit from the situation by taking over the fields abandoned by the less fortunate, and built up much larger properties for themselves.

Beginning with the churches, the landowners became poorer because they were unable to collect dues and rents, because fields ceased to be cultivated and villages were deserted, and also because they had to repair or rebuild farm buildings which were often destroyed by fire. Many nobles were ruined in this way, even when they did not have to pay heavy ransoms to the enemy. The high mortality and a low birth-rate contributed to the disappearance of a good number of ancient noble families; at Nîmes, for example, in the second half of the fourteenth century, the last noble houses, the traditional adversaries of the city council, died out. But a new nobility was formed from those who had been able to take advantage of the situation by service to the king, speculation or commercial profiteering.

The patriciate of the towns, made wealthy by exploiting the urban proletariat and the peasant population, and often allied by marriage with the nobility, tended to amalgamate with it, while the gulf between these 'magnates' and the other burghers widened. This was a further stage in a process which was already well marked from the middle of the thirteenth century in Italy in general and Florence in particular. The patricians aimed to keep the government of the towns in their hands; at Cologne, they formed the 'circle of the rich' (*Richerzeche*), at Lübeck, the 'society of the circle' (*Cirkelselschop*), and 'societies' in many other German and Italian towns.

The rich burghers, who devoted themselves exclusively to big business and certain occupations which were regarded as honourable, aspired both to oust the patriciate and to merge with it. Conflicts between opposing clans were always tearing towns apart. In France, where the barriers between the various

classes were less noticeable, the increase in wealth of this upper *bourgeoisie* was particularly striking; its members held the reins of urban administration, and tried to impose their will on the monarchy in fiscal matters in the States-General. The great burghers made loans to the town, as well as to the king. They were involved almost everywhere in the 'money business', bought fiefs and manors from ruined nobles, and went out round the towns collecting land, parcel by parcel, and amassing vast farms which they let out or cultivated directly. Finally they made further profits, according to region, out of vine plantations, cattle-raising or cattle-leasing contracts with the peasants.

Wherever it has been possible to study lists of taxes or land registers, it is clear that the mass of the population became poorer, that the numbers of hopelessly destitute people and beggars grew, and that the share of wealth in the hands of the richest people increased correspondingly.

The luxury trade gained in momentum at the very time when poverty was at its worst: clothes became increasingly expensive, consisting of Brussels

141 The world of luxury. Scene from the court of Philip the Good (detail).

142 The world of poverty. Beggars receiving alms; detail of a miniature from a fifteenth-century French manuscript.

scarlet, silk cloths stitched with gold, and heavy robes of velvet lined with costly fur; jewellery from Paris and Cologne, tapestries from Paris, Tournai or Arras, in which mixed gold and silk thread were sometimes used for exquisite detail, French and Italian Gothic ivory work, English alabaster, rings and jewels set with diamonds, rubies and pearls, illuminated manuscripts, elaborately sculptured tombs which sometimes amounted to veritable chapels, all went to swell the trade. Everything bore witness to the madness of unbridled luxury which bewitched the wealthy in a world of frightful poverty, and when they themselves were threatened with death at every instant. The less rich did their utmost to emulate the opulence of the great.

The luxury of the rich and the poverty of the rest of the population explain the explosions of popular fury which unleashed class hatred and class warfare over the whole of Europe in the later Middle Ages, dividing burghers against nobles, and peasants against lords. Since the trades had finally been organized on a hierarchical pattern, and access to mastership was more and more    229 frequently, if not legally, reserved to the sons of masters, strife broke out between the rich tradesmen and the patriciate, while serious conflicts developed between rich and poor trades – *arts majeurs* and *arts mineurs*, *populo grasso* and *populo minuto*. Even within the same corporation, journeymen and masters became increasingly conscious of the divergence of their interests, and organized themselves into distinct and opposing groups.

A notable feature of these social conflicts was that they occurred at about the same time in different geographic areas. They always corresponded to a time of grave crisis, when fiscal pressure, or unreasonable demands from the lords, weighed heavily on the taxpayers, who could no longer face up to their own problems because of the declining revenue from agriculture, unemployment, industrial over-production, and excessive competition. The breaking-point was often reached simultaneously in several places: an urban revolution or a peasant revolt soon found an echo, and it is symptomatic that in spite of the tenuous link between the people of the towns and the countryside, these crises often affected the rural and urban classes at the same time.

The first social crises had appeared in the middle of the classical Middle Ages: they had been violent between 1240 and 1250 and between 1278 and 1282, affecting the population of the industrial towns in particular. In the reign of Philip the Fair, there had been sudden strains, in which the weakenings and strengthenings of the currency played an important part, but with the anger of the 'trades' directed primarily against the patriciate of the great 'lineages'. The most serious event occurred in 1296, when the industrial population of Flanders rose against the patricians, who called in the French king's help: this was the first of the long series of royal interventions in the Low Countries, and at Courtrai in 1302 the small burghers of the Flemish proletariat gained their first victory over the French knights and the great burghers of Flanders. The embittered struggle of the *petits* against the *grands* ended in the downfall of the Ghent lineages, but it also led to popular representation at the Council of Liège. At Magdeburg the heads of ten trades were burnt alive in a riot. In 1312, at the 'Liège Matins', 200 patricians were executed or burnt in the church and ten out of the fourteen sheriffs perished.

After the preceding events, it was decided to collect the royal fines in the countryside of Flanders, and this provoked one of the most violent explosions of the Middle Ages. From 1323 to 1328, the peasants rose in western Flanders, received the support of the proletarians of Ypres and Bruges, and fell upon the nobles, the wealthy and those who did not work with their hands. The church, as collector of tithes, was attacked and the stocks in its granaries distributed to the poor. Atrocities were committed throughout the country. The king of

France had to intervene again to bring the revolt to an end in 1328, at the cost of merciless repression. In the Flemish towns, and in particular at Ghent, more or less perpetual disturbances continued among the fullers' and weavers' trades, epitomized by the dictatorship of Jacob van Artevelde, and his assassination in 1345.

After the defeat of John the Good and the crushing of the knights at Poitiers, the country revolted against the fiscal pressure which became greater despite the ruin of trade and the devastation of the countryside, and despite the decimation of the population as a result of the Great Plague. This revolutionary mood resulted in the triple crisis of the States-General, the Parisian revolution with Etienne Marcel, and the 'Jacquerie'. Brutal rioting broke out in the Beauvais district, Vexin, the plain of France, and Brie, at the end of May 1356. The hatred of the non-nobles for the nobles, involving the whole population, was expressed in the pillage and destruction of noble houses, and the assassination of knights and members of their families. The reaction of the various classes was that the king of Navarre's men and the partisans of the Dauphin, although enemies, formed an alliance to meet the onslaught of the Jacques: they crushed their bands, then pursued them and fired their villages, carrying the butchery into the towns which, like Corbeil, had sympathized with them.

After a short crisis around 1367–69, the most serious social conflicts which were experienced in the Middle Ages occurred one after another in the years 1378–82. The textile workers of Florence, the *Ciompi*, seized power from the government, set up one of their number, a wool-carder, as chief magistrate, and persecuted the nobles. Flanders rose up again under the leadership of the Ghent weavers, and the movement was crushed only by an intervention of the royal army at Roosebeke (1382). With cries of 'Vive Gand', violent riots broke out at Rouen (the 'Harelle'), Paris ('les Maillotins'), Montpellier, Béziers, and in Catalonia. The 'Tuchins' of Languedoc were driven by poverty, the havoc caused by the large brigand-bands, and by taxation, to take to the *maquis* or '*touche*'. They organized themselves into groups, indulged in banditry over a wide area extending as far as Velay and Carcassès, and even seized towns where they set up an egalitarian form of government. Disturbances broke out in various towns of the empire, in particular Lübeck, where the revolution led by the butchers ended in a bloodbath (1384), and as far away as Prague.

So far, England had succeeded in avoiding social disturbances, due to the king's resolutely maintained authority and the 'Statute of Labourers' which the royal commissioners enforced throughout the realm; but in 1381 a new tax, the 'poll tax', sparked off trouble. The people of the south and west, whose livelihood was seriously affected by the decline of agriculture, hurled them-selves on the lords' manors and the churches, extorted freedom charters from their masters, burnt the manorial archives, and even seized London, under the command of their leader Wat Tyler. This 'labourers' movement' was doubtless not unconnected with the innovatory sermons of Wycliffe, and it was the first peasants' revolt where social and religious elements were found in conjunction – a pattern which recurred in the time of Hus and Luther.

There was a fresh series of social troubles at the beginning of the fifteenth century. In 1405, under the leadership of the butchers, the patriciate of Metz was overthrown and many of its members executed. Then the Catalan pea-sants, who were utterly destitute, rose up in 1409 and led a terrible *jacquerie*. From 1408 to 1416, the people of Lübeck usurped the functions of govern-ment; in Paris the 'Cabochiens' forced their plan for the reorganization of the kingdom by means of a riot, making provision for purging the administration, election to public offices, reparations and forced loans from those who had profited by the financial confusion, monetary reform, and so forth (1413). A little later, after the condemnation of John Hus at the Council of Constance (1415), the national peasant uprising of Bohemia broke out, devastating the country – and forging the Czechs into a nation.

The last important crises of the fifteenth century occurred between 1431 and 1437. There were communistic insurrections in Forez (1431) and Catalonia; *maquis* were formed in lower Normandy against the English garrisons, and the French lords who were in favour of collaborating with them. But this time the northern countries were primarily affected by the national rebellion of the miners and peasants of central Sweden around Engelbrekt (1434), the raids of the Norwegians on the fairs of Oslo (1436), the uprising of the Finnish peasants, over whom a certain David proclaimed himself king (1438), and disturbances in the rural areas of Jutland (1441).

These events serve to illustrate the progress of ideas. In the thirteenth century, social disturbances had been primarily urban in character. From the beginning of the fourteenth century, as a result of excessive taxation and the luxury of the aristocracy and the 'magnates', the conflicts became harsher, hatred was exacerbated, in the countryside as in the towns, and the flames spread all over Europe. In the fifteenth century, class warfare was accompanied by nationalism, in the Norman *maquis* as well as in Scandinavia and Bohemia. In the sixteenth century, with the Reformation, peasant uprisings took another turn, and became still more revolutionary – as already foreshadowed by the crisis of Wat Tyler and Wycliffe – under the leadership of Thomas Münzer at Mühlhausen and during the 'Peasants' War'.

Underpopulation had been the dominant feature of Europe in the fourteenth century and during a large part of the fifteenth. The Great Plague and the epidemics which followed it had reduced the population to a third or perhaps half of its level at the beginning of the fourteenth century. Vast areas had been ravaged by war and guerrilla bands, and deserted by their inhabitants. The expansion of stock-raising and transhumance had also been a contributory factor in the depopulation of certain districts. Other areas, however, had continued their economic development, notably the Hanseatic countries and central and eastern Europe. From the beginning of the fifteenth century, northern and central Italy, too, had surmounted the crisis. Even in the areas where depression seemed extreme, the displacement of the population had to some extent contributed to the rise of new industrial centres or the industrialization of certain rural areas.

The second half of the fifteenth century was marked by an economic recovery which gradually gave new life to the areas which had previously been devastated, while expansion continued in the regions which were in the course of development. The combination of these two factors caused an unprecedented economic boom, and the economy continued to improve right up to about 1550–60, as a result of technical progress and the great geographical discoveries. The situation was set fair for the development of modern civilization.

As had happened after the crisis of the ninth- and tenth-century invasions, the population explosion provided the motive force for the economy. The watershed seems to have been reached just in the middle of the fifteenth century, and here the cessation of Anglo-French hostilities was the crucial event. Its effects began to appear in a number of households around 1470. But where the events of war had ceased earlier – in Brittany, the Massif Central, the Alpine region and upper Provence – there was clearly a considerable population migration even in the previous generation towards richer regions which had been devastated.

Two examples may be quoted of regions from which many of the inhabitants emigrated despite a relatively modest growth in population: in the north, the rural population of the three castellanies of Lille, Douai and Orchies only increased from 9,500 households to 11,500 between 1469 and 1485, that is, by 21 per cent; while the province of Le Faucigny saw its population increase by 40 per cent between 1481 and 1518.

We may contrast these regions with two others where there was considerable immigration. In lower Provence, the bailiwick of Barjols, which was particularly affected by the demographic depression, jumped from 560 households to 1,428 between 1470 and 1518; we may estimate that the population of lower Provence as a whole doubled between 1471 and 1540. Several provostships increased the number of their inhabitants three-fold, and some of the parishes even five-fold during this period. Similarly in the Ile-de-France, one of the provinces which had been most extensively laid waste, the population density of the parishes in the deanery of Montmorency was not more than about 4 to 5 households per square kilometre around 1470, and it fell to 2 households per square kilometre in the 13 parishes of the deanery of Châteaufort. In 1520, however, a section of the parishes which was dependent on the abbey of Saint-Denis achieved a density of 30 to 38 households per square kilometre, a sizeable figure corresponding to a density of 120–180 inhabitants per square kilometre. Virtually all the places in this region that had been inhabited at the beginning of the fourteenth century were reoccupied at this time and the plots of land seem to have been divided up between a considerable, and perhaps excessive, number of tenants.

The increase in the population was partly due to the inhabitants returning to their villages of origin, and to the high birth-rate; partly to immigration from other regions. The small towns, which were artificially swollen during times of trouble, quickly gave up their excess population again to the neighbouring countryside: in Brabant, for example, the population in the nineteen small towns, expressed as a proportion of the population of the Duchy, fell steadily from 29·3 per cent in 1437 to 14·7 per cent in 1496, while that of the countryside rose from 53·2 per cent to 60·9 per cent; the remainder were concentrated in the very large towns.

The same feature is found all over France: it was very rare for villages to be abandoned completely. In the areas which were most affected (the Bordelais, Quercy, Provence), the lords and the abbeys concentrated on attracting immigrants and issuing them with 'rehabitation charters' for the ancient villages; elsewhere, collective leases were arranged. The areas which had a start in the demographic recovery, namely Brittany, the lower Loire regions, Artois, Flanders and Liguria, sent considerable contingents to the devastated areas from about 1450. There was thus a great ferment of population, and the mountain regions, the Massif Central, Dauphiné and upper Provence, which had been less affected by the demographic decline in the previous century, lost their population at this period to richer areas. With renewed security, the villages perched on hilltops in the French Midi began to descend along the slopes and into the plain, and the settlements of the western regions tended to spread out to an even greater extent. The nobles left their fortresses for more

143 Cafaggiolo, one of the villas of the Medici family, in the Mugello valley near Florence. It was designed by Michelozzo for Cosimo in the mid-fifteenth century.

pleasant residences, castles in the plains and fine town houses. The Tuscan hills and the Venetian countryside were strewn with 'villas'.

Around the rebuilt villages, land won back from waste was once again sown with wheat to meet the needs of the population. In Provence, for example, from the end of the troubles (which came here earlier than elsewhere), land which had formerly been planted with vines or olives was converted back again into arable. In 1421 Marseilles relaxed the rules prohibiting the export of corn, and in 1437 the interdict on this trade was revoked.

From 1452, whole boatloads of cereals went down the Seine to Rouen, and from this we may conclude that corn, coming from the upper Seine region, arrived at Paris in sufficient quantities to permit the authorization of its passage beyond the capital towards Normandy. Soon even Normandy, which was one of the most devastated provinces, and the last to suffer from the calamities of war, exported grain again: in 1478 the port of Rouen was authorized to send out 22,000 hl. (60,522 bushels) of wheat, which was exported from the kingdom in 52 ships.

The commercial rise of France was still more remarkable and rapid than the rise of her agriculture. It started first in Languedoc and Provence, which were freed from the spectre of war at the earliest date. The fortunes of Marseilles had reached rock-bottom in 1423, when the city was taken by the Catalans and sacked; now the farming of *poids et casses* taxes, reflecting the world trade of the city, which had fallen to 80 livres in 1409, went up to 100 livres in 1438, 150 in 1441, 225 in 1445, and 320 in 1465; the number of transactions had therefore quadrupled in half a century, even before the union of Provence with the kingdom of France.

The situation was similar in the Mediterranean ports of the kingdom, Narbonne and Montpellier, which alone had preserved close relations with the countries of the Orient. Jacques Cœur, a rich burgher of Bourges, who had further increased his wealth by manufacturing the royal coins at Bourges and Saint-Pourçain, went to Damascus and Beirut in 1432–33, on board a galley from Narbonne. Upon his return, he founded a counting-house at Montpellier which became the base of his operations in the Mediterranean. The exceptional success of this man, who was made mint-master of Paris in 1436 by Charles VII, his treasurer in 1437, and was ennobled by him in 1440, is interwoven with the economic recovery of the kingdom, for he handled every type of trade which was a factor in the resumed activity of the national economy as a whole. His business was first of all centred in the Mediterranean. His galleys, sailing from Aiguesmortes and Montpellier, Marseilles, Collioure, Barcelona or Naples,

144 The house of the great French merchant, Jacques Cœur, at Bourges, 1442–53.

fanned out across the sea, loaded with linens, cloths and silver, and brought sugar, spices and silk back from Egypt, Syria and Cyprus. In fact he was the only French merchant of the Middle Ages to succeed in making the presence of French galleys felt in oriental seas; he was instrumental in opening the first French consulate in Alexandria in 1445.

To supply his business, he launched into the textile trade at Rouen and Bourges, and the linen trade at Troyes, and then into leathers and furs, which led him to found banks in Rouen and Bruges and to send his ships into the Atlantic. From there he went on to buy wool from Scotland and England via the port of La Rochelle, and became involved in the salt trade of Poitou and Brittany. His interest in the salt-taxes led him to organize the 'Rhône salt-haulage', and the business which this generated led him to apply himself to finance and exchange on the great money-markets of Avignon, Geneva and Lyons. In order to trade in the east, where the currency was silver, and copper metal was at a premium, he obtained a concession of the silver and copper mines in Forez and Beaujolais. In 1449, he was in a position to lend the king the 200,000 gold crowns which enabled him to reconquer Normandy. His vast fortune included investments in land comprising more than thirty important estates, and was estimated by contemporaries at a million gold crowns when he was arrested in 1451, his goods sequestrated and he himself condemned.

Jacques Cœur embodied in a striking manner the great economic impetus which drove the kingdom forward. But the progress of this imposing merchant's affairs already illustrates the shift in the French economy's centre of gravity: he began by making his fortune in Mediterranean trade, and, following the classical medieval system, subsequently became increasingly interested in the trade of the north. From the reign of Louis XI, and particularly at the end of the fifteenth century, Paris became the undisputed capital of the kingdom, supported by a network of great regional metropolises: Rouen, Troyes, Orléans, Nantes and Lyons. The king intervened with the full weight of his authority to give Lyons and its fairs a pre-eminent role, and he banned French merchants from visiting Geneva. He also tried to give new life to the Troyes and *Lendit* fairs, and his efforts at making the *Lendit* fairs more the centre of the French textile industry were completely successful.

Two sets of figures aptly indicate the rise of the *Parisian* market: in the middle of the fifteenth century, the textile industry of Paris was ruined; less than a century later, the Parisian dyers and cloth-finishers brought cloth production in northern France under central control and set up a commercial organization. About 500,000 pieces of cloth were treated in the Gobelin and Canaye workshops in Paris. The number of 'French companies', from which

unaffiliated merchants had to seek permission at Paris in order to trade on the Seine, illustrates the same point: the number of permits issued by these companies varied from 48 to 82 a year between 1453 and 1457 and from 142 to 188 between 1458 and 1462. In 1533 they had risen to 891.

Though ruined after the departure of the English, *Rouen* experienced renewed prosperity as an importer of corn from the Parisian basin. Its trade in herrings, for example, rose from 900 tons a year in 1451 to 7,524 in 1515.

*Bordeaux* had suffered greatly from the Hundred Years' War, during which its vineyards were ravaged, and still more from the aftermath of war which interrupted its traditional contacts with England. Then, from 1450 to 1475, 5,000–6,000 tuns of wine alone left the port each year; after the treaty of Picquigny with the English (1475) the number went up to 8,000–10,000 tuns; from the beginning of the sixteenth century it rose to 20,000–30,000 tuns, with a peak of 80,000 tuns in the course of the century. Bordeaux was not, however, engaged exclusively in the wine trade: it exported corn from Aquitaine, and, like La Rochelle, became one of the outlets for pastel, which brought great prosperity to the Toulouse region at this time. The total of 310 ships visiting Bordeaux in 1481 should be compared with a figure of 587 vessels which took on cargoes of wine there in 1509 and 2,666 vessels entering the port in 1562.

To keep pace with this economic development, the Breton navy expanded considerably. Taking advantage of the neutrality of the Duchy during the wars, the difficulties encountered by the other fleets and the remarkable expansion of business (salt and linens) in the region, it eventually dominated the maritime routes from Portugal to the North Sea. Then, towards the end of the fifteenth century, Norman sailors again appeared on the international maritime scene. At the beginning of the sixteenth century, Breton and Norman ships sailed along the coasts of Africa in company with the Portuguese and towards the Icelandic fishing-grounds with the Hanseatics, before launching out along with the Basques towards the shores of the New World.

The renewed drive of the French economy should be specially emphasized, since for a century and more the enfeeblement of France, the most densely populated country in Europe, was primarily responsible for the recession in a large part of the European economy. Its resurrection was reflected in a general rise in prosperity.

The political power of the Hanse declined to a certain extent, and it was evidently powerless to prevent the rise of the Dutch and English fleets in the Baltic, or the diversion of the Breton navy towards Spain and Portugal. However, the towns and districts which were dependent on it continued their economic progress. Danzig exported 10,000 tons of rye a year during the years

239

145 Carving of ship, from a lintel in Jacques Cœur's house.

1470–75; 20,000 in 1490–92; and the trade reached a peak of 100,000 tons in the course of the sixteenth century. Consignments of iron from Sweden rose from about 2,500 tons at the end of the fifteenth century to 6,000 tons a century later. Similarly, consignments of wax, which were imported into London by the Hanseatic counter every year, rose from about 50 tons in the middle of the fifteenth century to 100 tons in 1475–79, and 840 tons in 1528–29.

For the merchants of southern Germany who competed with the Hanseatics on their own ground, this was a period of dazzling success. Even before the middle of the fifteenth century, the Great Company of Ravensburg and the merchants of Constance had begun to lay siege to the Mediterranean, and especially the Spanish markets, by way of Venice, or Genoa and Savona, or by Geneva, Dauphiné and Port-de-Bouc. The merchants of Augsburg and Nuremberg followed suit. The name of Fugger is itself symbolic, since this family combined the profits of an intensive commercial and banking business in all the important centres, from Lübeck to Venice and from Rome to London, with gold, silver, copper and iron mining in Hungary, the Tyrol and Carinthia; they finally carved out a real financial empire for themselves, especially in Spain.

The Dutch became formidable rivals to the Hanseatics. In particular their navy increasingly dominated the Atlantic, visiting the Portuguese salt-marshes or those of the Bay, Bordeaux, La Rochelle and Bristol; it went right up the Baltic to buy grain directly, flouting the privileges of the towns. The cloth trade of Leyden and 's Hertogenbosch, the fairs of Deventer, and the markets of Amsterdam and Kampen, achieved a position of growing importance in north-western Europe.

Antwerp, with its neighbouring ports sited at the mouths of the great rivers – Middelburg, Bergen-op-Zoom, Veere, Arnemuiden – tended to replace Bruges as the key junction of the international economy; its financial role was unrivalled.

The commercial expansion of the English cloth industry, which had begun at the end of the fourteenth century, continued and accelerated considerably at the end of the fifteenth century and beginning of the sixteenth. Around 1470, the total exports of cloths from English ports rose to about 40,000 pieces; 46,000 pieces went out through the port of London alone in 1500, and 75,000 in 1525, reaching 132,767 in 1550. From the beginning of the fifteenth century, the English navy started to expand, and, from then on, it competed with the Hanseatic ships right along the Baltic, discharging cargoes of salt and southern produce, and taking on grain and fish; it also competed with the Breton and Basque navies on their own ground, and occasional ships went as far as the Mediterranean. In 1446 an English wool convoy sailed for Pisa.

146 Relief of scales, by Adam Krafft, 1497, which was originally on the public weigh-house of Nuremberg.

Italians continued to predominate at Southampton. At London, however, the Hanseatic privileges were abolished in 1447 and subsequently the Hanse failed to regain the privileged position it had held for two centuries. But the volume of trade with Hanseatic countries did not suffer as a result – rather the reverse. At Bristol the famous Merchant Adventurers' Company was founded, also in 1447, and, from that time forward, this port became the true centre of the national economic expansion. Starting by acting as a channel for the products of England itself (cloths and wools, iron and coal) and exploiting those of Ireland close by (wool, woollen cloth, butter, lard, etc.), its merchants launched into the conquest of foreign markets, Lisbon, Cádiz, Seville, and especially Bilbao, the economy of which received a valuable boost as a result. Their contacts with the Iberian peninsula finally encouraged English sailors and merchants to enter the Mediterranean in force from about 1511; exchanging roles with the Italians, who had exploited the English markets for two centuries, they brought their cloths and corn from the northern countries to Italy.

Finally, on a more modest scale, English fishermen flocked in growing numbers to the fishing grounds, venturing always further afield – as far as Iceland and even, at the very end of the century, to the banks of Newfoundland, whose cod from then on provided Europe with a new source of supply.

In the Mediterranean region, the situation in the fifteenth century was also, for the most part, favourable. Venice had ceased to be a city-state, and was now a territorial state, at the height of its maritime and economic power. The fall of Constantinople was only a minor accident as far as Venice was concerned, since as a result of its shrewd policy in the east, it hardly suffered from Turkish domination in the eastern Mediterranean, and was able to maintain its political influence for a very long time while even bettering its economic position. Venice retained its leading role in the spice markets at Alexandria and Beirut, and in fact monopolized the trade in Damascus and Hama cotton, conveying it to the textile centres of Lombardy and southern Germany, whose agent it had become. Its interests led Venice to develop the mineral resources of its mainland territories and its possessions in the Balkans, as well as the products of its colonial domains, Crete and Cyprus, lands of wine, salt and sugar.

Genoa, with its independence lost, and its power on the Riviera overthrown, was chased from its oriental colonies, and survived only by leaning on the capital and the industry of Milan, which was expanding rapidly. Genoa had a period of great prosperity since it had succeeded in changing the direction of its interests in the course of the fourteenth century: when it was expelled from its bases in Aragon and exposed to the Catalan raids, it had made a bid for the ports of Málaga, Seville, Cádiz and Lisbon. Proceeding beyond Barcelona, it

147 Christ with the symbols of artisans, from an Italian fresco.

acquired a commanding position on the route to England and Flanders, and by using ships of a greater tonnage than had been developed so far, it brought these countries a wide range of goods, in particular the alum of Asia Minor, and subsequently of Tolfa, without which the textile industry of the north would not have been able to function. The Genoese, who gave Castile Columbus, were well prepared for playing a leading role in the finances of the new Spanish empire.

Finally Florence became the most important financial power of the west at the time of the Medici bank. It was enabled to do so by reason of its banking networks, its vast capital, and the expertise of its financiers. At the beginning of the fifteenth century Florence bought up its old rival Pisa, which resumed its previous trade with North Africa and Egypt, and subsequently, foreshadowing Leghorn, turned towards the Atlantic.

The sailors of Ragusa, which was a meeting-place of the Turkish and Christian worlds, and the outlet for the Balkan mines, began to assume the role of carriers in the Mediterranean. Due to the good relations which they maintained with the new masters of Constantinople, they were to continue in this for three centuries, while the Basque and Cantabrian fleets supplied tramp ships for the western powers.

In southern Italy, the extension of stock-raising continued in Apulia and in the *latifondi* of the Roman Campagna: the herds on the *Tavoliere* of Apulia increased during the sixteenth century from 1,500,000 to 5,500,000 head. The growth of the population of Sicily was as yet far from cancelling out the surplus of its wheat production, and its exports of corn reached their peak in 1532 with 520,000 quintals (about 1,023, 574 cwt.).

148 Florentine banking scene; woodcut from an Italian manuscript, 1490.

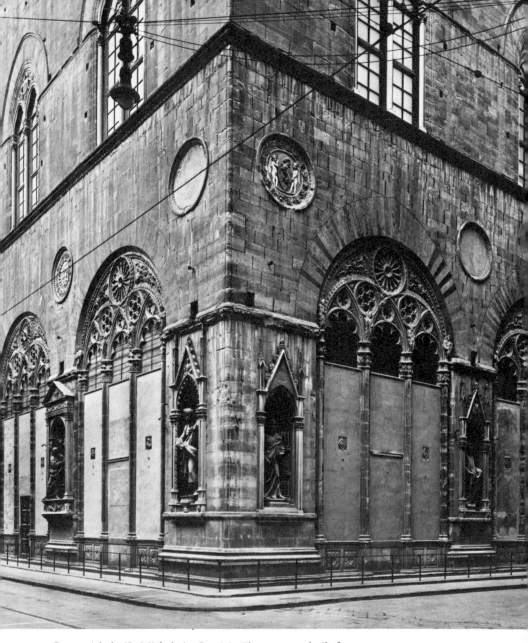

149 Orsanmichele (S. Michele in Orto) in Florence was built from 1337 to 1343 as a grain-market in the form of a huge tower of over 120 feet, the upper storey serving as warehouse. It was later altered into a church for the Artists' Guild.

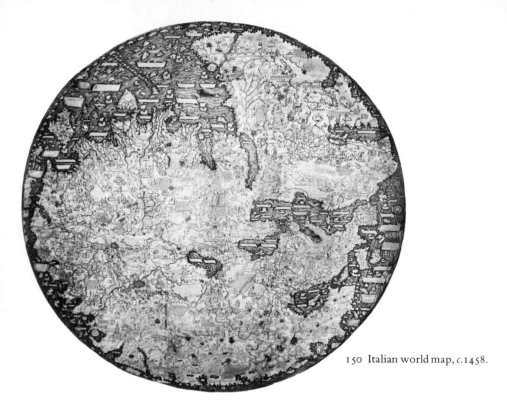

150 Italian world map, *c.*1458.

THE AGE OF DISCOVERY

The second half of the fifteenth century shares with the nineteenth the privilege of having provided civilization with an impressive series of technical achievements and geographical discoveries, which gradually revolutionized the economy.

Two schools of engineers, one German and the other Italian, made considerable technical progress. The Germans were concerned more with military problems, the Italians more with the arts. Of the latter, the most famous is of course Leonardo da Vinci (1452–1519), whose researches brought the encyclopædic bent of fifteenth-century technicians to its highest point.

The most spectacular invention of this period, and the most important for its intellectual consequences, was clearly *printing*. From the beginning of the fifteenth century, various researches had paved the way for the crucial discovery of movable metal type. Its invention is attributed to Gutenberg and dated around 1440. But the book which is allegedly the first to have been printed, the famous Forty-two-line Bible of Mainz, bears no date, and the

151 The 42-line Gutenberg Bible.

first book which is dated, the Psalter of the same town, was printed in 1457. In the last quarter of the century the progress of printing was overwhelming: the number of 'incunabula' editions which were produced before 1500 in 236 towns has been estimated at 35,000. New technical developments in the engraving of the characters and the manufacture of oily ink and sized paper contributed to its success. The printing press, which was originally similar to those used for making wine and cider, was perfected, notably by the use of the moving platen.

In the technical field proper, the beginning of the fifteenth century saw the appearance of the connecting-rod, which enabled continuous circular motion to be transformed into alternating rectilinear motion, and vice versa. When combined with an improved gear-system it had many applications, beginning with the suction- and force-pump and the modern saw. Drawings survive from the last quarter of the fifteenth century which illustrate new technical progress including hydraulic turbines, various types of weight-raising machinery, and finally windmills with rotating caps.

The technology of mines and metallurgy made great strides. From the end of the fourteenth century, galleries took the place of simple mine-shafts reached by ladders, and at the beginning of the following century their shoring was improved. Drawings dating from the end of the century show minerals being transported along the galleries in small wagons running on rails, and being raised by means of a pulley-system, with horses providing the motive power.

As we have noted, the blast furnace made its appearance most probably at the very end of the fourteenth century in the Liège district, but it became widespread only at the end of the fifteenth century, together with casting, which revolutionized metal working. The copper industry, which helped to make the fortunes of Jacques Cœur and the Fuggers, also made great progress at this time, but bronze advanced even further, because of its suitability for casting. Bronze cannon appeared in the middle of the fifteenth century, permitting the development of artillery, since gunpowder was also improved by the use of saltpetre which began to be manufactured at this time. From then on the cannon became an essential instrument of warfare.

Machine tools were completely revolutionized by the invention of machines for boring, polishing, drilling, and piercing wood and metal. The spinning-wheel had appeared in the fourteenth century, but was not developed commercially for a long time; it was now perfected and became widespread, together with wool-carding. Manuscript illustrations also show machines for milling silk.

152 Typical Venetian goblet of the late fifteenth century.

'Venetian' crystal is said to have been invented at Murano in 1443; kali, imported from Egypt, replaced potash when the industry spread to Venice. Flat glass for window-panes helped to improve living conditions, and glass mirrors plated with lead became widespread.

This period was perhaps even more notable for its great public works. In Holland a start was made on the polders, from 1435 onwards, using a new technique: the area to be drained was cut off by means of high dykes, and the interior criss-crossed with canals. About the same time, locks were built on the Juine, near Etampes, and on the Eure between Nogent and Chartres; canals with locks were dug, especially in Piedmont and in Venetia. The flow of the Loire was regulated, and several of its tributaries made navigable. Improved conditions were created for shipping by digging and dredging harbours. Bridges were built with a wider span, and sound foundations were made for their piers, which stood in the water, by building a shell-framework and using machines with chains and buckets to drain the water from the shell. In France, the communications network was reorganized, taking the form of a system of roads radiating from Paris, Lyons and Toulouse. Louis XI ordered the construction of a tunnel under Monte Viso, at a height of 2,000 metres, connecting Dauphiné with the Marquisate of Saluzzo. In 1480, in the Tyrol, gunpowder was used for the first time to blast a route for a road.

All these works helped the flow of traffic, and the institution of the royal post in France by Louis XI is symptomatic of the improved conditions on the roads. In the field of transport, chain- or webbing-suspension for carriages and mobile fore-carriages, which were introduced from the beginning of the fifteenth century, enabled heavier loads to be transported.

At sea, new types of vessels made their appearance or became more widespread. The pattern of shipping in the Atlantic, where ships of large beam tended to oust the medieval *kogge*, spread to the Mediterranean. Genoa gave up using galleys completely and Venice adopted a new type, which was longer and of greater tonnage. The oar of the classical galley was now only auxiliary to the sail, and the tonnage of the Genoese ships continued to increase, reaching more than 1,000 metric tons around 1460. The ships' hulls became stronger, with higher superstructures; the sails were square and placed one above another, and from this time they were distributed over several masts. At the same time, the adoption of the caravel type of boat, with its remarkable sailing qualities, together with the progress of cartography and astronomy, was one of the determining factors in the success of the Portuguese navigators.

Spurred on by its prince, the genius Henry the Navigator, Portugal embarked on a methodical programme of voyages of discovery. Ceuta was seized in 1415, Madeira and the Azores occupied in 1420 and 1431 respectively. Portuguese ships ventured further and further along the coasts of Africa, as far as Guinea, the land of gold and long pepper under the command of Cadamosto, with Bartholomew Diaz as far as the Cape of Good Hope in 1486, and with Vasco da Gama as far as India in 1498, under king Emanuel I, thus retracing the spice route to its source. This was an event of great importance, since at that time the traditional *status quo* in Mediterranean Europe was reversed: the Mediterranean became a closed lake, while the ocean opened up unlimited possibilities. Soon the thousand-year-old Central Asian routes lost their *raison d'être*, and the current of trade with the Far East ceased to flow towards Egypt, which gradually became devitalized as a result. On the day of the victory of Diu (1509), Arab trade in the Indian Ocean was relegated into second place by the competitive enterprise of the Portuguese.

153 Detail of a Portulan chart dated 1456.

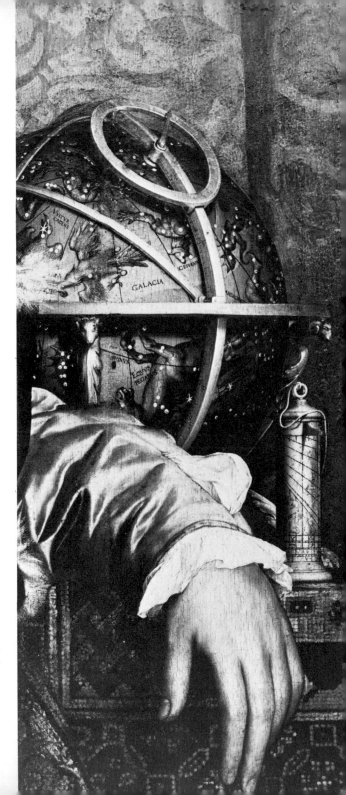

154 Symbols of world exploration; detail from Holbein's *The Ambassadors*, 1533.

155 Portrait of Henry The Navigator (1394–1460) with his device, *Talan de bien faire* ('gift for doing good'), from a contemporary Portuguese manuscript.

156 Belem tower in Lisbon.

From 1501, pepper carried by the Portuguese reached Antwerp; in 1503 the Welsers of Augsburg turned from Venice to Lisbon; in 1504 five Portuguese ships entered Falmouth, laden with 380 tons of pepper. The glut of spices caused a catastrophic fall in their price in every market-town, and king Emanuel had to fix an official price for pepper: that same year the Venetian galleys returned from Alexandria and Beirut empty, having failed to find their usual cargo. A page in the history of international economy had been turned. For though Venice was not doomed at this stage – it made several comebacks in the sixteenth century – the city of the doges was actually reduced to stagnation while the rest of the world was experiencing a headlong economic expansion.

157 The arms of Christopher Columbus, from the title-page of a fifteenth-century Italian manuscript.

158 Woodcut from the title-page of a Florentine edition (1493) of Columbus's letter announcing his discovery of the West Indies.

In 1492 Christopher Columbus, whose birthplace was Genoa, discovered America while seeking another route to the spices of the Indies. The future of Spain now lay beyond the seas, while in Spain itself Islam was driven from Iberian soil by the conquest of Granada. From the time of Columbus' second voyage, the Catholic kings set up an administration at Seville to control trade with the recently discovered lands. In 1503 Ferdinand built the *Casa de la Contratación* to house it; ten caravels set sail for the coast of the isthmus of Panama. The sixteenth century was the century of gold and silver which flowed across Spain and, channelled by the Italian, German and Dutch banks, transformed the very foundations of the European economy.

The future of Europe no longer lay in the confined seas of its birth, but across the oceans, where the western powers went to found their colonies. The economic expansion which began in the middle of the fifteenth century continued to grow with increasing vigour in every field, right up until modern times.

# BIBLIOGRAPHY

## GENERAL WORKS OF REFERENCE

### INTERNATIONAL CONGRESSES
Apart from the five-yearly International Congress of Historical Sciences, the proceedings of the International Conferences on Economic History have been published. The first of these conferences was held at Stockholm in 1960, the second at Aix-en-Provence in 1962, and the third at Munich in 1965.

### GENERAL BIBLIOGRAPHICAL WORKS
There is no complete bibliography of medieval economic history; but extremely elaborate bibliographical notes are contained in the three volumes of the *Cambridge Economic History of Europe*, and in J. Heers, *L'Occident aux XIVe et XVe s.* (Paris 1963); for Italy, see A. Sapori, *Studi di storia economica* (2nd ed. Florence 1947).

### GLOSSARIES
The following can be consulted:
A.-M. Bautier, 'Contribution à un vocabulaire économique du Midi de la France', in *Archivum mediae et infime latinitatis* (Bulletin du Cange 1956–60).
F. Edler, *Glossary of medieval terms of business. Italian series 1200–1600* (Cambridge, Mass. 1934).
Reference might also be made to the index (on weights and measures, merchandise, etc.) in the edition by A. Evans of *La pratica della mercatura* by Francesco Balducci Pegolotti (Cambridge, Mass. 1936).

### GENERAL MANUALS
The *Cambridge Economic History of Europe* is the best general work: vol. I (3rd ed.): *The Agrarian Life of the Middle Ages* (Cambridge 1961) ed. M. M. Postan; vol II: *Trade and industry in the Middle Ages* (Cambridge 1952) edd. M. M. Postan and E. E. Rich; vol. III: *Economic organization and policies in the Middle Ages* edd. E. E. Rich and E. Miller. This collective work, a result of the collaboration of specialists, is of uneven value; most of the first volume is the same as the 1941 edition. In the second volume the chapters devoted to Italy and England are of particular interest; but the book is not always accurate on Germany, and especially on France and Spain.
See also:
H. Pirenne, *Economic and social history of medieval Europe* (London 1936). A brilliant synthesis, which formed a turning-point in historiography and gave rise to many valuable criticisms; it remains of value today, particularly for north-west Europe.

### INDIVIDUAL COUNTRIES
DENMARK
E. Arup, O. H. Larsen and A. Olsen, *Dänische Wirtschaftsgeschichte* (Jena 1933).
ENGLAND AND SCOTLAND
E. Lipson, *The economic history of England*, vol. I: *The Middle Ages* (11th ed. London 1956).

GERMANY
H. Bechtel, *Wirtschaftsgeschichte Deutschlands von der Vorzeit bis zum Ende des Mittelalters* (Munich 1951). Outstanding.
F. Lütge, *Deutsche Sozial- und Wirtschaftsgeschichte* (2nd ed. Berlin-Göttingen 1960). Especially important for rural history.
ISLAM
D. and J. Sourdel, *La civilisation de l'Islam omassique* (Paris 1968). See also the articles in *L'Encyclopédie d'Islam* (and, above, the section on Spain).
ITALY
A. Doren, *Italienische Wirtschaftsgeschichte*, vol. I (Jena 1934).
G. Luzzatto, *An Economic History of Italy* (New York 1961).
A. Sapori, *Studi di storia economica medievale* (3rd ed. Florence 1955). A collection of the author's articles, with an excellent bibliography.
LOW COUNTRIES
J. F. Niermeyer, *De wording van onze volkshuishouding Hoofdlijnen uit de economische geschiednis der noordelijke Nederlanden in de Middeleeuwen* (The Hague 1946).
POLAND
Two important and fundamental articles are:
H. Lowmianski, 'Economic problems of the early feudal Polish State', in *Acta Poloniae historica*, 1960.
M. Malowist, 'The economic and social development of the Baltic countries from the 15th to the 17th century', in *Economic History Review*, 1959.
SPAIN
J. Vicens Vives, *Historia social y económica de España y América* (Barcelona 1957).
J. Vicens Vives, L. Suarez Fernandez and C. y Carrere, *La economia de los paises de la corona de Aragón en La Baja Edad Media* (Madrid 1957). Important.
P. Vilar, *La Catalogne dans L'Espagne moderne* (3 vols. Paris 1962). Essential.
For Muslim Spain, see the writings of E. Lévi Provençal:
*Histoire de l'Espagne musulmane* (3 vols. Paris 1950–53).
*L'Espagne musulmane au Xe s.: institutions et vie sociale* (Paris 1932).
*La civilisation arabe de L'Espagne* (Paris 1948).

### CHRONOLOGICAL
ANTIQUITY
T. Frank, *Economic history of Rome* (2nd ed. Baltimore 1927).
——— (ed.), *Economic Survey of Ancient Rome* (4 vols. and index Baltimore 1933–40).
F. M. Heichelheim, *Wirtschaftsgeschichte des Altertums* (Leiden 1938).
K. Remondon, *La crise de L'Empire romain de Marc-Aurèle à Anastase* (Paris 1964).
M. Rostovzeff, *Social and economic history of the Roman Empire* (2nd ed. Oxford 1957).
THE EARLY AND THE CLASSICAL MIDDLE AGES
A. Dopsch, *Die Wirtschaftsentwicklung der Karolingerzeit, vornehmlich in Deutschland* (2nd ed. 2 vols. Weimar 1921).

———, *Economic and social foundations of European civilization* (2 vols. Vienna 1923–24).

R. Latouche, *The birth of the western economy* (New York 1961).

J. Le Goff, *La civilisation de l'Occident médiéval* (Paris 1964). An admirable synthesis, based on the personal researches of the author.

R. S. Lopez, *Naissance de l'Europe* (Paris 1962). An excellent summary by a specialist.

F. Lot, *The end of the ancient world and the beginnings of the Middle Ages* (London 1931).

E. Salin, *La civilisation mérovingienne, d'après les sepultures, les textes et le laboratoire* (4 vols. Paris 1949–59).

J. W. Thompson, *Economic and social history of the Middle Ages* (2nd ed. New York 1969).

THE FOURTEENTH AND FIFTEENTH CENTURIES

J. Heers, *L'Occident aux XIV^e et XV^e s. Aspects économiques et sociaux* (2nd ed. Paris 1966). The best summary of the period.

H. A. Miskimin, *The economy of early Renaissance Europe, 1300–1460* (New Jersey 1969). A synthesis of the author's work.

M. Mollat, P. Johansen, M. M. Postan, A. Sapori and C. Verlinden, 'L'économie européene aux deux derniers siècles du Moyen Age', in *Relazioni del X Congresso Internazionale di Scienze Storiche* (vol. VI, pp. 801–957) (Florence 1955). A review of recent work, especially on commercial history.

F. Braudel, *Civilisation matérielle et capitalisme* (XV^e–XVIII^e s.) (Paris 1967).


DEMOGRAPHY

A survey of recent research into medieval demography was supplied by C. Cipolla, J. Dhondt, M. M. Wolff and P. Wolff in vol. I, pp. 55–80, of the *Rapports of the Ninth International Congress of Historical Sciences* (Paris 1951). Since then an enormous amount of work has been done in this field. For towns, an excellent summary, if already somewhat dated, is R. Mols, *Introduction à la démographie historique des villes d'Europe du XIV^e au XVIII^e s.* (3 vols. Louvain 1954–56). Vol. III has a very important bibliography. See also J. C. Russell, *Late ancient and medieval population* (Philadelphia 1958).

GENERAL DEMOGRAPHIC DEVELOPMENT

L. Genicot, 'Sur les témoignages d'accroissement de la population en Occident du XI^e au XIII^e s.', in *Cahiers d'histoire mondiale*, 1953.

M. M. Postan, 'Some evidence of declining population in the later Middle Ages', in *Economic History Review*, 1950.

J. Z. Titow, 'Some evidence of the XIIIth century population increase', in *Economic History Review*, 1961–62.

BELGIUM

M. A. Arnould, *Les dénombrements de foyers dans le comté de Hainaut* (XIV^e–XVI^e s.) (Brussels 1945).

FRANCE

From a large number of recent works the most important are:

E. Baratier (ed.), *La démographie provençale du XIII^e au XVI^e s.* (Paris 1961).

J. Glenisson and E. Carpentier, 'La démographie française au XIV^e s. . . . Bilans et méthodes', in *Annales. Economie. Sociétés. Civilisations*, 1963.

The basis (disputed but nevertheless fundamental) of all estimates of medieval French demography remains the work of F. Lot, in particular: 'L'état des paroisses et des feux de 1328,' in *Bibliothèque de l'Ecole des Chartes*, 1929; and *Recherches sur la population et la superficie des cités remontant à la période gallo-romaine* (4 vols. Paris 1945–54), a work of unequal value.

GERMANY

E. Keyser, *Bevölkerungsgeschichte Deutschlands* (3rd ed. Leipzig 1943).

GREAT BRITAIN

J. C. Russell, *British medieval population* (Albuquerque 1948). Fundamental.

HUNGARY

G. Györffy, 'Einwohnerzahl und Bevölkerungsgeschichte in Ungarn bis zum Anfang des XIV. Jahrhunderts', in *Etudes historiques publiées par la commission nationale des historiens hongrois* (Budapest 1960).

ITALY

K. J. Beloch, *Bevölkerungsgeschichte Italiens* (3 vols. Berlin–Leipzig 1937–61).

POLAND

E. Vielrose, *Die Bevölkerung Polens vom X. bis XVIII. Jahrhundert* (Marburg 1958).

SWITZERLAND

H. Ammann, 'Die Bevölkerung der Westschweiz im ausgehenden Mittelalter', in *Festschrift Friedrich Emil Welti* (Aarau 1937).

———, 'Die Bevölkerung von Stadt und Landschaft Basel am Ausgang des Mittelalters', in *Basler Zeitschrift für Geschichte und Altertumskunde*, 1950.

L. Binz, 'La population du diocèse du Genève à la fin du Moyen Age', in *Mélanges d'histoire économique et sociale en hommage au professeur A. Babel* (Geneva 1963).


FAMINES AND EPIDEMICS

E. Carpentier, 'Famines et épidémies dans l'histoire du XIV^e s.', in *Annales. Economie. Sociétés. Civilisations*, 1962, stresses the importance of climatic evolution. Cf. E. Le Roy Ladurie, *Histoire du climat depuis l'an mil* (Paris 1967).

On famines see:

H. H. Curschmann, *Hungernöte im Mittelalter. Ein Beitrag zur deutschen Wirtschaftsgeschichte* (Leipzig 1900).

H. Van Werveke, 'La famine de l'an 1316 en Flandre et dans les régions voisines', in *Revue du Nord*, 1959.

Much has been written on plagues, including the following titles:

E. Carpentier, *Une ville devant la peste: Orvieto et la peste noire de 1348* (Paris 1962).

J. Schreiner, *Pest og prisfall i sen middelalderen et problem i norsk historie* (Oslo 1948). A French résumé has been published in *Excerpta nordica*, 1950.

H. van Werveke, *De zwarte dood in de Zuidelijke Nederlanden (1349–57)* (Brussels 1950).


POPULATION MOVEMENTS

Much has been written on the *Drang Nach Osten*:

R. Boutruche, 'Les courants de peuplement dans l'Entre-deux-mers', in *Annales d'histoire économique et sociale*, 1935.

C. Higounet, 'Mouvements de population dans le Midi de la France . . .', in *Annales. Economie. Sociétés. Civilisations*, 1953.

——, 'L'occupation du sol entre Tarn et Garonne au Moyen Age', in *Annales du Midi*, 1953.

R. Kotzschke, *Quellen zur Geschichte der ostdeutsche Kolonisation* (2nd ed. Leipzig 1931).

## DESERTED VILLAGES

One of the subjects most studied in the last decade. *Villages désertés et histoire économique XIᵉ–XVIIIᵉ s.* (Paris 1965) is a fundamental collective review of research covering the whole of Europe.

The following can also be consulted:

W. Abel, *Die Wüstungen des ausgehenden Mittelalters* (2nd ed. Jena 1955).

M. Beresford, *The lost villages of England* (Lutterworth 1954).

H. Pohlendt, *Die Verbreitung der mittelalterlichen Wüstungen in Deutschland* (Göttingen 1953).

W. Rusinski, 'Wüstungen. Ein Agrarproblem des feudalen Europas', in *Acta Poloniae historica*, 1962.

## RURAL HISTORY

Research has been reorientated, especially for the ninth to thirteenth centuries, by one of the best recent works:

G. Duby, *L'économie rurale et la vie des campagnes dans l'occident médiéval (France, Angleterre, Empire IXᵉ–XVᵉ s.)* (2 vols. Paris 1962), with an English translation, *Rural economy and country life in the medieval West* (Columbia, South Carolina 1968). Neglects Mediterranean Europe; an important bibliography.

See also:

B. H. Slicher Van Bath, *The agrarian history of Western Europe, A.D. 500–1850* (London 1963).

## BELGIUM

L. Genicot, *L'économie rurale namuroise au Bas Moyen Age (1199–1429)*, vol I: *La seigneurie foncière*; vol. II: *Les hommes, la noblesse* (Namur-Louvain 1943–60).

Among numerous studies of the temporal possessions of the abbeys is:

D. Van Derveeghde, *Le domaine de l'abbaye du Val-Saint-Lambert de 1202 à 1387* (Brussels 1955).

## BYZANTIUM

P. Lamerle, 'Esquisse pour une histoire agraire de Byzance. Les sources et les problèmes', in *Revue historique*, 1958. Important.

G. Rouillard, *La vie rurale dans l'Empire byzantin* (Paris 1953).

See also:

G. Ostrogrorsky, *Quelques problèmes d'histoire et de la paysannerie byzantine* (Brussels 1956).

G. Tchalenko, *Villages antiques de la Syrie du Nord* (3 vols. Paris 1953).

## ENGLAND

J. E. T. Rogers, *History of agriculture and prices in England 1259–1703* (5 vols. Oxford 1886–92).

E. A. Kosminsky, *Studies in the agrarian history of England in the XVIIIth century* (Oxford 1956); cf. 'The evolution of feudal rent in England from the XIth to the XVth century', in *Past and Present*, 1955.

P. Vinogradoff, *The growth of the manors* (3rd ed. London-New York 1951).

On Domesday Book, see H. C. Darby et al., *The Domesday Geography* (4 vols. Cambridge 1952–62).

The importance of the sources available has made the study of landed property (granges, manors, estates) one of the most significant aspects of English economic history:

R. H. Hilton, *The economic development of some Leicestershire estates in the 14th and 15th centuries* (Oxford 1947).

E. Miller, *The abbey and bishopric of Ely. The social history of an ecclesiastical estate from the 10th century to the early 14th century* (Cambridge 1951).

J. A. Raftis, *The estates of Ramsey abbey. A study in economic growth and organization* (Toronto 1957).

J. M. W. Bean, *The estates of the Percy family, 1416–1537* (Oxford 1958).

G. A. Holmes, *The estates of the higher nobility in 14th century England* (Cambridge 1957).

## FRANCE

M. Bloch, *Les caractères originaux de l'histoire rurale française* (2nd ed. 2 vols. Paris 1956) (with notes by R. Dauvergne). Fundamental.

M. Devèze, *La vie de la forêt française au XVIᵉ s.* (2 vols. Paris 1961). Partly replaces A. Maury's classic work, *Les forêts de la Gaule et de l'ancienne France* (2nd ed. Paris 1867).

R. Dion, *Histoire de la vigne et du vin en France des origines au XIXᵉ s.* (Paris 1969).

R. Grand and R. Delatouche, *L'agriculture au Moyen Age. De la fin de L'Empire romain au XVIᵉ s.*, vol. III: *L'agriculture à travers les âges* (Paris 1950). Excellent chapters in a generally disappointing work.

C. Higounet, 'Les forêts de l'Europe occidentale du Vᵉ au XIᵉ s.', in *Agricultura e mondo rurale in Occidente nell'alto Medio Evo* (Spoleto 1966), pp. 343–98.

Of the numerous important regional studies, see:

Y. Bezard, *La vie rurale dans le sud de la région parisienne de 1450 à 1560.* (Paris 1929).

R. Boutruche, *Une société provinciale en lutte contre le régime féodal. L'alleu en Bordelais et en Bazadais du XIᵉ au XVIIIᵉ s.* (Rodez 1943).

——, *La crise d'une société: seigneurs et paysans du Bordelais pendant la guerre de cent ans* (Paris 1947).

A. Deleage, *La vie rurale en Bourgogne jusqu'au début du XIᵉ s.* (3 vols. Mâcon 1941).

G. Duby, *La société aux XIᵉ et XIIᵉ s. dans la région mâconnaise* (Paris 1953). Essential.

——, 'Recherches récentes sur la vie rurale en Provence au XIVᵉ s.', in *Provence historique*, 1965.

——, 'Techniques et rendements agricoles dans les Alpes du Sud en 1338', in *Annales du Midi*, 1958.

R. Fossier, *Les hommes et la terre en Picardie jusqu'à la fin du Moyen Age* (2 vols. Paris 1969). The best regional monograph.

G. Fournier, *Le peuplement rural en Basse-Auvergne durant le Haut Moyen Age* (Paris 1962). Very important for the early Middle Ages.

I. Guerin, *La vie rurale en Sologne aux XIVᵉ et XVᵉ s.* (Paris 1960).

C. E. Perrin, *Recherches sur la seigneurie rurale en Lorraine d'après les plus anciens censiers (IXᵉ–XIIᵉ s.)* (Strasbourg 1935).

T. Schlaffert, *Le Haut-Dauphiné au Moyen Age* (Paris 1936).

——, *Cultures en Haute-Provence. Déboisements et pâturages au Moyen Age* (Paris 1959).

Of the few local studies on the manor see:

C. Higounet, *La grange de Vaulerent* (Paris 1965).

——, 'Les types d'exploitations cisterciennes et prémontrées du XIIIᵉ s. et leur rôle dans la formation de l'habitat et des paysages ruraux', in *Annales de l'est,* 1959.

### GERMANY

W. Abel, *Agrarkrisen und Agrarkonjunktur in Mitteleuropa von XIII. bis zum XIV. Jahrundert* (Jena 1935).

G. Franz (ed.), *Deutsche Agrargeschichte*: vol. II, W. Abel, *Geschichte der deutschen Landwirtschaft vom frühen Mittelalter bis zum XIX. Jahrhundert* (Stuttgart 1962); vol. III, F. Lütge, *Geschichte der deutschen Agrarverfassung . . .* (Stuttgart 1963); vol. IV, G. Franz, *Geschichte des Bauernstandes . . .* (Stuttgart 1963; revised ed. 1967).

G. von Below, *Geschichte der deutschen Landwirtschaft des Mittelalters in ihren Grundzügen . . .* (ed. F. Lütge) (Jena 1937).

P. Dollinger, *L'évolution des classes rurales en Bavière depuis la fin de l'époque carolingienne jusqu'au milieu de XIIIᵉ s.* (Paris-Strasbourg 1949).

F. Lütge, *Die Agrarverfassung des frühen Mittelalters im mitteldeutschen Raum, vornehmlich in der Karolingerzeit* (Jena 1937).

### ITALY

F. M. De Robertis, 'La produzione agrizola in Italia dalla crisi del IIIs. all'età dei Carolingi', in *Annali della Fac. di Economia e commercio della Univ. di Bari,* 1948.

D. Herlihy, 'The history of the rural seigneury in Italy, 751–1200', in *Agricultural History Review,* 1959.

——, 'Church property on the continent, 701–1208', in *Speculum,* 1961.

E. Sereni, *Storia del paesaggio italiano* (Bari 1961), translated as *Histoire du paysage italien* (Paris 1965).

### THE LEVANT

J. Prawer, 'Etude de quelques problèmes agraires et sociaux d'une seigneurie croisée au XIIIᵉ s.', in *Byzantion,* 1952 and 1953.

### RUSSIA

J. Blum, *Lord and peasant in Russia from the IXth to the XIXth century* (London-Princeton 1961).

### LAND-HOLDING

I. Imberciadori, *Mezzadria classica toscana,* con documentazione inedita dal IX al XIV sec. (Florence 1951).

L. Merle, *La métairie et l'évolution agraire de la Gâtine poitevine, de la fin du Moyen Age à la Révolution* (Paris 1959).

G. Sizard, *Le métayage dans le Midi toulousain à la fin du Moyen Age* (Toulouse 1956).

P. Toubert, 'Les statuts communaux de l'histoire des campagnes lombardes au XIVᵉ s.', in *Ecole française de Rome. Mélanges d'archéologie et d'histoire,* 1960.

### STOCK-RAISING

The ninety-second national congress of French learned societies, meeting at Strasbourg in 1967, took as its theme *L'élevage au Moyen Age*; its proceedings were published in the *Bulletin philologique et historique du comité des travaux historiques et scientifiques,* 1967. The ninety-third congress, which met in 1968 at Tours, discussed *L'alimentation au Moyen Age* (and, in particular, meat consumption); its proceedings were published in the same journal in 1968. See also:

A. Filangieri, 'La "Dogna delle pecore" di Puglia e la struttura economico-agraria del Tavogliere', in *Rivista di economia agraria,* 1950.

J. Klein, *The Mesta, a study in Spanish economic history, 1273–1836* (Cambridge, Mass. 1920).

This topic has received relatively little study: see also the section above on deserted villages, and the section below on the wool trade.

### URBAN HISTORY

The International Commission for the History of Towns is publishing for each country a *Bibliographie d'histoire des villes* and, in addition, collections of town-plans. Of the former, the volumes on France (edd. P. Dollinger and P. Wolff), Great Britain (by C. Gross) and Switzerland (by P. Guyer) have already appeared. The volume on Germany (by E. Keyser) is in the course of publication, as is a critical examination of the sources.

Excellent guides to the history and organization of towns in the various parts of Europe appear in 'La Ville', in *Recueils de la société Jean Bodin,* vol. VI: *Institutions administratives et judicaires* (Brussels 1954); vol. VII: *Institutions économiques et sociales* (Brussels 1955); vol. VIII: *Droit privé* (Brussels 1956).

### GENERAL WORKS

E. Ennen, *Frühgeschichte der europäischen Stadt* (Bonn 1953). Cf. T. Mayer, 'Zur Geschichte der Stadt im Frühmittelalter', in *Schweizerische Zeitschrift für Geschichte,* 1954.

T. Mayer (ed.), *Studien zu den Anfangen des europäischen Stadtwesens* (Lindau-Constance 1953).

H. Pirenne, *La ville et les institutions urbaines* (2 vols. Paris-Brussels 1939). A reprint of the author's classic writings.

F. Rörig, *Die europäischen Stadt und die Kultur des Bürgertums im Mittelalter* (Göttingen 1955).

*La città nell'alto Medioevo* (Spoleto 1958). An important publication of the Centro Italiano di Studi sull'Alto Medioevo.

ENGLAND

C. Stephenson, *Borough and town. A study of urban origins in England* (Cambridge, Mass. 1933).

FRANCE

E. Chapin, *Les villes de foires de Champagne, des origines au début du XIVᵉ s.* (Paris 1937).

P.-A. Fevrier, *Le développement urbain de la Provence, de l'époque romaine à la fin du XIVᵉ s.: archéologie et histoire urbaine* (Paris 1964).

262

F.-L. Ganshof, *Etude sur le développement des villes entre Loire et Rhin au Moyen Age* (Paris-Brussels 1944).

F. Vercauteren, *Etudes sur les civitates de la Belgique Seconde. Contribution à l'histoire urbaine du Nord de la France de la fin du III^e s. à la fin du XI^e* (Brussels 1934).

GERMANY

E. Keyer, *Stadtgründungen und Städtebau in Nordwestdeutschland im Mittelalter* (2 vols. Remagen 1958).

H. Planitz, *Die deutsche Stadt im Mittelalter. Von der Römerzeit bis zu den Zunftkämpfen* (Graz-Cologne 1954). An important survey.

G. Vollmer, *Die Stadtentstehung am unteren Niederrhein* (Bonn 1952).

L. von Winterfeld, 'Städtewesen und Bürgertum als geschichtliche Kräfte', in A. von Brandt and W. Koppe (edd.), *Gedächtnisschrift für Fritz Rörig* (Lübeck 1953).

ITALY

G. Mengozzi, *La città italiana nell'alto medio evo. Il periodo longobardofranco* (2nd ed. Florence 1951).

SPAIN

J. M. Lacarra, *El desarollo urbano de las cuidades de Navarra y Aragón en la Edad Media* (Saragossa 1950).

### INDIVIDUAL TOWNS

ENGLAND

J. W. F. Hill, *Medieval Lincoln* (Cambridge 1948).

FRANCE AND BELGIUM

B. Guillemain, *La cour pontificale d'Avignon 1309-76. Etude d'une société* (Paris 1962).

C. Higounet (ed.), *Histoire de Bordeaux*; vol. II: C. Higounet, *Bordeaux pendant le Haut Moyen Age* (Bordeaux 1963); vol. III: Y. Renouard (ed.), *Bordeaux sous les rois d'Angleterre* (Bordeaux 1965); vol. IV: R. Boutruche (ed.), *Bordeaux de 1453 à 1715* (Bordeaux 1966).

H. van Werveke, *Gand. Esquisse d'histoire sociale* (Brussels 1946).

J. Schneider, *La ville de Metz au XIII^e et XIV^e s.* (Nancy 1950).

P. Wolff, *Histoire de Toulouse* (Toulouse 1959); cf. J. H. Mundy, *Liberty and political power in Toulouse, 1050-1230* (New York 1954).

GERMANY

E. Keyser (ed.), *Deutsches Städtebuch* (3 vols. Stuttgart-Berlin 1939-52). Publication of this historical encyclopaedia of German towns has been interrupted.

H. Meinert, *Frankfurts Geschichte* (Frankfurt-am-Main 1949).

W. Reinecke, *Geschichte der Stadt Lüneburg* (Lüneburg 1933).

L. von Winterfeld, *Geschichte des freien Reichs- und Hansestadt Dortmund* (2nd ed. Dortmund 1956).

W. Zorn, *Augsburg. Geschichte einer deutscher Stadt* (Augsburg 1955).

ITALY

R. Cessi, *Storia della Repubblica di Venezia* (2 vols. Milan 1944-46).

R. Davidsohn, *Geschichte von Florenz* (4 vols. Berlin 1896-1927).

——, *Forschungen zur älteren Geschichte von Florenz* (4 vols. Berlin 1896-1908).

Fondazione Treccani degli Alfieri per la Storia di Milano, *Storia di Milano* (16 vols. Milan 1953-62).

J. Heers, *Gênes au XV^e s. Activité économique et problèmes sociaux* (Paris 1961).

D. Herlihy, *Pisa in the early Renaissance. A study of urban growth* (New Haven 1958).

——, *Medieval and Renaissance Pistoia. The social history of an Italian town, 1200-1400* (New Haven-London 1967).

V. Vitale, *Brevario della storio di Genova. Lineamenti storici ed orientamenti bibliografici* (2 vols. Genoa 1955).

SPAIN

R. Carande, 'Sevilla, forteleza y mercado', in *Annuario de historia del derecho español*, 1924.

### TOWN-PLANNING

P. Lavedan, *Histoire de l'urbanisme* (2 vols. Paris 1926-41).

L. Torres Balbas, 'Les villes musulmanes d'Espagne et leur urbanisation', in *Annales de l'institut d'études orientales* (Algiers 1942-47).

——, *Resumen historico del urbanismo en España* (Madrid 1954).

T. F. Tout, *Medieval town planning* (Manchester 1934).

### THE URBAN ECONOMY

FRANCE

P. Wolff, *Commerces et marchands de Toulouse (vers 1350-vers 1450)* (Paris 1954). One of the best French studies.

GERMANY

B. Kuske, *Köln, das Rhein und das Reich. Beiträge aus fünf Jahrzehnten wirtschaftsgeschichtlicher Forschung* (Cologne-Graz 1956).

ITALY

A. Doren, *Studien aus der florentiner Wirtschaftsgeschichte* (2 vols. Stuttgart 1901-08).

R. S. Lopez, *Studi sull'economia genovese nel Medio evo* (Turin 1936); cf. 'Aux origines du capitalisme génois', in *Annales d'histoire économique et sociale*, 1937.

C. M. Cipolla, 'L'economia milanese, 1350-1500', in *Storia di Milano*, 1955.

C. Violante, *La società milanese nell'età precomunale* (Bari 1953).

R. Cessi, *Politica ed economia di Venezia nel Trecento* (Rome 1952). A collection of the author's writings.

G. Luzzatto, *Studi di storia economica veneziana* (Padua 1954). A collection of the author's writings.

SWITZERLAND

H. Ammann, *Schaffhauser Wirtschaft im Mittelalter* (Thayngen 1948).

——, 'Freiburg als Wirtschaftsplatz im Mittelalter', in *Gedenkenband zur 800. Jahrfeiere Freiburg* (Freiburg 1957).

A. Babel, *Histoire économique de Genève des origines au début du XV^e s.* (2 vols. Geneva 1963).

J.-F. Bergier, *Genève et l'économie européene de la Renaissance*, vol. I (Paris 1963). Important.

### COMMERCE

### THE EARLY MIDDLE AGES

See the essential works, already mentioned, of A. Dopsch, R. Latouche and H. Pirenne. The more important of the many contributions to this subject are listed as follows:

263

F. Carli, *Storia del commercio italiano. Il mercato nell'alto evo* (Padua 1934).

F. J. Himly, 'Y a-t-il emprise musulmane sur l'économie des Etats européens du VIIIᵉ au Xᵉ s.' in *Schweizerische Zeitschrift für Geschichte*, 1955.

H. Jankuhn, *Haithabu. Eine germanische Stadt der Frühzeit* (3rd ed. Neumünster 1956).

P. Le Gentilhomme, *Le monnayage et la circulation monétaire dans les royaumes barbares en Occident (Vᵉ–VIIIᵉ s.)* (Paris 1946). Important.

J. Lombard, 'L'oz musulman du VIIᵉ au XIᵉ s.', in *Annales. Economie. Sociétés. Civilisations*, 1947.

——, 'Mahomet et Charlemagne: le problème économique', in *Annales. Economie. Sociétés. Civilisations*, 1948. A brilliant thesis, nevertheless open to criticism.

A. Verhulst, *Der Handel im Merowingerreich* (Stockholm 1970).

### FROM THE TWELFTH TO THE FIFTEENTH CENTURY

**BELGIUM**

E. Commaert, *Les Français et le commerce international à Anvers (fin de XVᵉ–XVIᵉ s.)* (Paris 1961).

R. Doehaerd, *L'expansion économique belge au Moyen Age* (Brussels 1946).

——,*Etudes anversoises. Documents sur le commerce international à Anvers, 1488–1513* (3 vols. Paris 1962–63).

J. A. Goris, *Etude sur les colonies marchandes méridionales (Portugais, Espagnols, Italiens) à Anvers de 1488 à 1567. Contribution à l'histoire des débuts du capitalisme moderne* (Louvain 1925).

**ENGLAND**

A. Beardwood, *Alien merchants in England, 1350 to 1377. Their legal and economic position* (Cambridge, Mass. 1931).

E. M. Carus-Wilson, *The overseas trade of Bristol in the later Middle Ages* (Bristol 1937).

——, *Medieval Merchant Venturers* (London 1954).

E. M. Carus-Wilson and O. Coleman, *England's export trade, 1275–1547* (Oxford 1963).

E. E. Power and M. M. Postan, *Studies in English trade in the XVth century* (London 1933).

A. A. Ruddock, *Italian merchants and shipping in Southampton, 1270–1600* (Southampton 1951).

J. de Sturler, *Les relations politiques et les échanges commerciaux entre le duché de Brabant et l'Angleterre du Moyen Age. L'étape des laines anglaises et les origines du développement du port d'Anvers* (Paris 1936).

**FRANCE**

J. Bernard, *Navires et gens de mer à Bordeaux (vers 1400–vers 1500)* (3 vols. Paris 1968).

V. Chomel and J. Ebersolt, *Cinq siècles de circulation internationale vue de Jougne. Un péage jurassien du XIIIᵉ au XVIIIᵉ s.* (Paris 1951).

G. Rambert (ed.), *Histoire du commerce de Marseille*, vol. I: R. Busquet, *L'antiquité*, and R. Pernoud, *Le Moyen Age jusqu'en 1291*; vol. II: E. Baratier, *De 1291 à 1423*, and F. Reynaud, *De 1423 à 1480*; vol. III: R. Collier and J. Billioud, *1480–1599* (Paris 1949–57).

M. Mollat, *Le commerce maritime normand à la fin du Moyen Age* (Paris 1952).

J. Touchard, *Le commerce maritime breton à la fin du Moyen Age* (Paris 1967).

**GERMANY AND THE BALTIC**

During the last century, the Verein für Hansische Geschichte has published the sources of Hanseatic history (in particular the *Hanse-Recessen* and the *Hansische Geschichtsquellen*), memoirs and texts (*Quellen und Darstellungen zur Hansische Geschichte*), booklets devoted to individual studies (*Pfingstblätter* and *Volkshefte*), and an extremely important journal (*Hansische Geschichtsblätter*). See also:

K. Holbaum, K. Kunze and W. Stein, *Hansisches Urkundenbuch* (Leipzig-Halle 1876–1907).

The most important general works are:

E. Daenell, *Die Blütezeit der deutschen Hanse. Hansische Geschichte von der zweiten Hälfte des XIV. bis zum letzten Viertel des XV. Jahrhunderts* (2 vols. Berlin 1905–06). Fundamental.

P. Dollinger, *La Hanse, XIIᵉ–XVIIᵉ s.* (Paris 1964). An excellent summary with a bibliography.

F. Rörig, *Hansische Beiträge zur deutschen Wirtschaftsgeschichte* (Breslau 1928).

——, *Vom Werden und Wesen der Hanse* (Leipzig 1940).

The most important detailed studies of Hanseatic history are:

W. Koppe, *Lübeck-Stockholmer Handelsgeschichte im XIV. Jht.* (Neumünster 1963).

G. Lechner, *Die hansischen Pfundzollisten des Jahr 1368* (Lübeck 1935).

H. Nirrnheim, *Das hamburgische Pfundzollbuch von 1369* (Hamburg 1910).

——, *Das hamburgische Pfundzollbuch von 1399 und 1400* (Hamburg 1930).

On other areas of German trade see:

F. Bastian, *Das Runtigerbuch (1383–1407) und verwandtes Material zum Regensburger – Süddeutschen Handel- und Münzwesen* (3 vols. Regensburg 1935–44).

A. Dietz, *Frankfurter Handelsgeschichte* (4 vols. Frankfurt-am-Main 1910–25).

B. Kuske, *Quellen zur Geschichte des Kölner Handels und Verkehrs im Mittelalter* (4 vols. Bonn 1917–34).

K. O. Müller, *Quellen zur Handelsgeschichte der Baumgartner von Augsburg 1480–1570* (Wiesbaden 1954).

A. Schulte, *Geschichte des mittelalterlichen Handels und Verkehrs zwischen Westdeutschland und Italien, mit Ausschuss von Venedig* (2 vols. Leipzig 1900). Essential.

——, *Geschichte der grossen Ravensburger Handelsgesellschaft, 1380–1530* (Stuttgart-Berlin 1923).

O. Stolz, *Quellen zur Geschichte des Zollwesens und Handelsverkehr in Tirol und Voralberg vom XIII. bis XVIII. Jht.* (Wiesbaden 1955).

On the Fuggers see:

R. Ehrenberg, *Das Zeitalter der Fugger, Geldkapital und Kreditverkehr im XVI. Jht.* (3rd ed. 2 vols. Jena 1922).

G. Frh. von Pölnitz, *Jakob Fugger. Kaiser, Kirche und Kapital in der oberdeutschen Renaissance* (2 vols. Tübingen 1949–52). Essential.

——, *Anton Fugger I, 1453–1535* (Tübingen 1958).

A. Schulte, *Die Fugger in Rom, 1495–1523* (2 vols. Leipzig 1904).

**ITALY AND THE MEDITERRANEAN LANDS**

R.-H. Bautier, 'Les relations commerciales des Occidentaux

avec les pays d'Orient au Moyen Age', in *Congrès international d'histoire maritime*, 1969.

G. I. Bratianu, *Recherches sur le commerce des Génois dans la Mer Noire au XIII^e s.* (Paris 1929).

——, *Les Vénitiens dans la Mer Noire au XIV^e s.* (Bucharest 1939).

J. Day, *Les douanes de Gênes* (Paris 1965).

R. Doehaerd, *Les relations commerciales entre Gênes, la Belgique et l'Outremont, d'après les archives notariales génoises aux XIII^e et XIV^e s.* (3 vols. Brussels 1941).

R. Dochaerd and C. Kerremans, *Les relations commerciales entre Gênes, la Belgique et l'Outremont, d'après les archives notariales génoises de 1400 à 1440* (Brussels 1952).

W. Heyd, *Histoire du commerce du Levant au Moyen Age* (2 vols. Paris 1885).

F. C. Lane, *Venetian ships and shipbuilding of the Renaissance* (Baltimore 1934).

R. S. Lopez, *Storia delle colonie genovisi nel Mediterraneo* (Bologna 1938).

——, *Genova marinara nel Duecento: Benedetto Zaccaria* (Messina 1933).

A. Schaule, *Handelsgeschichte der romanischen Völker des Mittelmeergebiets bis zum Ende der Kreuzzüge* (Munich-Berlin 1906).

H. Simonsfeld, *Der 'Fondaco dei Tedeschi' in Venedig* (3 vols. Stuttgart 1887).

L. de Sturler, *Les relations commerciales entre Gênes, la Belgique et l'Outremont de 1320–1400* (2 vols. Brussels 1969).

F. Thiriet, *La Romanie vénitienne au Moyen Age. Le développement et l'exploitation du domaine colonial vénitien (XII^e–XV^e s.)* (Paris 1959).

The records of Genoese notaries after 1154 contain a large quantity of documents dealing with Mediterranean commerce; their minute-books from the twelfth and the beginning of the thirteenth century have been systematically published, in addition to hitherto unpublished documents on relations between Genoa and Sardinia, Corsica, Tuscany, Piedmont and the Orient. Equally valuable for the history of international commerce are the published Venetian sources (the proceedings of the Councils and of the various courts, financial documents, records of Cretan notaries, etc.).

THE MUSLIM EAST

C. Cahen, 'Orient latin et commerce du Levant, ou notes sur l'histoire des Croisades et de l'Orient latin', in *Bulletin de la Faculté des Lettres de Strasbourg*, 1951.

——, 'Douanes et commerce dans les ports méditerranéens de l'Egypte mediévale, d'après le Minhadj d'Al-Makhzumi', in *Journal of Economic and Social History of the Orient*, 1964.

——, 'Quelques problèmes concernant l'expansion économique musulmane au Haut Moyen Age', in Centro Italiano di Studi sull'alto Medioevo, *L'Occidente e l'Islam nell'alto medio evo* (Spoleto 1964).

G. S. P. Freeman Grenville, *The medieval history of the coast of Tanganyika with special reference to recent archaeological discoveries* (London-New York 1962).

SPAIN

C. Carrere, 'Le droit d'ancrage et le mouvement du port de Barcelone', in *Estudios de Historia moderna*, 1953.

C.-E. Dufour, *L'Espagne catalane et le Maghreb aux XIII^e et XIV^e s.* (Paris 1966).

## MERCHANTS, COMMERCIAL AND BANKING ORGANIZATIONS

A. Sapori, *Le marchand italien au Moyen Age* (Paris 1952) is a general guide with a bibliography and can be supplemented by:

J. Le Goff, *Marchands et banquiers du Moyen Age* (Paris 1956).

Y. Renouard, *Les hommes d'affaires italiens du Moyen Age* (Paris 1949).

Of numerous monographs, the following are of particular importance:

M. Chiaudano, *Studi e documenti per la storia del diritto commerciale italiano nel sec. XIII* (Turin 1930).

F. C. Lane, *Andreà Barbarigo, merchant of Venice, 1418–1449* (Baltimore 1944).

F. Melis, *Aspetti della vita economica medievale. Studi nell'Archivo Datini di Prato* (Siena 1962). Very important.

I. Origo, *The Merchant of Prato* (London 1957).

V. Renouard, *Les relations des papes d'Avignon et des compagnies commerciales et bancaires de 1316 à 1378* (Paris 1941).

W. E. Rhodes, 'Italian bankers in England and their loans to Edward I and Edward II', in *Historical essays by members of Owens College*, edd. T. F. Tout and J. Tait (Manchester 1902).

R. de Roover, *Money, banking and credit in medieval Bruges. Italian merchant-bankers, Lombards and money-changers* (Cambridge, Mass. 1948). Very important.

——, 'The story of the Alberti Company, 1302–1348', in *The Business History Review*, 1958.

——, *The rise and decline of the Medici Bank* (Cambridge, Mass. 1963).

A. Sapori, *La crise delle compagnie mercantili dei Bardi e dei Peruzzi* (Florence 1926).

——, *I libri di commercio dei Peruzzi* (Milan 1934).

——, *I libri della ragione bancaria dei Gangiflazzi* (Milan 1946).

——, *La campagnia dei Frescobaldi in Inghilterra* (Florence 1947).

——, *I libri degli Alberti del Giudice* (Milan 1952).

These important works are complemented by the author's articles, particularly those in *Studi di storia economica*. See also *Studi in onore di Armando Sapori* (Milan 1957).

## INTERNATIONAL COMMERCE

The following medieval trading manuals are particularly useful:

A. Borlandi, *Il manuale di mercatura di Saminiato de Ricci* (Genoa 1963).

L. Chiarini, *El libro di mercatantie et usanze de' paesi*, ed. F. Borlandi (Turin 1938).

K. O. Müller, *Welthandelsbräuche (1480–1540)* (Wiesbaden 1962).

F. B. Pegolotti, *La practica della mercatura*, ed. A. Evans (Cambridge, Mass. 1936).

CLOTH

H. Ammann, 'Deutschland und die Tuchindustrie Westeuropas', in *Hansische Geschichtsblätter*, 1954.

R.-H. Bautier, 'La place de la draperie brabançonne et plus particulièrement bruxelloise dans l'industrie textile du Moyen Age', in *Bulletin de la société royale d'archéologie de Bruxelles*, 1961.

E. M. Carus-Wilson, 'Trends in the export of English woollens in the XIVth century', in *Economic History Review*, 1950. Important.

J. Laurent, *Un grand commerce d'exportation au Moyen Age: la draperie des Pays Bas en France et dans les pays méditerranéens, XIIᵉ–XVᵉ s.* (Paris 1935). Very important.

M. M. Postan, 'Etudes anglaises sur les "Customs Accounts" principalement au sujet de la laine', in *Sources de l'histoire maritime* (Paris 1962).

A. Sapori, *Una compagnia di Calimala ai primi del Trecento* (Florence 1932).

METALS

R. Sprandel, 'Le commerce du fer en Méditerranée orientale au Moyen Age', in *Actes du VIIIᵉ congrès international d'histoire maritime* (Bayreuth 1966).

SALT

*Le rôle du sel dans l'histoire* (Paris 1968). The proceedings of an international colloquy held at Paris.

A. R. Bridbury, *England and the salt trade in the late Middle Ages* (Oxford 1955).

V. Rau, *A exploração e o comércio de sal de Setúbal* (Lisbon 1951).

SLAVES

C. Verlinden, *L'esclavage dans l'Europe médiévale*, vol. 1: *Péninsule iberique, France* (Bruges 1955). See numerous articles by the same author.

SPICES, DYES AND FURS

F. Borlandi, 'Note par la storia della produzione e del commerco di una materia prima: il guado nel Medio evo', in *Studi in onore di G. Luzzatto* (Milan 1949).

G. Caster, *Le commerce du pastel et de l'épicerie à Toulouse de 1450 à environ 1561* (Toulouse 1962).

J. Delumeau, *L'alun de Rome, XVᵉ–XIXᵉ s.* (Paris 1962).

E. M. Veale, *The English fur trade in the later Mediaeval Age* (Oxford–New York 1966).

WINE

H. Ammann, *Von der Wirtschaftsgeltung des Elsass im Mittelalter* (Lahr 1956).

J. Craeybeckx, *Un grand commerce d'importation: les vins de France au anciens Pays Bas (XIIIᵉ–XVIᵉ s.)* (Paris 1959).

V. Renouard, 'Le grand commerce des vins de Gascogne au Moyen Age', in *Revue historique*, 1959.

WOOL

R. Bigwood, 'La politique de la laine en France sous les règnes de Philippe le Bel et ses fils', in *Revue Belge de Philologie et Histoire*, 1936–37.

E. Power, *The wool trade in English medieval history* (Oxford 1941).

The work of the first seminar of economic history, held at Prato, devoted to the production of and trade in wool, is at present in the course of publication.

## FAIRS

*La Foire. Recueil de la Société Jean Bodin* (Brussels 1953). A collection of works on different countries.

P. Huvelin, *Essai historique sur le droit des marches et des foires* (Paris 1897). Out of date but irreplaceable.

F. Borel, *Les foires de Genève au XVᵉ s.* (Geneva 1892).

F. Bourquelot, *Etude sur les foires de Champagne aux XIIᵉ, XIIIᵉ et XIVᵉ s.* (Paris 1865).

G. Des Marez, *La lettre de foire à Ypres au XIIIᵉ s.* (Brussels 1907).

## TRANSPORT

The only general work deals with Germany:

F. Bruns and H. Weczerka, *Hansische Handelsstrassen. Atlas, Textband und Register* (3 vols. Cologne–Graz 1962–67).

See also:

R.-H. Bautier, 'Recherches sur les routes de l'Europe médiévale', in *Bulletin philologique et historique*, 1960.

M. P. Charlesworth, *Trade routes and commerce of the Roman Empire* (Cambridge 1926). Essential.

M.-C. Daviso di Charvensod, *I pedaggi delle Alpi occidentali nel Medio evo* (Turin 1961).

J. Hubert, 'Les routes du Moyen Age', in *Les routes de France depuis les origines* (Paris 1959).

L. Vazquez de Parga, J. M. Lacarra and J. Uria Riu, *Les peregrinaciones a Santiago de Compostela* (3 vols. Madrid 1959). Essential.

## FINANCE

### MONEY

A basic bibliography of coinage appears in P. Grierson, *Coins and medals. A select bibliography* (London 1954).

The proceedings of the Congresso internazionale di numismatica (Rome 1961) can also be consulted.

On money, currency circulation and precious metals see:

M. Bloch, *Esquisse d'une histoire monétaire de l'Europe* (Paris 1954).

E. Bridrey, *La théorie de la monnaire au XIVᵉ s.: Nicole Oresme. Etude d'histoire des doctrines et des faits économiques* (Paris 1906).

R. Cessi, *Problemi monetari venezani fino a tutto il sec. XIV* (Padua 1937). Important.

C. M. Cipolla, *Studi di storia della moneta*, vol. 1: *I Movimenti dei cambi in Italia dal sec. XIII al XV* (Pavia 1948).

A. Grünzweig, 'Les incidences monétaires internationales des mutations monétaires de Philippe le Bel', in *Le Moyen Age*, 1953.

H. Laurent, *La loi de Gresham au Moyen Age. Essai sur la circulation monétaire entre la Flandre et le Brabant à la fin du XIVᵉ s.* (Brussels 1953).

R. S. Lopez, 'Settecento anni fa: il ritorno all'oro nell'Occidente duecentesco' (Naples 1953). An essential work, which has been summarized as 'Back to Gold 1252', in the *Economic History Review*.

A. Luschin von Ebengreuth, *Allgemeine Münzkunde und Geldgeschichte des Mittelalters und der neueren Zeit* (2nd ed. Munich 1926). Important.

A. Nagl, 'Die Golwahrung und die handelsmässige Gelrechnung im Mittelalter', in *Numismatische Zeitschrift*, 1895. Important.

F. de Sauley, *Recueil de documents relatifs à l'histoire des monnaies frappées par les rois de France* (4 vols. Paris 1879–92).

F. Spooner, *L'économie mondiale et les frappes monétaires en France, 1493–1680* (Paris 1956). Important for the end of the Middle Ages and the sixteenth century.

*Moneta e scambi nell'alto Medio evo* (Spoleto 1961) is a very important collection of work on the early Middle Ages.

On the late empire, and the byzantine, islamic and mongol east see:

R. P. Blake, 'The circulation of silver in the Moslem East down to the Mongol epoch', in *Harvard Journal of Asiatic Studies*, 1937.

J.-P. Callu, *Genio populi romani 295–316. Contribution à l'histoire monétaire de la Tetrachie* (Paris 1960).

——, *La politique monétaire des empereurs romains de 238 à 311* (Paris 1969).

R. A. Carson, P. V. Hill and J. P. C. Kent, *The late Roman bronze coinage (A.D. 324–498)* (London 1960).

H. Franke, *Geld und Wirtschaft in China unter den Mongol Herrschaften* (Leipzig 1949).

L. C. West and A. C. Johnson, *Currency in Roman and Byzantine Egypt* (Princeton 1944).

D. A. Zakythinos, *Crise monétaire et crise économique à Byzance du XIIIe au XVe s.* (Athens 1938).

## PRICES AND WAGES

W. H. Beveridge, 'The yield and the price of corn in the Middle Ages', in *Economic Journal (Historical Supplement)*, 1929.

——, 'Wages in the Winchester manors', in *Economic History Review*, 1936.

C. M. Cipolla, *Money, prices and civilization in the Mediterranean world* (Princeton 1956).

N. S. B. Gras, *The evolution of the English corn-market from the XIIth to the XVIIIth cent.* (Cambridge, Mass. 1926).

E. J. Hamilton, *Money, prices and wages in Valencia, Aragon and Navarra 1351–1500* (Cambridge, Mass. 1936).

H. van Houtte, *Documents pour servir à l'histoire des prix de 1385 à 1794 (Brussels 1902)*.

H. A. Miskimin, *Money, prices and foreign exchange in XIVth century France* (New Haven-London 1963).

A. F. Pribram, *Materialen zur Geschichte der Preise und Löhne in Oesterreich* (Vienna 1938).

J. E. T. Rogers, *A history of agriculture and prices in England* (4 vols. Oxford 1866–82).

C. Verlinden, *Documents pour servir à l'histoire des prix et des salaires en Flandre et en Brabant (XVe–XVIIIe s.)* (Bruges 1959).

H. van der Wee, *The growth of the Antwerp market and the European economy*, vol. I: *History of prices and wages in Brabant (XIVe–XVIe s.)* (Leuven 1963).

## BANKING, EXCHANGE AND ACCOUNTANCY

F. C. Lane, 'Venetian bankers, 1496–1533. A study in the early stages of deposit bankings', in *The Journal of Political Economy*, 1937.

R. de Roover, 'Aux origines d'une technique intellectuelle: la formation et l'expansion de la comptabilité à partie double', in *Annales d'histoire économique et sociale*, 1937.

——, *L'évolution de la lettre de change (XIVe–XVIIIe s.)* (Paris 1953).

——, 'The development of accounting prior to Luca Pacigli, according to the account books of medieval merchants', in *Studies in the history of accounting* (London 1957).

——, *The Bruges money market around 1400* (with a statistical supplement by H. Sardy) (Brussels 1968).

A. P. Usher, *The early history of deposit banking in Mediterranean Europe* (Cambridge, Mass. 1943).

T. Zerbi, *La banca nell'ordinamento finanziario visconteo: dai mastri del banco Giussano . . . (1356–58); Aspetti economico-tecnici del mercato di Milano nel Trecento; Il mastro a partita doppia di una azienda mercantile del Trecento* (3 vols. Milan 1935–36).

——, *Le origini della partita doppia. Gestioni aziendali e situazione di mercato nei secc. XIV e XV* (Milan 1952).

## CREDIT

Much has been written on the 'Lombards' and on usury, less on the various credit techniques:

G. Bigwood, *Le régime juridique et économique du commerce de l'argent dans la Belgique du Moyen Age* (2 vols. Brussels 1921–22).

L. Gauthier, *Les Lombards dans les deux Bourgognes* (Paris 1927).

R. Genestal, *Le rôle des monastères comme établissements de credit, étudié en Normandie du XIe à la fin du XIIIe s.* (Paris 1901).

J. Heers, 'Le prix de l'assurance maritime à la fin du Moyen Age', in *Revue d'histoire économique et sociale*, 1959.

B. N. Nelson, *The idea of usury* (Princeton 1949).

A.-M. Patrone, *Le casane astigiane in Savoia* (Turin 1959).

P. Petot, *La constitution de rente aux XIIe et XIIIe s. dans les pays coutumiers* (Paris 1928).

G. Sicard, *Aux origines des sociétés anonymes: les moulins de Toulouse au Moyen Age* (Paris 1953).

J. Strieder, *Studien zur Geschichte kapitalistischer Organisationsformen. Monopole, Kartelle und Aktiengesellschaften im Mittelalter und zu Beginn der Neuzeit* (2nd ed. Munich 1925).

### JEWISH MONEY-LENDERS AND MERCHANTS

The following are fundamental:

H. Gross, *Gallia judaica* (Paris 1897).

I. Elbogen, A. Freimann and H. Tykocinski, *Germania judaica*, vol. I (Breslau 1934); vol. II in *Zeitschrift für Geschichte der Juden in Deutschland*, 1937.

J. Aronius, *Regesten zur Geschichte der Juden von fränkischen und deutschen Reiche bis zum 1273* (Berlin 1887–1902).

M. Wiener, *Regesten zur Geschichte der Juden in Deutschland während des Mittelalters* (Hannover 1862).

Regional and local studies are frequent, in particular:

M. Ciardini, *I banchieri ebrei in Firenze nel sec XV.* (Borgo San Lorenzo 1907).

R. W. Emery, *The Jews of Perpignan in the XIIIth cent. An economic study based on notarial records* (New York 1959).

A. A. Neuman, *The Jews in Spain*, vol. I (Philadelphia 1949).

L. Rabinowitz, *Jewish Merchant Venturers* (London 1948).

J. Stengers, *Les Juifs dans les Pays Bas Au Moyen Age* (Brussels 1950).

See also G. Caro, *Sozial- und Wirtschaftsgeschichte der Juden im Mittelalter* (2 vols. Frankfurt-am-Main 1920–24) and the same author's 'Die wirtschaftliche Tätigkeit der Juden im frühen Mittelalter', in *Vierteljahrschrift für Sozial- und Wirtschaftsgeschichte*, 1912. In addition, Isaac Loeb has written many articles in the *Revue des études juifs*.

## INDUSTRY

The only general history is a dated work on England:

T. Salzman, *English industries of the Middle Ages* (2nd ed. Oxford 1923).

## MINING AND METALLURGY

A recent fundamental work, including a bibliography, is R. Sprandel, *Das Eisengewerbe im Mittelalter* (Stuttgart 1968). See also:

O. Johannsen, *Geschichte des Eisens* (3rd ed. Düsseldorf 1953).

J. U. Nef, 'Silver production in Central Europe (1450–1618)', in *The Journal of political economy*, 1941.

——, *The rise of the British coal industry* (2 vols. London 1932).

M. Yans, *Histoire économique du duché de Limbourg sous la maison de Bourgogne: les forêts et les mines* (Brussels 1932).

## TEXTILES

E. Coornaert, *La draperie-sayetterie d'Hondschoote (XIV$^e$– XVIII$^e$ s.)* (Paris 1930).

——, 'Draperies rurales, draperies urbaines. L'évolution de l'industrie flamande au Moyen Age et au XVI$^e$ s.', in *Revue belge de Philologie et d'Histoire*, 1950. Important.

A. Doren, *Studien aus der Florentiner Wirtschaftsgeschichte*, vol. I: *Die Florentiner Wollentuchindustrie vom XIV. bis zum XVI. Jht.* (Stuttgart 1901).

G. Espinas, *La draperie dans la Flandre française au Moyen Age* (2 vols. Paris 1923). Important.

G. Espinas and H. Pirenne, *Recueil de documents relatifs à l'histoire de l'industrie drapière en Flandre* (4 vols. Brussels 1906–24). Essential.

U. Gualazzini, *Rapporti fra capitale e lavoro nelle industrie tessili lombarde del Medio evo* (Turin 1932).

G. de Poerck, *La draperie médiévale en Flandre et en Artois. Technique et terminologie* (3 vols. Bruges 1951).

E. Sable, *Histoire de l'industrie linière en Belgique* (Brussels 1945).

H. Sagher, 'L'immigration des tisserands flamands et brabançons en Angleterre sous Edouard II', in *Mélanges d'histoire offerts à H. Pirenne* (Brussels 1926).

——, *Recueil de documents relatifs à l'histoire de l'industrie drapière en Flandre. Le Sud-Ouest de la Flandre, depuis l'époque bourguignonne*, vol. I (Brussels 1951).

L. Zanoni, *Gli Umiliati nei loro rapporti con l'eresia, l'industria della lana ed i comuni, nei secc. XII et XIII* (Milan 1911).

## LABOUR HISTORY

The *Histoire générale du travail*, edited by L.-H. Pariac, is a collective work; see vol. I: *L'âge de l'artisanot: Le Moyen Age*, P. Wolff (Paris 1960).

See also:

P. Toissonnade, *Le travail dans L'Europe chrétienne du Moyen Age (V$^e$–XV$^e$ s.)* (2nd ed. Paris 1931).

——, *Essai sur l'organisation du travail en Poitou* (2 vols. Paris 1900).

E. Coornaert, *Les corporations en France avant 1789* (Paris 1941).

A. Doren, *Deutsche Handwerker und Handwerkerbruderschaften im mittelalterlichen Italien* (Berlin 1903).

——, *Das Florentiner Zunftwesen vom XIV. bis zum XVI. Jht.* (Stuttgart-Berlin 1908).

F. Favresse, *Etudes sur les métiers bruxellois du Moyen Age* (Brussels 1961).

C. Gross, *The Gild Merchant. A contribution to British municipal history* (2 vols. Oxford 1890).

M. S. Leicht, *Operari, artigiani e agricultori in Italia del sec VI al XVI* (Milan 1946).

G. Michwitz, *Die Kartelfunktionen der Zunfte und ihre Bedeutung bei der Entstehung des Zunftwesens* (Helsinki 1936).

## SOCIAL CLASSES

For the nobility and the peasantry, see the section above on rural history, especially those works dealing with the landowners and rural life, and those by Boutruche, Duby and Genizot. See also M. Bloch, *La société féodale* (2 vols. Paris 1939–40, with a new ed. 1949), and R. Boutruche, *Seigneurie et féodalite*, vol. I (Paris 1959), both classics with ample bibliographies. For artisans and the urban working class see the section on labour history, above; for the bourgeois and patrician classes see urban history, above, as well as the following works:

F. Blockmans, *Het Gentsche stadspatriciat tot omstreeks 1302* (Ghent 1938). A French summary appeared in *Revue du Nord*, 1938.

G. Espinas, *Les origines du capitalisme*, vol. I: *Sire Johan Boinebroke . . .* (Lille 1933); vol. II: *Sire Jehan de France . . .* (Lille 1936).

J. Febvre, J. Lestocquoy and G. Espinas, 'Fils du riches ou nouveaux riches. Les origines du patriciat urbain . . .', in *Annales. Economie. Sociétés. Civilisations*, 1946.

S. Lerner, *Die Frankfurter Patriziergesellschaft* (Alten Limpurg 1952).

J. Lestocquoy, *Patriciens du Moyen Age: les dynasties bourgeoises d'Arras de XI$^e$ au XV$^e$ s.* (Arras 1945).

N. Ottokar, *Il comune di Firenze alla fine del Dugento* (Florence 1926).

S. C. Thrupp, *The merchant class of medieval London* (Chicago 1948).

P. Wolff, *Les estimes toulousaines des XIV$^e$ et XV$^e$ s.* (Toulouse 1956).

References should also be made to the work, already mentioned, of G. Luzzatto on Venice and of A. Sapori on Florence and the cities of Tuscany. On officialdom see B. Guenee, *Tribunaux et gens de justice dans le bailliage de Senlis à la fin du Moyen Age (vers 1380–vers 1500)* (Paris 1963).

## SOCIAL ANTAGONISMS AND THE CLASS STRUGGLE

G. Des Marez, *Les luttes sociales en Flandre au Moyen Age* (Brussels 1900).

R. H. Hilton and H. Fagan, *The English rising of 1381* (London 1954).

P. Lindsay and R. Groves, *The Peasants' revolt of 1381* (London 1950).

M. Malowist, 'Le commerce de la Baltique et le problème des luttes sociales en Pologne aux XV$^e$ et XVI$^e$ s.', in *La Pologne au X$^e$ Congrès international des sciences historiques à Rome* (Warsaw 1955).

M. Mollat and P. Wolff, *Ongles bleus, Jacques et Ciompi: les revolutions populaires en Europe aux XIV$^e$ et XV$^e$ siècles* (Paris 1970).

N. Rodolico, *Il popolo minuto. Note di storia fiorentina, 1343–78* (Bologna 1899).

——, *I Ciompi. Una pagina di storia del proletariato italiano* (Florence 1945).

F. Vercauteren, *Luttes sociales à liège, XIII<sup>e</sup> et XIV<sup>e</sup> s.* (Brussels 1943).

J. Vicens Vives, *Historia de los remensas en el s. XV* (Barcelona 1945).

——, *El gran sindicato remensa, 1488–1508* (Madrid 1954).

P. Wolff, 'Les luttes sociales dans les villes du Midi français, XIII<sup>e</sup>–XV<sup>e</sup> s.', in *Annales. Economie. Sociétés. Civilisations.*

### PUBLIC FINANCE

G. Nobili Schiera has compiled a selective bibliography of publications between 1950 and 1960 on administrative and financial history, and an exhaustive one for 1961 onwards, in the *Annali della Fondazione italiana per la storia amministrativa* for 1964, 1965 and 1966. J. Favier, 'L'histoire administrative et financière du Moyen Age depuis dix ans', in *Bibliothèque de l'Ecole de Chartes* provides an excellent summary of recent works.

On urban history, see above, and also the proceedings of the 1964 international colloquy 'Pro civitate': 'L'impôt dans le cadre de la ville et de L'état', in *Pro Civitate, Collection histoire*, 1966.

In addition to the third volume of the Cambridge Modern History, B. Lyon and A. Verhulst, *Medieval Finance. A comparison of financial institutions in Northwestern Europe* (Bruges 1957) should be mentioned.

### ENGLAND

C. Dietz, *English public finance, 1485–1641* (2nd ed. London 1962).

V. H. Galbraith, *The making of Domesday book* (Oxford 1961).

N. S. B. Gras, *The Early English customs system* (Cambridge, Mass.-London 1918).

S. K. Mitchel, *Studies in taxation under John and Henry III* (New Haven 1914).

——, *Taxation in medieval England* (New Haven-London 1951).

J. H. Ramsey, *A history of the revenues of the kings of England, 1066–1399* (2 vols. Oxford 1925).

A. Steel, *The receipt of the Exchequer, 1377–1485* (Cambridge 1954).

J. F. Tout, *Chapters in the administrative history of medieval England* (6 vols. Manchester 1920–33).

G. Unwin (ed.), *Finance and trade under Edward III* (Manchester 1918).

J. F. Willard, *Parliamentary taxes on personal property, 1290 to 1334. A study in medieval English financial administration.* (Cambridge, Mass. 1934).

### FRANCE

L. Borrelli de Serres, *Recherches sur divers services publics du XIII<sup>e</sup> au XVIII<sup>e</sup> s.* (3 vols. Paris 1895–1909).

G. Dupont-Ferrier, *Etudes sur les institutions financières de la France à la fin du Moyen Age* (2 vols. Paris 1930–32).

——, *Les origines et le premier siècle du cour du Trésor* (Paris 1936).

R. Gandilhon, *Politique économique de Louis XI* (Rennes 1941).

M. Rey, *Les finances royales sous Charles VI: les causes du déficit, 1388–1413* (Paris 1965).

——, *Le domaine du roi et les finances extraordinaires sous Charles VI* (Paris 1965).

J. R. Strayer and C. H. Taylor, *Studies in early French taxation* (Cambridge, Mass. 1939).

M. Mollat, 'Recherches sur les finances des ducs Valois de Bourgogne', in *Revue Historique*, 1958.

### THE ORIENT

F. Dolger, *Beiträge zur Geschichte der byzantinischen Finanzverwaltung, besonders des X. und XI. Jhts.* (Leipzig-Berlin 1927).

H. Glykatzi-Ahrweiler, 'Recherches sur l'administration de l'Empire byzantin aux IX<sup>e</sup>–XI<sup>e</sup> s.', in *Bulletin de correspondance hellénique*, 1960

E. Stein, *Untersuchungen zur spätbyzantinischen Verfassungs-und Wirtschaftsgeschichte* (Hannover 1925).

### THE PAPACY

J. Favier, *Les finances pontificales à l'époque du grand schisme d'Occident, 1378–1409* (Paris 1966).

W. E. Lunt, *Financial relations of the papacy with England to 1327* (Cambridge, Mass. 1939).

—— *Papal revenues in the Middle Ages* (2 vols. New York 1934).

### SCIENCE, TECHNOLOGY AND INVENTION

G. Beaujouan, 'Medieval science in the Christian West', in R. Taton (ed.), *A General History of the Sciences*, vol. 1: *Ancient and Medieval Science* (London-New York 1963).

J. M. Millas Vallicrossa, *Estudios sobre historia de la ciencia española* (Barcelona 1949).

——, *Nuevos estudios . . .* (Barcelona 1960).

G. Sarton, *Introduction to the history of science*, vol. III: *Science and learning in the fourteenth century* (Baltimore 1950).

### GENERAL TECHNOLOGICAL HISTORY

B. Gille, 'Les origines de la civilisation technique: Le Moyen Age en Occident (V<sup>e</sup> s.–1359)', and 'Les premières étapes du machinisme: les XV<sup>e</sup> et XVI<sup>e</sup> s. en Occident', in M. Dumas (ed.), *Histoire Générale des Techniques* (2 vols. Paris 1962–65).

CLOCKS

E. Zinner, *Die ältesten Räderuhren und modernen Sonnenuhren* (Bamberg 1939).

ENGINEERS

B. Gille, 'Leonard de Vinci et son temps', in *Techniques et Civilisation*, vol. II (Paris 1952).

——, *Les ingénieurs de la Renaissance* (Paris 1964). Fundamental.

MILLS

A.-M. Bautier, 'Les plus anciennes mentions de moulins hydrauliques et de moulins à vent', in *Bulletin philologique et historique*, 1960.

E. M. Carus-Wilson, 'An industrial revolution of the XIIIth century', in *Essays in Economic History* (London 1954).

PAPER AND PRINTING

A. Blum, *Les origines du papier, de l'imprimerie et de la gravure* (Paris 1935).

——, *La route du papier. . . . De Chine en Occident* (Grenoble 1947).

L. Febvre and H. J. Martin, *L'apparition du livre* (Paris 1957).

PLOUGHING

A. G. Haudricourt and J.-B. Delamarre, *L'homme et la charrue* (Paris 1955).

F. G. Payne, 'The British Plough. Some stages in its development', in *Agricultural History Review*, 1957. For other agricultural techniques, see *Etudes rurales* and the writings of G. Duby.

EXPLORATION, NAVIGATION AND DISCOVERY

A basic work, with an ample bibliography, is P. Chanu, *L'expansion européene du XIII<sup>e</sup> au XV<sup>e</sup> s.* (Paris 1969). See also:

L. H. Parias (ed.), *Histoire universelle des explorations*, vol. I: R. Nougier, J. Beaujeu and M. Mollat, *De la préhistoire à la fin du Moyen Age*; vol. II: J. Amsler, *La Renaissance, 1415–1600* (Paris 1955).

C. Verlinden, *Les origines de la civilisation atlantique* (Neuchâtel-Paris 1966).

EXPLORATION IN ASIA

L. Olschki, *Marco Polo's precursors* (Baltimore 1943).

H. Yule, *The Book of Sir Marco Polo* (2nd ed. London 1903).

——, *Cathay and the way thither* (2nd ed. London 1913–16). Cf. P. Pelliot, *Notes on Marco Polo*, a posthumous work published by L. Hambis (Paris 1959).

NAVAL AND NAVIGATIONAL HISTORY

See the proceedings of the first, second and fifth international colloquia on maritime history:

*Le navire et l'économie maritime du XV<sup>e</sup> au XVIII<sup>e</sup> s.* (Paris 1957).

*Le navire . . . du Moyen Age au XVIII<sup>é</sup> s., principalement en Méditerranée* (Paris 1958).

*Les aspects internationaux de la découverte océanique aux XV<sup>e</sup> et XVI<sup>e</sup> s.* (Paris 1966).

A. Jal's *Glossaire Nautique* began to appear in 1970.

ANCIENT SHIPS

A. W. Brogger and H. Shetelig, *The Viking ships. Their ancestry and evolution* (Oslo 1951).

P. Heinsius, *Das schiff der hansischen Frühzeit* (Weimar 1956).

G. La Roërie, 'Les transformations du gouvernail', in *Annales d'histoire économique et sociale*, 1935.

R. J. Lefebvre des Noettes, *De la marine antique à la marine moderne* (Paris 1935).

R. Mauny, *Les navigations médiévales sur les côtes sahariennes antérieures à la découverte portugaise (1434)* (Lisbon 1960).

The basic bibliography on Portuguese discoveries is the *Bibliografia Henriquina* (2 vols. Lisbon 1960).

The chief works are:

A. Baião, *Historia da expansão no mondo* (3 vols. Lisbon 1938–40).

J. Cortesão, *Os descobrimentos portugueses* (2 vols. Lisbon 1960).

V. Magalhães Godinho, *Documentos sobre a expansão portuguesa* (3 vols. Lisbon 1943–45).

——, *A expansão quatrocentista portuguesa. Problemes das origines e da linha de evoluçao* (Lisbon 1944).

——, *Historia economica e social da expansão portuguesa*, vol. I: *Noroeste africano* (Lisbon 1947). Essential.

——, *O Mediterraneao saariano e as caravanas do ouro sec. XI–XV* (São Paulo 1956).

R. Ricard, *Etudes sur l'histoire des Portugais au Maroc* (Coimbra 1955).

——, *Etudes hispano-afriques* (Tetuán 1956).

J. M. da Silva Marques, *Descobrimentos portugueses* (3 vols. Lisbon 1944–49).

On the technical background to these discoveries, see articles by G. Beaujouan, E. Poulle and Ct. A. Teixeira da Motta in the proceedings of the colloquia mentioned above, and also:

L. Mendoza de Albuquerque, *Introdução a historia dos descobrimentos* (Coimbra 1962).

J. Bensaude, *L'astronomie nautique au Portugal à l'époque des grandes découvertes* (Bern 1912).

——, *Histoire de la science nautique portugaise à l'époque des grandes découvertes* (Geneva 1917).

# LIST OF ILLUSTRATIONS

271

273

274

275

# INDEX

284